CAMBRIDGE STATION

Fig. 1 : The splendid architectural facade of Cambridge Station (1846) was designed by Sancton Wood for the Eastern Counties Railway Company. Successor companies made various changes which this book explores. The London North Eastern Railway Company apparently felt a need to broadcast their stewardship, visible down Station Road as prospective passengers approached the Station.

CAMBRIDGE STATION

ITS DEVEOPMENT & OPERATIONS AS A RAIL CENTRE

Rob Shorland-Ball

PEN & SWORD
TRANSPORT

First published in Great Britain in 2017 by
Pen & Sword Transport
An imprint of Pen & Sword Books Ltd
47 Church Street
Barnsley
South Yorkshire
S70 2AS

ISBN 978 1 47386 904 2

Typeset in Palatino by Pen & Sword Books Ltd
Printed and bound by Imago Publishing Limited

Pen & Sword Books Ltd incorporates the imprints of Pen & Sword Archaeology, Atlas, Aviation, Battleground, Discovery, Family History, History, Maritime, Military, Naval, Politics, Railways, Select, Social History, Transport, True Crime, and Claymore Press, Frontline Books, Leo Cooper, Praetorian Press, Remember When, Seaforth Publishing and Wharncliffe.

For a complete list of Pen and Sword titles please contact
Pen and Sword Books Limited
47 Church Street, Barnsley, South Yorkshire, S70 2AS, England
E-mail: enquiries@pen-and-sword.co.uk
Website: www.pen-and-sword.co.uk

Contents

Acknowledgements 7

Abbreviations, Acronyms and Notes 9

Prelude 11

Chapter 1 Why Build a Railway to Cambridge? 13
East Anglia, the 'Eastern Counties' and Cambridge

Chapter 2 Eastern Counties Railway Company 18

Chapter 3 29 July 1845: Cambridge Station Train Services Begin 24

Chapter 4 GER - Great Eastern Railway Company 30

Chapter 5 GER and the Newmarket Railway Company's
Cambridge Branch 37

Chapter 6 GER's Branch Lines to and from Cambridge 47

Chapter 7 Cambridge Station as an Entrepôt 50

Chapter 8 'Four Railway Companies in a Tangle of Mutual
Inconvenience' 52

Chapter 9 How the Station was operated: 1845-1990s 57
Track layouts, platforms and passengers

Chapter 10 How the Station was operated: 1845 to the 1990s 72
Changing the station track layout – Signalling

Chapter 11 How the Station was operated: 1845 to the 1990s 80
Goods Sheds, Goods Yards and goods by rail

Chapter 12 How the Station was operated: 1845 to the 1990s 95
Cambridge Motive Power Depots

Chapter 13 How the Station was operated: 1845 to the 1900s 102
Industrial sidings in the Cambridge Station area

Chapter 14   The Royal Show in Cambridge   107
                1840; 1894; 1922; 1951; 1960 & 1961

Chapter 15   Cambridge University Railway Club - CURC   115
                Cambridge Station Traffic Survey
                06.00 to 00.00 Friday 27 October 1961

Chapter 16   A Goods Porter on Cambridge Station – 1958 to 1964   123

Chapter 17   BR Modernisation Plan and the 'Beeching Report':   132
                The Reshaping of British Railways

Chapter 18   Cambridge Station and the Privatisation of British
                Railways   137

Chapter 19   Re-shaping the Station setting and a new island platform   143

Chapter 20   Cambridge Station and rail services today   151

                Postlude   158

                List of Illustrations   169

                Notes   179

                Select Bibliography   181

                Index   183

ACKNOWLEDGEMENTS

I am very grateful to the following friends, colleagues and contacts whose support, help and knowledge have made this book possible. If I have missed some I hope I may be forgiven because the omission is not by malice but simply by forgetfulness amongst the 'clouds of witness' who have helped me. A paraphrase from Hebrews Chapter 12, verse 1, in the King James Bible (1611) advises us: 'Seeing we are compassed about with so great a cloud of witnesses … let us run with patience the race that is set before us.' I have run with patience, enjoyed the race, so thank you all:

John Scott-Morgan (my Commissioning Editor) was starter and coach for 'the race' and kind supplier of a number of images and contacts for others; Anthony (Tony) Kirby, railway historian and formerly Co-ordinator of Strategic Planning, Anglia Ruskin University, whose knowledge and enthusiasm have been invaluable; Michael Perrins, railway archivist and librarian, who has supplied images and sources of information and been a much-respected, and valued, proof-reader and critic.; Frank Paterson, former General Manager of BR Eastern Region which embraced Cambridge; William Parker, former Assistant to Cambridge Traffic Manager then King's Cross District Manager; Dave Harris, Co-ordinator, Midland Railway Study Centre, Derby; Dr John Gough, railway historian and author; Geoffrey Skelsey, Registrar of University of Cambridge, Fellow of St Catherine's College, railway historian and author; Chris Jakes, Local Studies Manager, Cambridge Library; Geraint Hughes, Partnerships Manager (Projects), Abellio Greater Anglia; Darren Kitson, railway historian and author; Steven Saunders, Secretary Railway Study Association; RSA members who contributed memories and images; Ralph Potter, former railway signal engineer; Graham Burling; BR Clerk at Longstanton near Cambridge then senior BR Officer; Paul Stannard, Area Customer Service Manager, Cambridge; Graham Berry, Train Dispatcher, Cambridge Station; Robert Stripe, Chairman Fen Line Users Association; Jonathan Denby, Head of Corporate Affairs, Abellio Greater Anglia; Adrian Shooter, friend and former CEO Chiltern Railways; Christopher Burton, member R&CHS; Tim Edmonds, Cambridge school-fellow (1960s) and railway historian; Michael Blakemore, Editor *BackTrack*; Vicky Stretch, Archivist Network Rail; all those who contributed memories of Cambridge Station which are in the

Postlude at the end of the book and are fully acknowledged there.

During Cambridge field work I visited the CB1 development, met Brookgate staff at their Project Offices in Station Road and learned much of the AGA plans from Geraint Hughes, Partnerships Manager for AGA; thank you to you all, and for permission to reproduce the images in Chapter 19.

And a final thank you to the many authors whose works I have consulted, whose knowledge and wisdom have underpinned my writing and from whom I have sometimes used (and acknowledged) edited or abridged quotations.

Images and permissions.

I have tried to contact all possible copyright holders and have checked any unacknowledged images with forensic image search engines. If any have been missed would those concerned please contact me.

Finally, I am a careful researcher, have tried to make this book as accurate as possible and the grammar and language correct and enjoyably readable. Any errors are my responsibility but , if you find an error, please contact me. I will be happy to respond and try answer to your concerns.

Fig. 2: Cambridge Motor Omnibus Company open-topped double deck bus on Station - Market Hill service, in the 1890s.

Fig. 2

ABBREVIATIONS, ACRONYMS AND NOTES

BoT	Board of Trade
BR	British Railways
BT	British Transport
CB1	Cambridge Station area redevelopment scheme
DMU	Diesel Multiple Unit
ECR	Eastern Counties Railway
FOC	Freight Operating Company
GER	Great Eastern Railway
GNR	Great Northern Railway
IECC	Integrated Electronic Control, Centre
ILN	Illustrated London News
L&NWR	London & North Western Railway
LMS	London Midland & Scottish Railway
LNER	London North Eastern Railway
MPD	Motive Power Depot
MR	Midland Railway
N&CR	Newmarket & Chesterford Railway
NR	Network Rail
NRM	National Railway Museum
ORR	Office of Rail and Road
OS	Ordnance Survey
PW	Permanent Way
R&CHS	Railway & Canal Historical Society
RASE	Royal Agricultural Society of England
RCH	Railway Clearing House
ROC	Regional Operating Centre
ROSCO	Rolling Stock Leasing Company
TOC	Train Operating Company
TPO	Travelling Post Office
UK	United Kingdom
VDU	Visual display unit

The University of Cambridge is a collegiate University, like Oxford and Durham Universities. The Vice Chancellor provides academic and administrative leadership to the whole of the University with a small personal secretariat. The primary governing body is Regent House which embraces the staff of both the University and of the thirty-one Cambridge Colleges. The Colleges each have their own administration and in this book the principal references are to Jesus College which owned much of the land that was sold to the ECR for railway development.

Wayleave: sometimes required to secure access across a piece of land. Possession of wayleave secured a right to use the surface of the piece of land but did not grant any right to minerals beneath the piece of land. A Wayleave often had to be purchased.

The Grouping: the Railways Act 1923 grouped most of the railway companies in the UK into four principal companies, LNER, LMS, SR and GWR

This book is an historical work so the pre-decimal form of UK currency and imperial measurements will be used where appropriate.

PRELUDE

Aside from the history and operation of railways, a long-term interest of mine has been the classical pipe organ. For me it is wonderful machine and an accomplished organist can make it 'speak' to produce glorious sounds – like the organ in Kings College Chapel, Cambridge. A Prelude & Fugue is organ music which introduces the subject, or theme, of the piece then develops the theme by interweaving the parts. My subject is Cambridge Station, developed in twenty chapters, and concluded with a Postlude. I hope my readers enjoy the 'music' I am making!

I grew up in Cambridge and Mr George Docking, Chief Controller for the Cambridge District, lived nearby. Mr Docking – described by Gerard Fiennes in *I Tried to Run a Railway* as a man of 'resource and sagacity' – was looking for young men (and some young women) who might join the Railway as Traffic Apprentices after completing University. Mr Docking knew I was very interested in railways so suggested I should start at the bottom and learn how the Railway worked before, perhaps, becoming a Traffic Apprentice. For seven years, I worked on Cambridge Station as a goods porter during every VI Form and then (Nottingham) University long vacations from 1958 to 1965. It was shift work

and I variously worked all three of the shifts – 06.00 to 14.00; 14.00 to 22.00 and, sometimes, 22.00 to 06.00, the night shift – so I saw a great deal of Cambridge as a working station. Particularly interesting for me were the additional jobs that the Down and Up end Inspectors required. They included: walking nearly two miles along the cess north of the station (and back) to deliver notices to: signal boxes; shunters' bothies; carriage cleaners' bothies; permanent way bothies when repairs or maintenance are in progress, the Coldham Lane Diesel Depot; re-painting the white lines along the platform edges (night shift only); cleaning up on the platform and the station yard after Chipperfield's Circus elephants had de-trained at Platform 3 and walked, trunk-to-tail, away to Midsummer Common and finally, checking that the HM the Queen's ice-packed fish boxes bound for Sandringham were in good order and surrounded by sufficient sawdust to absorb any leaking moisture.

I was, indeed, seeing the working railway from the bottom, as Mr Docking intended, and it was fascinating; it encouraged me to research the history of Cambridge Station and some of the results are here.

I have sustained my interest in railways and was very fortunate in 1987 to be appointed Deputy Head and Development

Project Director at the National Railway Museum. There I learned a lot more and had access to a substantial reference library. I worked on the Museum Steam Team which involved cleaning, oiling, coaling, sometimes driving in the Museum grounds as well as taking turns to ride on the footplate as an NRM representative during main-line charters. I also sustained my interest in Cambridge Station and was interested to discover that – as the select bibliography at the end of this book shows – very little has been published about the station and its operation.

I hope I can show that a single-sided station, served by and serving four competing railway companies for passenger and goods traffic, has an interesting story to tell. I believe in a holistic approach to my subject and to illustrating Cambridge Station as an important link in a complex chain of activities and services.

A concluding quote from Sergei Witte (Director of Department of Railway Affairs in Imperial Russia from 1899 to 1906) nicely makes my point:

> 'A railway is a ferment that causes cultural brewing and even if it encounters a completely wild population on its way it can quickly civilise it to the necessary levels.'[1]

Chapter 1

WHY BUILD A RAILWAY
TO CAMBRIDGE?

East Anglia, the 'Eastern Counties' and Cambridge

read Geography at university and my geographical mind-set encouraged me to ask why railway companies would choose to build railways to Cambridge, and beyond. I always thought of Cambridge as the front door to East Anglia and the map of UK regions around Cambridge illustrates this — **Fig. 3** below. Cambridge, in the nineteenth century, was a bridging-point on the River Cam with water connections via the Cam and Ouse to King's Lynn and the North Sea. It was a flourishing market town, its University a major seat of learning and of influence in London and among the so-called 'ruling classes'. Many such gentry had attended one of the Cambridge Colleges and often their male offspring were there too.

It may be argued from the map that Cambridge is not central but peripheral to East Anglia. It amused me to learn while working in Suffolk that, to Suffolk people, if Cambridge existed at all, it was the back door to East Anglia. So be it, but Cambridge was a relatively large town, a county head-quarters, and on a par with Norwich in Norfolk, Ipswich in Suffolk and Chelmsford in Essex. With the possible exception of Colchester, the only other largish towns were Kings

Lynn, Yarmouth and Lowestoft which were as peripheral to their counties as is Cambridge to East Anglia. The relative size of the coastal towns – including Ipswich which was, and is, a port – illustrated the importance to East Anglia of coastal traffic. The map in **Fig. 4** is redrawn and cropped from a more comprehensive early nineteenth century map and shows, as railway promoters believed, that the position of Cambridge offered a potential route northwards,

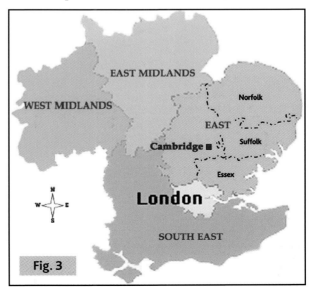

Fig. 3

south westwards towards London and east into East Anglia.

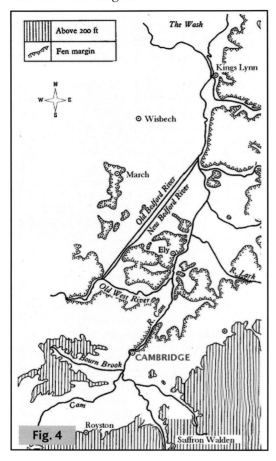

Fig. 4: Map showing River Cam plus tributaries and River Ouse illustrating Cambridge as a geographically favoured route centre.

The railway promoters knew that it was goods traffic which was likely to generate the most income to a developing railway, although marketing wisdom suggested that investors, tempted to support the railway by buying shares, would be more likely to favour swift personal transport. The alternatives were passenger boats on the rivers – slow, cold and meandering; or stage coaches – faster but often uncomfortable on poorly maintained roads.

The northerly route, perhaps via Ely, March and Wisbech to Kings Lynn, offered access to the rich agricultural products from the Fens. More importantly, as railways developed, much-needed industrial raw materials and coal could be brought into the eastern counties which was entirely lacking in them. Coal as a fuel for industry and for heating buildings could come from the Midlands and Yorkshire coal fields in railway wagons which, railway promoters suggested, could return with loads of East Anglian agricultural products.

The eastern routes to Norfolk, Suffolk and Essex could carry grain, potatoes, other vegetables and, from the coastal ports, fish.

Routes to London were obvious choices for many railway companies by the beginning of the Railway Age in the early nineteenth century. The city had been a hub since Roman times from AD 42 and in the next two centuries many of the major trunk roads were built out from London. By the nineteenth century, London was the capital of the British Empire and its population was over 6 million. The city was a government and administration hub and was leading the world as a diplomatic, commercial and financial centre. The early railways needed London support, money and parliamentary approval for their proposals. A problem, however, was finding sites for large terminal stations in London and the operating facilities required there.

This problem in London also faced the railways aiming for Cambridge and its industrial satellites. Many of these industrial villages have a tradition that goes back at least to the nineteenth century. Railway development could, and did, help many of these villages and industries. Histon's fruit preserves and jams (Chivers, then Cadbury Schweppes, then Premier Foods); Harston's chemicals (several companies); Sawston's paper-making (was Spicers) and tanning are examples of long-established industries. March had railway marshalling yards in the nineteenth century and Haverhill had a specialist textile industry (Gurteen & Sons) and now scientific instruments. Commuting is not itself an industry but, with the development of railway services and then the almost universal ownership

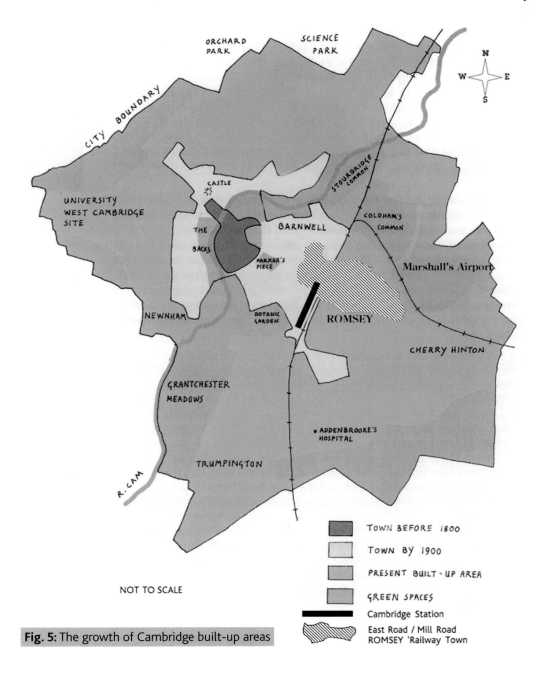

Fig. 5: The growth of Cambridge built-up areas

NOT TO SCALE

TOWN BEFORE 1800

TOWN BY 1900

PRESENT BUILT-UP AREA

GREEN SPACES

Cambridge Station

East Road / Mill Road
ROMSEY 'Railway Town'

of cars, people began to travel to work. Commuting has made many villages into urban communities and Cambridge has grown to employ many such commuters.

Cambridge has become the centre of a region around it, especially to west and south. The city is easily accessible from all the towns and villages of this region and lies beside roads linking Norwich to London and Ipswich to the Midlands so it is a transport hub and the railway network, though now less comprehensive than it was, began to provide fast services for passengers – commuters today – parcels and goods.

Cambridge Station opened on 29 July 1845 for train services from Bishopsgate station in London via Stratford and Bishop's Stortford. Lack of available building land in London and in Cambridge meant that Bishopsgate and Cambridge stations were not very convenient for passengers. Bishopsgate survived as a passenger station until 1875 then became a freight terminal. It was succeeded by Liverpool Street Station but in Cambridge the station remained on its original site and is still there today.

The arrival of a railway changed the shape of the town plan, originally growing along the roads and the River Cam. After 1845, the town extended along a different line, to and along the railway. The University was a powerful and rich player in facilitating changes to the town. For instance, the University bought forty acres of flat but poorly drained land south of Bateman Street for a Botanic Garden. The garden was created in 1831 by Professor John Stevens Henslow, a graduate of St John's College, Charles Darwin's mentor, and Professor of Botany, and was opened to the public in 1846. This development ensured that a more central site than the present Station was not available for railway development.

The railway companies intending to build to and through Cambridge were seeking land for a station. They wanted:

▸ access to the centre of the town which may be thought of as the Market Place.

▸ spaces open for development – such as Romsey Town and the villas along Station Road.

▸ an absence of existing buildings.

▸ dry, firm foundations for permanent way; and space for Cambridge Station buildings, and the other facilities a working railway needed such as goods yards, sidings, locomotive stabling and general maintenance for machinery and Way & Works.

At first, they sought in vain. In low-lying Cambridge, central land relatively near the river Cam was either already owned and built over by the town and the University or was too soggy for railway development. An additional problem in the existing built-up areas was that home-owners did not favour noisy, dirty and unattractive railways near their homes. To gain support the railway promoters promised a great increase in prosperity for Cambridge but the water-men feared that the railways would kill their trade on the Cam. Railway supporters suggested that the railway would feed the Cam and the Cam the railway but the water-men were right and trade deserted their river. In the Census Report of 1861 a footnote states that in St. Michael's parish '… many families have left as the Eastern Counties Railway is absorbing the trade of the Cam'. St. Michael's Parish was very central, extensive, and is now best distinguished by Great St Mary's Church beside the Market Place and the University's Senate House. Ideal in the railway promoter's minds for a station but quite unattainable.

Fig. 11 on page 27 shows the seventeen sites for a Cambridge station which no less than sixteen railway proposals suggested. None proved practicable or attainable. The site eventually agreed seemed to many railway supporters to be in the depths of the country. It was on agricultural land purchased from Jesus College, about one mile to the south and east of the Market Place but very soon the town reached the railway (**Fig. 5**). Building proceeded apace at first on the western side of the railway station towards the town centre: Mill Road, and East Road at right angles to it, were soon lined with houses and a maze of little streets between Hills Road and Newmarket Road was laid out. Soon, building crossed the railway, at first via a level crossing on Mill Road, so Romsey Town grew up between the tracks and Coldham's Brook to the east of the railway. Alongside the railway, industrial firms were attracted by the prospect of cheap land, cheap transport and some raw materials like chalk and clay for cement and tile works.

There was a rapid expansion of poorly-built houses east of the railway and of industries helped by railway links. After the First World War, road links and air transport developed.

To the west of the town, expansion was slower and building more open but, once College Fellows were allowed to marry and still retain their Fellowships, family houses were needed by them as well as rooms in colleges.

New streets often had small corner shops, and village stores became more important, but most Cambridge folk still came into the centre for shopping. Congestion there increased and the weekly markets, in front of the Guildhall in the Market Place, prospered. The town grew and the University expanded but the most fundamental changes to Cambridge – and to settlements throughout the UK – were not brought about by the railway

but the development of motor transport. The railway provided fast land transport for bulky goods for the first time and offered passenger travel. But it was a linear development, whereas a car-owning population needed a dense network of roads in an aereal development. The Cambridge built-up area expanded and the surrounding villages, like Girton, Newnham, Trumpington, Barnwell, Shelford, Cherry Hinton and Fulbourn became subsumed in the growing greater Cambridge.

London, too, became more accessible, by car for people, by lorry for cargoes of all sorts and in both cases without the potential inconveniences of the railway timetable or of double-handling for cargoes to specific road-accessible destinations. Cambridge could develop as an entrepôt and the railway at Cambridge Station played a part in this development but was increasingly facing competition for the swiftest, cheapest and most convenient method of travelling. Railway branches were built in the nineteenth century to connect some of the villages listed above so there were stations at Barnwell, Cherry Hinton, Fulbourn and Shelford to carry passengers, and goods, to and from Cambridge centre but – as the railway promoters had feared – Cambridge Station was at least one mile from the town centre.

In the town itself, public transport came to play an important part in linking the railway station to the town centre and elsewhere via the bus station which developed at Drummer Street near the centre of Cambridge. Horse-drawn, then electric, trams and soon motor-buses offered an alternative to the mile-long walk from Cambridge Station (see **Fig. 2**, page 8) to the centre of town and bicycles soon became a popular means of travelling about the town.

Chapter 2

EASTERN COUNTIES
RAILWAY COMPANY

Several railway companies were interested in reaching Cambridge and beyond – eastward and north-eastward into East Anglia for rich agricultural products; north and north-westward, especially for coal; and south-westward to London. Several detailed studies have explored and explained the history of railway promoters who included Cambridge in their prospectus and they are listed in the bibliography.

Some early prospective Cambridge-bound railways included: in 1821 – An Engine Railroad from Bishop's Stortford to Clayhithe Sluice; in 1827 – Northern Railroad Company from London Bridge to Cambridge and Cromford (High Peak, Derbyshire); in1834 – Grand North Eastern Railway from the City of London to the Town of Cambridge and to York; in 1836 – Great Northern Railway from London via Dunmow to Saffron Walden, Cambridge and York.

Significantly, these proposals were all London-based but ignored the potential wealth of East Anglia and were aiming for the north. Two specifically named York as a destination because York was, and is, an important north eastern hub for roads,

railways, businesses, the army and the Church.

An early railway company whose name did advertise its interest in East Anglia was the Eastern Counties Railway (ECR), incorporated on 4 July 1836. On the same date, the Northern & Eastern Railway (NER) was given Parliamentary authority for a fifty-three mile railway from the inner London borough of Islington to Cambridge. A subsequent lease to the ECR took these con-joined companies to Cambridge and Brandon in Norfolk. Cambridge Station was opened and train services began on 29 July 1845.

In 1851 the ECR published *The Eastern Counties Railway Illustrated Guide*. It explained to shareholders, and any other interested readers, the railway system the ECR now managed and its raison d' être. I quote some examples of the Company's florid prose.

The market for passenger traffic and the attraction of Cambridge as a seat of learning:

'Among the numerous causes which have, of late years, given such an impetus to the trade, commerce and still increasing prosperity of Great Britain, few have contributed more largely than the invention and construction of Railroads. By the heretofore unprecedented facilities they offer to locomotion, they have induced nearly all classes to travel, and have thus, through the increased opportunities afforded of acquiring information, the more general dissemination of knowledge, and the improved tone and expansiveness of thought so produced, been obviously one of the principal means of gaining for England her proud pre-eminence as possessing probably the most intelligent population in the world.'

The geographical attractions of the Cambridge route and of railway development in East Anglia:

'Upon glancing over the map of England, it will be immediately perceived that the country naturally divides itself into 3 distinct and characteristic provinces.

'From west to east they are [i] the mountainous, [ii] the hilly, and [iii] the flat.

'The flat, [iii] or eastern portion, has neither mountains nor hills, and even its trifling elevations sink at length into the immense marshes [the Fens] . . . This district is inhabited solely by an agricultural population.

'... the level nature of this flat district offered the greatest facilities for the construction of railways so, as early as 1836, Acts of Parliament were obtained for the formation of 2 distinct lines; one, in a northerly direction, towards Cambridge, called the Northern and Eastern; and the other, easterly, towards Colchester, called the Eastern Counties.'

The traffic which the railway generates:

'Passengers: 1,734,390 persons were carried in the 6 months ending January 4th 1851 over the 326 miles of Railway which the Company possesses. The classification and revenue arising from this 1¾ million passengers were as follows –

Fig. 6	Number	£	s	d
1st Class passengers	226,714	63,386	09	05
2nd Class passengers	801,541	83,733	19	01
3rd Class passengers	706,135	54,360	10	08

'Goods: In Cambridgeshire alone . . . the soil is exceedingly diversified – a strong black earth in the Fen districts and on the uplands gravel, loam, or clay [which] produces excellent wheat, yielding … 24 bushels per acre and on the Fen lands … 40 bushels per acre.

'[Elsewhere] … the dairy is the most important object of attention. Cottenham [parish] … feeds upwards of 1,800 cows … Willingham 1,200 … and Ely [is celebrated] for its garden vegetables.

'Considerable quantities of cattle and sheep are annually sent to the London market … as are also vast numbers of wild-fowl … thus furnishing the Metropolis with an article considered very luxurious.'

The ECR had already leased the NER and extended it to Cambridge. They took over the Norfolk Railway (NR); absorbed the East Anglian Railway (EAR) from 1 January 1852; assumed the working of the Eastern Union (EUR); and absorbed the Newmarket and Great Chesterford Railway (N&GCR), with its branch to Cambridge.

By 1856, ECR controlled 6,172 miles of track and by 1860 700¾ miles but it was not a financially stable or an efficient railway company. The complex railway politics which had brought about the successive amalgamations listed above had not yet brought about holistic management.

The Life & Times of the Great Eastern Railway 1839 – 1922 by Harry Paar and Adrian Gray, published in 1991 by Castelemead and now out of print, illustrates the sort of micro-management which often wasted the time of the ECR Board. For instance, meeting in July 1859, the Traffic & Permanent Way Committee debated the number of rats killed at various stations in June. Kennett on the Bury St Edmunds and Ipswich line recorded 150 deaths so at least the Company was taking care of their 'excellent wheat' traffic as some passed through Kennett Station.

The same ECR Chairman, Horatio Love, who was concerned about rat infestations, remained Chairman when the ECR and its constituent companies morphed into the Great Eastern Railway Company (GER) under the powers of the Great Eastern Railway Act 1862. The new company's system of just over 1,000 track-miles extended from London Liverpool Street Station through the north-eastern suburbs of London to East Anglia (see **Fig. 14**, page 31).

Before leaving the ECR and moving on to Cambridge Station in Chapter 3 and the Great Eastern Railway in Chapter 4, it is pertinent to the holistic story of Cambridge Station to look more closely at the railway company that placed Cambridge on the railway map. The ECR's principal offices were at Bishopsgate Station in London. Cambridge, as Chapter 1 has demonstrated, is on the western edge of the Eastern Counties. The ECR Board looked north eastward to towns like Wisbech and Kings Lynn and then further east to Norwich, Great Yarmouth, Ipswich and Harwich and anticipated growing revenues from passenger and goods traffic to and from these centres. However, it soon became apparent to potential customers and to ECR Shareholders that the Company was not living up to the promises of *The Eastern Counties Railway Illustrated Guide*.

When considering the early development of the ECR the *Railway Times* in 1838 explored the problem:

'There is this important peculiarity, too, in the Eastern Counties' line, that it does not, like many others, depend for success solely, or even principally, on the traffic that may be carried on between the places at the extremities of the line, London and Norwich and Yarmouth [but] there are limits to the increase from one town, but none whatever to the increase from an extensive tract of country, standing in need of nothing but the means of ready communication with the Metropolis to expand its energies.

'A moderate rise in twenty tributary streams will swell the main channel, into which they flow, into a deep and wide-spreading river.'

The ECR Board's management of their Railway was criticised and attacked by Shareholders and businesses in their area and in print in 1860 in an anonymous pamphlet, *The Eastern Counties Railway – Why Does it Not Pay?* published by Bailey Brothers in the 1860s. It is possible to find the text of this interesting book to read, free, online or there are modestly priced print-on-demand copies available from several major book suppliers. The book seems to be well-researched so I have drawn on it extensively in this chapter. Perhaps the author was a disappointed shareholder whose dividend never matched the company's promises or his expectations. Whoever he was, he wrote well and used publicly available data to answer the question his pamphlet poses. He claims that:

'ECR does not pay BECAUSE WE HAVE NEVER GOT THE TRAFFIC.

This, Proprietors, is the real secret of the Eastern Counties Railway: Your line does not pay because you have never yet secured a full proportion of the trade of your own district.'

The pamphlet extends to over 100 A4-sized pages of print and argues its case well. Cambridge, fortunately for this book, is considered to be well-placed:

'Cambridge is sufficiently near to Ely to be described as at the centre of our system. It is the object, of course, of every Railway Company to convey to and from the centre of its system to the points which are at the furthest extremities thereof. Our extremities may be described as Yarmouth, Peterborough, and London.'

In subsequent chapters I shall illustrate the traffic centrality of Cambridge Station and its function as an entrepôt. Alas, however, our disgruntled shareholder writing in 1859 was not satisfied with passenger services between Cambridge and London:

The Table in **Fig. 7**, with details supplied by the disgruntled shareholder, shows how Cambridge was served –

'Excluding the Parliamentary, Stopping, and Night Mail trains Cambridge is thus served by 4 trains yet is only 57½ miles from London.

'This is better than the Norwich services, but the distance is much shorter.

'What is the inducement to travel on our Line? We neither accommodate the public in regard to trains, or times, or rates of speed, or fares. Our tables seem devised to keep people off the line …

'Instead of offering the smallest inducement to the public to travel, we seem to keep them at bay, as if we were not dependent upon the public for our profits. Clearly, if we do not cultivate our traffic, we cannot expect our Line to pay …'

Unfortunately, we learn from this extensive diatribe, goods traffic is no better:

'I desire to consider the position of our Goods Traffic.

'Now the three great counties of the East of England, and indeed all the counties from which we derive any profits whatsoever, are essentially agricultural. We have no coal pits, no iron works, no manufactories of great importance in the Eastern Counties.

'[Goods Traffic figures show that] the ECR will be found to include in the goods traffic of the Line [up to] 200,000 tons, or only 20% of the 1,000,000 tons cereals produced annually within its district, and of which all but a very limited proportion is sent for consumption to different parts of the United Kingdom.

'If this is so; if we only carry 20% of the staple commodity of the district through which we have an entire monopoly of railway traffic, what becomes of the 80% which we do not carry ?'

The answer, we are told, is that the grain is carried by sea so water-borne

Fig. 7	MORNING – AM			AFTERNOON – AM			
Departure from London	06.27am	08.00am	10.57am	02.30pm	04.05pm	05.00pm	08.40pm
Arrival at Cambridge	10.10am	10.05am	01.20pm	05.40pm	07.00pm	06.55pm	11.25pm
Class	*Parly*	*1st & 2nd*	*Mail*	*1st & 2nd*	*Stopping*	*Express*	*Night Mail*
Journey time	3hr 43 min	2hr 05 min	2hr 23 min	3hr 10 min	3hr 55 min	1hr 55 min	2hr 45 min

competition is one reason why the ECR 'does not pay'.

'On the river Stort I am credibly informed that they send to London no less than 260,000 sacks of corn and 9,000 sacks of flour annually, bringing back 24,000 sacks of other corn and 10,000 tons of coals, besides other loading.

'Our Line runs from the Thames along the very banks of the River Stort. The trade, therefore, of this river, which we ought to command and make tributary to us throughout its course, exceeds 18,000 tons annually to London, and 13,000 tons from London; total, 31,000 tons which, at 2s. 6d. a ton, would pay us £4,000 per annum. 'The tolls from the traffic of the river Stort amount now to £2,000 per year and you are aware that 'tolls' do not include rates for carriage, or various other profits which a Railway Company derives from traffic.

The disgruntled Shareholder then illustrates the volume of fish traffic which travels by fast clipper cutters from the fishing smacks which catch the fish off Yarmouth and Lowestoft direct up the Thames to Billingsgate Market.

Fortunately, the Great Eastern Railway, and subsequently LNER and BR, recovered and expanded upon much of this 'lost' traffic including the fish from East Coast ports but that was still a little while away.

Some quotations from Great Eastern Railway Society Journal Special No 5: *Eastern Counties Railway 150th Anniversary*. Summer 1989, take the points further as Alan Wright, author of the *GERS Journal Special* poses similar questions to our disgruntled shareholder: why the Eastern Counties Railway? Was the ECR a railway which should never have been built? Was the ECR ever economic to run and why did it ever get built? What could the promoters of the railway have hoped to gain? Alan answers them in a more measured and, usefully for this book, a more analytical and contemporary twentieth century spirit.

Alan explains that the ECR was not a 'bubble' company; the 1834 Prospectus contained a list of towns which would be passed through by the proposed line or be near to the proposed line and within an available distance of the line. The Prospectus also contained a table showing the populations of the places and districts through which the ECR would pass in Essex, Suffolk and Norfolk. It is clear from this that only twenty per cent of the population of these counties – which effectively, with the omission of Cambridgeshire, constituted 'East Anglia' or the 'Eastern Counties' – lived in towns through which the railway was to pass and less than ten per cent lived in places near to the proposed railway. Of the towns directly served by the line, Norwich represented nearly forty per cent of the total population.

The fare was to be 2d per mile, making the fare for a return journey from Norwich to London about £1.15s.0d (about £90.00 today). At that time an average farm labourer's wage was equivalent to 1d to 12d per week and the majority living in East Anglia then were on labourer's wages or even a charge on the parish. Although a justification for the railway was said to be its passenger-carrying capacity, any investor analysing the potential as set out in the Prospectus would have had reason to question this.

The 1834 Prospectus then developed the commercial potential:

'Wherever railways abound most, there the greatest rise in the value of land has been observed and the most rapid strides have been made in agriculture, manufacturing and commercial property.'

Proof of this statement was given by reference to the development of the trade in the industrial north. The Prospectus made much of the potential for movement of agricultural produce but, yet again, the ECR gave the prospective investor cause to reconsider with the statement 'the large manufacturing town of Norwich has not, during the last 134 years, so much as doubled itself, while the population of Lancashire has been multiplied during the same period 9-fold.'

Nonetheless, the Prospectus must obviously have encouraged a number into investing in the ECR. Some undoubtedly were attracted by the promise of a 'dividend of upwards of 18%' and hints of even more within the text of the Prospectus.

Interestingly, investment was not forthcoming from those living in East Anglia and who could be considered to perhaps best know the new railway's potential. By September 1836 'little more than one 1/12th' of the issued shares had been taken up locally, in spite of considerable effort by the Chairman and Directors in 1835 to encourage local support by meetings held in important towns along the proposed route. The real investment was from northern industrial areas where merchants had already successfully invested in railways; 'upwards of one third' of the ECR funding was to come from such sources.

Much of the above comment is based on the 1834 Prospectus which has to be regarded as setting out what the ECR may have been. The final ECR was an amalgamation of other lines and had a wider coverage and longer track mileage than ever envisaged. Generally, the ECR seems to have been a railway which was operated as a hobby by a collection of gentlemen and run by the senior officers for their own various benefits. It undoubtedly had potential but this was never developed. It was held back by petty rivalries and jealousies between it and other companies operating in East Anglia and outside. Railway politics were allowed to influence too many decisions. In truth, because of the size of the population and the lack of any heavy industry, there was a limited market for a railway in East Anglia.

Nonetheless, there was a need and the building of a line was justified. What was wanted, but was not provided, was a modest and efficiently run operation which would attract custom. This also needed good marketing back-up to capture the trade which went by sea and road. But this did not happen because either the directors did not understand the need, or the officers did not see a need or were possibly only interested in areas for their own benefit.

Chapter 3

29 JULY 1845: CAMBRIDGE STATION TRAIN SERVICES BEGIN

The Eastern Counties Railway – with the North Eastern Railway – had parliamentary authority to build a railway to Cambridge, and beyond into Norfolk. However, an early problem in Cambridge was finding a site for the new station. The ECR Board were anxious that it should be as central as possible. The town had grown around a central market place and the University owned a great deal of land in and immediately around the town so a central station site might be difficult to secure. **Fig. 5**, at the end of Chapter 1 illustrates the lop-sided development of the built-up areas in Cambridge. University expansion, the coming of the railway and the growth of industry changed the shape of the town.

The ECR, seeking a Cambridge station site, were faced with a town that by 1845 lay almost wholly to the west of the railway, so the prospect of a really central station site was remote. It has often been stated that the University was opposed to railway development. I do not believe that it was, *per se*, opposed to the railway development but it was an influential and powerful body in the town and in the country. Its power enabled the insertion of some restrictive clauses in several local

Railway Acts which are frequently quoted as examples of university opposition. There is, however, little evidence that many of the clauses were enforced and some may be seen as contemporaneous concern for undergraduate morals and Sunday observance.

Indeed, Jesus College archives reveal a reason why a college, if not the university, might welcome ECR's need to purchase land for a station site and a wayleave for the railway to continue northwards and eastwards. Jesus College owned much of the land east of the present railway including an area called Radegund Manor in the vicinity of what became Romsey on the **Fig. 5** map .

The College website – www.jesus.cam. ac.uk/about-jesus-college/old-library-archives - includes some history drawn from the College archives so we learn that a nineteenth century Master, Dr William French, negotiated the sale of part of the Radegund Manor field land to ECR in1846. Dr French was anxious to have the station where it is because the sale afforded an opportunity to develop college land still in agricultural use. A condition of the sale of the station site was the construction of Station Road and the opening up of new housing sites on the

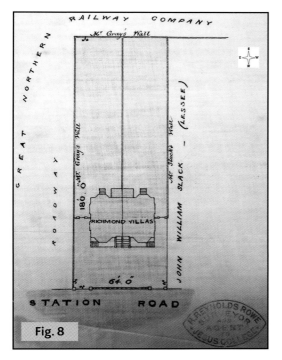

Fig. 8

to both the GER and the GNR. The total sales proceeds were £18,903 17s 6d, or just under £25m in 2017 money, so Dr French had secured a very good deal for his College.

Fig. 8 is from Jesus College Archives and illustrates the type of substantial villas which, from Dr. French's time onward were to line Station Road. **Fig. 9** is from the Plan which accompanies the Agreement in the Archives which Dr. French signed on behalf of Jesus College. I have added two explanatory notes in green.

The new station building, perhaps to ensure that it was architecturally appropriate to Dr French's proposed developments, was an impressive building and the *Illustrated London News* of the time praised it: 'The general effect is exceedingly chaste and appropriate.' The building is described in Gordon Biddle's *Britain's Historic Railway Buildings – An Oxford Gazetteer of Structures and Sites* OUP 2003. The book is recognised as a magesterial record, Pevsner-like in its

road frontage. After Dr French's death in 1849, building leases were granted in Station Road and Hills Road. There were further sales in the 1850s and the 1870s

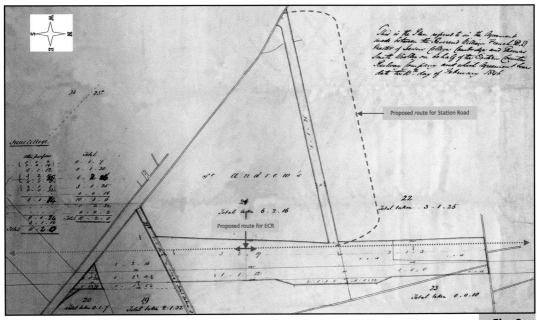

Fig. 9

comprehensive scholarship, and saying this about Cambridge station:

'Although the design of Cambridge Station is attributed to Francis Thompson, Sancton Wood and Henry Hunt also played a part. The precise extent of their contributions has not been fully established.

'The building is in buff brick with stone dressings and the frontage comprises an elegant colonnade of 15 Romanesque arches, like an Italian loggia, on square columns with plain capitals beneath an ornamental frieze and a deep dentilled cornice. Originally pantiles on the shallow-pitched roof peeped over the edge. The arch spandrels contain roundels bearing the arms of the University and its colleges, seemingly in random order.

'The design was continued around each end of the building, where road vehicles could enter and leave the colonnade by a broad, matching arch, and pedestrians by a narrower one alongside. The back, [the track side], incorporated a long, narrow train-shed under the same roof, covering the single track and narrow platform which

extended out at each end through similar pairs of arches. There was no colonnade, however; the rear elevation comprised a plain brick wall relieved by blind arcading and doorways, matching the front only in number.'

Fig. 10, from the *Illustrated London News* 2 August 1845, page 73, shows the trackside of the station and includes an Up train. Unfortunately, the artist, perhaps anxious to illustrate a train as well as the new station building, places the train on a through road and incorrectly shows the up end water crane off the platform and where the platform track should be, passing through the narrow train shed arch which Biddle describes. Potential passengers appear to be marooned on a platform some distance from their train.

Illustrated London News illustrations may be valuable as a source of reference but they need to be examined carefully because the artist may, as in this case, be knowledgeable about buildings but less so about the technology of railways. For instance, an *Illustrated London News* artist's view of an ECR train in the Lea Valley in 1830, drawn before the railway opened, shows a train carrying some

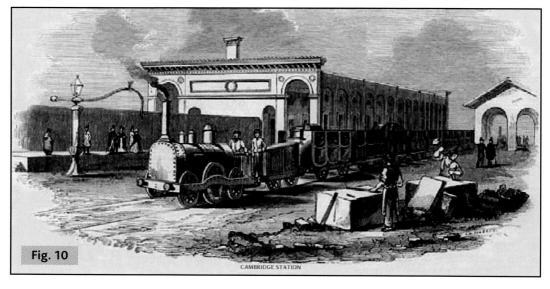

Fig. 10

CAMBRIDGE STATION

passengers. It is hauled by an 0–4–0 tender locomotive, with an open footplate like the train at Cambridge Station, but with no crew. Doubtless the disgruntled shareholder from Chapter 2 would have been concerned to learn of ECR driverless trains.

The disgruntled shareholder does not comment on the architectural splendour of Cambridge Station but he probably knew, and we know with historical hindsight today, that the ECR estimates of anticipated building costs were wildly ambitious. A proposed main line of 126 miles from London to Norwich and on to Yarmouth was estimated to cost £1.6m, but by 1845 that main line had only reached Colchester (52 miles) at a cost of £3m. Another main line had reached Cambridge, and beyond into Norfolk by 1845 but by negotiated arrangements and leases between ECR, the NER, and Norwich & Brandon Railway line.

The cost of Cambridge Station had to include the site purchase from Jesus College as well as architectural fees and building costs for passenger access and facilities; goods facilities and a Motive Power Depot plus associated engineering and maintenance requirements. I have not discovered a detailed breakdown of these costs but even the disgruntled shareholder admitted that Cambridge 'is sufficiently near to Ely to be described as at the centre of our system'. And Cambridge Station has survived on its original site and with its colonnaded facade to attract intending passengers; today it is a Grade II Listed building and handles over 10 million passengers each year.

If Cambridge was the centre of ECR operations it was also a town to which other railway companies were drawn but often discouraged because central station sites were not available. A brief listing of

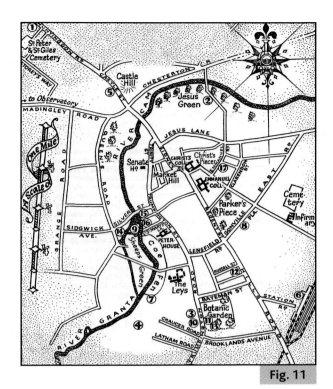

Fig. 11

other sites proposed for railway stations in Cambridge illustrates the interest, and the problem.

The numbers listed below are on the map, **Fig. 11**, slightly adapted from the Oleander Press 1976 reprint of *Railways to Cambridge: actual and proposed*. Canon Reginald D Fellows. Oakwood Press, 1948:

01 1834 Grand Northern & Eastern Railway

02 1836 Great Northern Railway

03 1836 Cambridge & Bury St Edmunds Railway

04 1836 Northern & Eastern Railway
    1836 Great Eastern & Western Junction Railway
    1841 East Anglian Railway
    1843 Thetford & Cambridge Railway

05 1841 Great Northern Railway (revised plans)

06 1844 Eastern Counties Railway – Cambridge Station opened in 1845

07 1844 Cambridge & Lincoln Railway

08 1846 additional station proposed by Mayor's Committee

09 Eastern Counties Railway (proposed additional station)

10 1846 Cambridge & Oxford Railway

11 1847 Royston & Hitchin Railway

12 1848 Royston & Hitchin Railway

13 1850 Cambridge & Shepreth Junction Railway

14 1848 Cambridge & Oxford Railway

15 1851 Royston & Hitchin Railway

16 1846 Cambridge & Oxford Railway

17 1864 Great Northern Railway

Fortunately for Cambridge, and because of the influence of the University and the City Councillors, only one of these proposed stations was built. As subsequent chapters illustrate, Cambridge Station was shared relatively amicably by other railway companies who were interested in the traffic they might generate with a line to – or running powers to – Cambridge Station.

The coming of the railway developed the town plan (**Fig. 5**, page 15) but the new 'Railway Town' buildings were less architecturally handsome than the station building, many University buildings and much of the post-Medieval town.

Originally Cambridge grew around the River Cam bridging-point, onto the slightly higher land north and west of the river and along the river itself – the 'Backs' of many of the Colleges. The river was an important route to and from Kings Lynn.

In the Census Report of

1861 a footnote states that in St Michael's parish 'many families have left as the Eastern Counties Railway is absorbing the trade of the Cam.' The decline of population in the riverside parishes of the old town was, however, more than balanced by the rise in new areas to the west of the railway. The town plan shows some of the early development in yellow and names and shades the Romsey area. This and along Mill Road, west and east of the Station, was where many of the early and numerous staff required for the developing Railway lived. Much of this eastern area was ready for rebuilding in the 1960s. The original 'railway' houses were run up as quickly and as cheaply as possible. They were not built to last and they have proved to be weak structures rapidly outmoded. In some parts reconstruction on modern lines has begun but progress has been slow.

Nevertheless there is a lot of Mill Road community interest in their houses and the railway history which explains them. *Poem for Railway House* by Dean Parkin, is from a poet supporting the HLF-grant-aided Mill Road History Project in 1965:

'Engine cleaner, Railway Servant, Shunter, Railway Porter,

Platelayer, Bricklayer, Signalman, Engine Fitter's Foreman,

Fig. 12

All lived here … (**Fig. 12**)'

And they all worked on the Railway and lived in houses like the row of 'Railway Cottages' adjoining Mill Road bridge. Originally Mill Road crossed the railway on a level crossing but the quality of these houses, and the light they received, was much reduced when Mill Road Bridge and its sloping approaches were built in 1890.

Mill Road level crossing and bridge were, and are, at the 'country end' of Cambridge Station. A housing-style contrast at the London end of the station is in Station Road, the wide, spacious road which leads from Hills Road directly to the front facade of the station. A condition from Jesus College on the sale of the station site was the construction of Station Road and the opening up of new housing sites.

Superficially the houses in the architect's drawing (**Fig. 9**, page 25) and the **Fig. 13** picture seem similar but the Station Road houses in **Fig. 13**, taken in 2002, are three-storey buildings with their own access along the row, separated from the traffic on Station Road by a private roadway and a wall. By the date of the photograph, most of these Victorian town houses, with easy access to trains to London for business and pleasure, had been converted to offices, or sub-divided

Fig. 13

into apartments. Nonetheless, they are still elegant properties and the nearness to the Station may still be a business advantage for the offices.

Chapter 4

GER – GREAT EASTERN RAILWAY COMPANY

The Great Eastern Railway Company was incorporated by the Great Eastern Railway Act of 7 August 1862. The purpose of the Act was: 'To amalgamate the Eastern Counties, the East Anglian, the Newmarket & Chesterford, the Eastern Union and the Norfolk Railway Companies, and for other purposes.'

The ECR had previously leased and absorbed the constituent companies which morphed into the GER in 1862 but the ECR was never financially stable and lacked holistic management. The GER Act was an expression of Parliamentary good sense in bringing together in one company a diverse miscellany of management and operational practices. A letter to *The Times* in March 1851 epitomises a widely-publicised view of the ECR:

'… a living embodiment of folly, fraud, delusion, recklessness and suffering; its name is identified with chicanery, mismanagement and confusion [with] reckless disregard of the Sabbath [and] total indifference to the comfort, convenience or moral welfare of the poor as regards 3rd Class trains …'

As with media coverage today, there were half-truths here but, as the disgruntled shareholder in Chapter 2 stated, the ECR 'Did not Pay'. William Makepeace Thackery (1811-63), the Victorian novelist, is reported to have made the sardonic remark about the ECR, '… a journey on the Eastern Counties [Railway] must have an end at last.' The early railways were frequently criticised or ridiculed so the ECR was not alone. The *Spectator* journal, 12 October 1889, in reviewing *The Railways of England* (W N Acworth. John Murray, 1889) mentions the East Coast route to Scotland which excited even more ridicule than the ECR:

'A line of railway by the coast . . . seems almost ludicrous, and one cannot conceive for what other reason it can have been thought of except that passengers by the railway, if any, might have the amusement of looking at the steamers on the sea and reciprocally the passengers by sea might see the railway carriages.'

So as the successor company to the ECR the GER was unlikely to have an easy journey.

There were advantages for the new Company's and Fig.14 illustrates the geographical extent of the GER system. Over 1,000 track-miles extended from

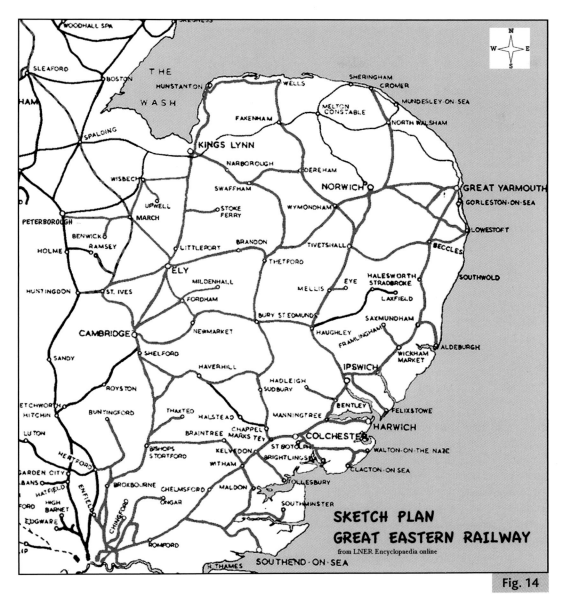

SKETCH PLAN
GREAT EASTERN RAILWAY
from LNER Encyclopaedia online

Fig. 14

London Liverpool Street Station through the north-eastern suburbs of London to East Anglia where the GER had an almost 100 per cent monopoly of rail transport provision The GER directors, like their predecessors on the ECR Board, had northerly and north-westerly ambitions. In time, liaisons with the GNR created a joint line to Doncaster, via Spalding, Lincoln and Gainsborough.

But there were disadvantages too. Much of the Works and Way which GER acquired and had to operate was cheaply built, especially a number of timber bridges, and had been lacking effective maintenance. Perhaps the company's near monopoly in East Anglia reflected the absence of a manufacturing or minerals base upon which to develop traffic. The GER served a predominantly rural area, with few large towns which had developed alternative means of transport, especially along the coast, because the ECR had failed to meet their needs.

It seemed unlikely that any new company could swiftly restore the damages done by the ECR and its successive Chairmen:

> 'Petition … complaining of the conduct of George Hudson, Esquire, a Member of the House, and Chairman of the Eastern Counties Railway Company, and praying for inquiry, and that he may be expelled from being a Member of the House.
>
> 'Petition of Proprietors of the Eastern Counties Railway, complaining of the conduct of George Hudson, Esquire, and David Waddington, Esquire, Members of the House, and Chairman and Deputy Chairman of the Board of Directors . . . and praying for inquiry.'
>
> *Hansard* 1849: HC Deb 17 May 1849 Vol. 105 cc 581-9

On 2 July 1867, the GER company was placed in receivership but, as sometimes happens, the right man became a champion of a beleaguered business. He was Samuel Laing MP (1812-97), graduate and Fellow of St. John's College Cambridge and former Finance Minister for India. He agreed to join the GER board of directors if his responsibility could principally be limited to financial business. He was elected to what at that time was called the Direction on 17 February 1867 so, with an Official Receiver in place by July, Laing's expertise was much needed.

The Direction called a meeting of all the preference shareholders and then made an application to Parliament in a Bill to raise £3m of additional debenture stock on terms which would give these shareholders significant control over the company's business. Both Houses passed the GER Bill and it received Royal Assent on 26 August 1867.

Slowly but surely, the additional shares were subscribed; the company had reached a turning-point in its history and began to prosper. It was never especially rich, for reasons already explained, but it gained a reputation for efficiency under a succession of able and well-connected Chairmen: Lord Cranbourne, the Most Honourable 2nd Marquess of Salisbury KG PC (1868-71); Lightly Simpson (1871-4) engineering graduate, Trinity College Cambridge; Charles H Parkes (1874-93); Lord Claud Hamilton (1893-1923).

On 1 Jan 1923, the GER became part of the London and North Eastern Railway Company so Claud Hamilton saw 'his' company into the Grouping of Railway Companies. He retired after the last meeting of the GER Board on 20 February 1923 and died in 1925 aged 82. He was the longest serving GER director – for all but ten years of the company's existence – and he had been Vice Chairman to Charles Parkes from 1874 until he succeeded to the Chairmanship in 1893.

Hamilton is known to many railway enthusiasts by the class of locomotives built for the GER which was named after him (**Fig. 15**). These locomotives were fine machines and liked by footplate crews but more significant to the prosperity of the GER were Hamilton's achievements in improving the Company's business and service. He oversaw the development of continental traffic, especially after the opening of Parkeston Quay at Harwich in 1882. Receipts rose from some £131,000 in 1881 to £269,000 in 1897. In 1898 GER obtained the contract for the carriage of Dutch mails. The opening of the Great Northern & Great Eastern Joint line from March to Doncaster in 1882 which enabled GER to begin carrying coal from Derbyshire and South Yorkshire to London was also during his tenure. The

Fig. 15: GER 'Claud Hamilton' D15 Class 4-4-0 1858 (re-numbered 8858 by LNER then 2549 in 1946) heading a London passenger train on Platform 1, Cambridge Station circa 1920.

improvement of hotel, restaurant and restaurant car services was a particular interest of Hamilton's as Chairman of the Hotels Committee for the whole of its forty-eight year existence. The principal change was the direct employment of catering staff, rather than sub-contracting. This improved the quality of service offered.

Bringing GER services 'in house' was typical of Hamilton's approach to staff management so GER staff trusted him to be just and fair in dealing with them even though he was antipathetic to trade unions. As a 'GER Signalman' wrote in a letter to *The Times* in 1907,. '… any complaint we might make … would …receive careful and courteous consideration .[and] his Lordship's refusal to grant recognition to the Societies [Trade Unions] is heartedly endorsed by a large number of railwaymen …'

My information on Lord Hamilton has been largely culled from an excellent article by Reg Davies in the GER Society Journal 2009: *Lord Claud John Hamilton 1843 – 1925: Soldier, Railway Chairman and Sportsman – A character sketch* and, in sincerely thanking Reg, I can do no better than to quote his concluding paragraph:

'Perhaps the last words are best left to the GER Magazine. Its first issue of 1911 profiled the Chairman and concluded he had 'a busy life … varied interests [and a] high sense of public service, combining … the best traditions of the old nobility with the energy and progress of the … business man.

To conclude this chapter I am indebted to the GER Society's Magazines and Journals, in particular C H Jeune's article *The Great Eastern Railway's Coat-of-Arms* published in the magazine in May 1911 and 'revived' in the Society's Journal 32. I have culled it considerably because the author has an expertise in heraldry which I lack but I commend the full article to interested readers.

The device used by the Great Eastern Company and illustrated in Fig.16 is not, strictly speaking, a coat of arms. The Great Central is the only pre-1923 Grouping railway company that can rightly boast of an escutcheon as it obtained a grant of armorial bearings on 25 February 1898. According to the conventions of English heraldry, the Great Eastern device – comprising, as it does, the arms of a number of corporations -- is unorthodox for, if a grant were made, such a combination could be recognised only by means of quarterings on a single shield. The design was not intended merely as a cognizance for the Company but as a compliment to the areas served by the Railway. Possibly to prevent jealousy, the various shields were used complete within a garter.

The device was designed by Mr Henry Parker of the GER Carriage Department in 1862. I have indicated arms of the County of Middlesex in Fig.16 with an orange arrow and the shields continue clockwise thus: the boroughs of Maldon and

The GER heraldic device.

Fig. 16

Ipswich; the city of Norwich; the boroughs of Cambridge, Hertford, Northampton; the device used by the town of Huntingdon, with the arms of the city of London in the centre.

The following are the heraldic descriptions of the shields on the Company's device:

'MIDDLESEX: *Gules, 3-seaxes barways proper, pommels and hilts to the dexter or*
'ESSEX is represented by the arms of the town of Maldon: *Party per pale azure and argent, on the dexter side 3 lions passant guardant in pale or, and on the sinister on waves of the sea in base proper a ship of 1 mast sable, the mast surmounted by a fleur de lis gold, and from the masthead a pennon flotant gules, the sail furled argent, and from a turret at the stern a flagstaff erect surmounted by a fleur de lis of the 6th, and there from a banner of the 1st charged with 3 lions passant guardant of the 3rd.*

'SUFFOLK is represented by the arms of the Borough of Ipswich: *Party per pale gules and azure, on the dexter side, a lion rampant guardant or, and on the sinister 3 demi-hulks of ships of the same conjoined to the empalement line*

The author of the article asks us to note that 'In Mr. Parker's original memorandum the lion is correctly shewn as guardant, that is the lion's head faces the viewer, but on his sketch, and on the Company's device at the present day, the lion's face is in profile.

'NORFOLK is represented by the city of Norwich: *Gules, castle domed argent, in base a lion passant guardant or*

It is a reflection of the original Eastern Counties which the ECR, and then the GER, served that Essex, Suffolk and Norfolk are listed in alphabetical order but are preceded by Middlesex wherein was a part of Liverpool Street Station and the GER principal offices. Once these counties have been complimented there is a curious omission of the counties of Cambridgeshire and Hertfordshire but Northamptonshire is 'in' though with a cautionary warning from the author:

'It must be admitted that the Company had not the same grounds for including the arms of Northampton as they had to include those of the other towns cited. The lines of the Great Eastern Company do not reach the town of Northampton, nor do they even enter the County of that name. Peterborough station, close to the borders of Northamptonshire, is in the County of Huntingdon.'

To resume the circling of the GER Company device:

'CAMBRIDGESHIRE, not named as a County but is represented by the arms of the town of Cambridge: *Gules, a bridge throughout fesseways, surmounted by 3 towers, in chief a fleur de lis or, between 2 roses argent, the base barry wavy argent and azure thereon 3 ships each with 1 mast and yardarm and sail furled sable.*'

'HERTFORDSHIRE, not named as a County, is represented by the arms of the town of Hertford: *Argent, a hart lodged on water proper.*'

'NORTHAMPTONSHIRE is represented by the arms of the town of Northampton: *Gules, on a mount vert a tower triple-towered in a pyramidical form argent, and supported by 2 lions rampant guardant or, in the portway of the tower a portcullis.*'

'HUNTINGDONSHIRE, not named as a County, is represented by a device commonly used by the town of Huntingdon: *A landscape with a tree in the centre, on the dexter side of which a bird is perched; on the sinister side is a huntsman blowing a horn, in his sinister hand a bow and arrow; on the dexter side a stag courant pursued by 2 hounds; all proper.*'

And in the centre, the coat of arms forming a hub of the company's design and the hub of the Nineteenth century world is the City of London wherein was the remainder of Liverpool Street Station:

'THE CITY OF LONDON: *Argent, a cross gules, in the 1st quarter, a sword in pale point upwards, of the last.*'

The red cross in the centre of the GER device represents St. George, the patron saint of England, and the sword is the emblem of St. Paul the Apostle, the patron saint of London,

Visitors to London today may see cast iron statues of heraldic beasts on metal or stone plinths that mark the boundaries of the City of London. An heraldic dragon holds a shield showing the cross of St George and the sword; on the dragon's back is a wing. This, plus the cross and

Fig. 17

is embossed or printed on certain of the Company's notepaper, is on the buttons of the staff uniforms and is used in connection with the steamboats and hotels, as well as on the tarpaulins of the Goods Department. **Fig. 17** is a typical example.

The Great Eastern Railway Company established a proud record, for punctuality, for installing mechanical lock-and-block signalling before any similar type of safety precaution on other railways, and was among the first Railway Company to abolish extra fares on express trains. Into BR days, Lord Claud Hamilton's name and reputation was remembered in the naming of a new District head-quarters office block in Station Road, Cambridge, as Hamilton House.

And BR adopted the slogan 'Progress – by Great Eastern' for the Great Eastern Line.

sword, were adopted by the ECR and was used by the GER.

This device, rudely referred to as the 'bat's wing' sometimes carries the sword but usually the cross. The device

Chapter 5

GER AND THE NEWMARKET RAILWAY COMPANY'S CAMBRIDGE BRANCH

The Newmarket and Chesterford Railway – later the Newmarket Railway – Company takes the Cambridge Station story back to the ECR days and illustrates the rivalries which existed between different Railway Companies trying to enhance their development prospects.

Fig. 18 illustrates the course of the original railway and the proposed extensions which will be explained later. The Prospectus of the Newmarket and Chesterford Railway with a branch to Cambridge appeared in *Herapath's Journal* on 4 and 11 October, 1845 by which date Cambridge Station was open and ECR train services were operating. Newmarket, only thirteen miles east of Cambridge, had no railway connection although the town was home to all the major British racing and training stables. There was constant inward/outward traffic in horses going to and coming from race meetings all over the country but until the railway came these transfers were slow and difficult.

By 1840, there were seven annual meetings in Newmarket on the town's two race courses: the Rowley Mile and the July Course. Race meetings attracted huge crowds, including many wealthy people and even more working-class visitors.

The dynamics of the 'Railway Mania' encouraged promoters to propose new schemes and Newmarket seemed to be a worthwhile goal.

By 31 October 1845, the project had received the support of the social and political influence of the ducal house of Rutland who owned the Cheveley Park Estate near Newmarket. Lord George Manners (then only 25 years of age), sometime MP for Cambridgeshire and son of the 5th Duke of Rutland, became Chairman of the Company's Committee of Management. Robert Stephenson directed the construction of the Railway.

John Villiers Shelley MP and member of the Jockey Club explained why the racing fraternity were keen to have a railway link with London:

> 'The Jockey Club felt that a railway to Newmarket would not only be a great convenience to parties anxious to participate in the truly British sport of racing but would enable Members of Parliament to superintend a race and run back to London in time for the same night's debate.'[1]

Inspired by such ideals, favoured by the local landowners, the company's Bill was unopposed and received the Royal

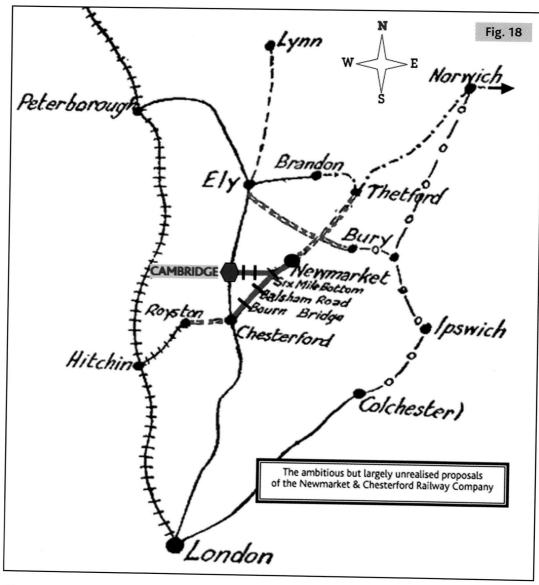

Fig. 18

The ambitious but largely unrealised proposals
of the Newmarket & Chesterford Railway Company

Newmarket Rly ···················· ▬▬▬	Eastern Union Rly ------- ------ --o—o—
ditto Proposed ------- --- ▬▬▬	East Anglian Rly ------------- _ _ _ _
Eastern Counties Rly ------------ ▬▬▬	Great Northern Rly ------------ +++++
Norfolk Rly - - - - - - - ▬·—·▬	

assent on 16 July 1846. Construction was
started immediately on the main line from
Chesterford to Newmarket and this line
opened to goods traffic on 3 January and
to passenger traffic on 4 April 1848.

Meanwhile, the Newmarket Railway
Directors were exploring substantial
expansions, not least because the main line
alone was unlikely to generate sufficient
traffic and income to sustain the Railway

and pay any dividends to shareholders. In June 1847, the railway obtained Acts to extend from Newmarket to Bury St Edmunds, with a branch to Ely and to make a line from Newmarket to Thetford (10 & 11 Vict. c. 12 and c. 20). Only the line to Bury St Edmunds was subsequently constructed as a separate undertaking and it was eventually taken over by the ECR. The Thetford extension, if constructed, would have provided a through route from London to Norwich, via Newmarket and connection with the Norfolk Railway which ran from Brandon to Norwich. The Norfolk Railway continued to Yarmouth so, in theory, the Newmarket Railway might have carried fish traffic to London.

However, hindsight – and to sustain a fish analogy – shows us that the Newmarket Railway was a tiddler negotiating with a pike. The ECR was already leasing the Norfolk Railway from May 1848 and was a very powerful company in East Anglia. The ECR also had an interest in taking over the Newmarket Railway to divert London-Newmarket and eastwards traffic via Cambridge.

The Newmarket Railway's 'main line' was generating so little income that the Committee of Management succumbed to the pike; the ECR took over control of the traffic from 2 October 1848 but even the pike was not sufficiently powerful to swim against the ECR shareholders tide. An agreement between the Newmarket Railway and the ECR had to be formalised at the next ECR Shareholders' General Meeting in February 1849. But the ECR Chairman, George Hudson (the so-called Railway King), did not attend the meeting. The meeting ejected him from the Chairmanship *in absentia* and refused to consider an agreement with the Newmarket Railway because it seemed that the line was very nearly bankrupt.

We know today that the ECR, in working the Newmarket Railway, had been starving and bleeding it. The ECR sought to charge 1s. 5d. a mile for locomotive power; (on the South Western Railway the charge was only 9d. and on the Brighton line 8½d). The ECR also charged the Newmarket Railway £600 a year for the management or rather – as the Chairman of the Newmarket Railway did not scruple to call it – the mismanagement of the line.

As a result, three months working to 4 January 1849, showed a gross profit to the Newmarket Company of only £704, out of which they had to pay bond interest of £2,000. The Newmarket Railway's financial problems were rendered all the more difficult because the ECR held on to even this small balance of £704 on the ground of alleged other claims. In addition, the Newmarket Company had to defray out of capital the cost of maintaining their permanent way and stations and owed their contractor, and many debenture holders, a considerable sum.

On 30 June 1850, the Newmarket Committee of Management closed their Railway to all traffic; the Cambridge branch was not complete and Newmarket was again without a railway connection. All the engines and rolling stock went to the ECR under what the Newmarket Directors called 'an equitable arrangement' but which looks uncommonly like a case of the ECR astutely taking the locomotives and rolling stock in part-settlement of a bad debt.

At this hopeless moment, a vigorous personality, Mr Cecil Fane, who held the office of a Commissioner in Bankruptcy, took control of the Newmarket Railway. Robert George Cecil Fane (1796-1864) was educated at Charterhouse and Oxford. He was called to the Bar at Lincoln's Inn in 1821 and in 1831 was appointed one of six Commissioners of Bankruptcy.

He had already been chairman of a

committee appointed on 22 March 1849, to investigate the work of the Newmarket Railway Company. His committee had urged the immediate pressing on with the Cambridge branch as the Newmarket Railway Company's one hope of salvation.

When however, at the Extraordinary Meeting of 27 July, 1850, the directors told the story of their defeatist policy of closing the line in the previous month, without even having called the shareholders together on the matter, Mr Commissioner Fane rose in his wrath and tore the Committee of Management to shreds. He showed that if running the line would probably entail a loss, keeping it shut would mean a larger loss. He criticised the mistake of making, as the pivot of the line, Chesterford, a small village, and not Cambridge, a large town, and robustly denounced the bungling of the various negotiations with the ECR and the Directors' tactless handling of Mr Jackson, the contractor and debenture holder.

So the shareholders, by a large majority, cast out Lord George Manners and his Committee of Management, and Mr Commissioner Fane with his chosen directors formed a board to reign in their stead. The result was magical. The line was re-opened from Chesterford to Newmarket on 9 September 1850, with rolling stock borrowed from the ECR

But better still, Fane made an arrangement with the ECR to accommodate, when opened, the Cambridge branch at Cambridge Station and so avoid the expense of a separate station and staff there. In addition, Mr Fane got Mr Jackson, the contractor, to agree to complete the line to Cambridge for a sum not exceeding £9,000, on being furnished with a certain quantity of rails and sleepers which, Fane stated, the Company would have at its disposal.

This last phrase covers an ingenious move by Mr Fane's. The original main line from Chesterford to Newmarket was laid as double track. A single line was ample for the traffic so Mr Fane had one set of rails and sleepers lifted from Chesterford to the junction with the Cambridge branch. This provided some eleven miles of rails and sleepers for the branch to Cambridge – and some £7,000 worth of rails in-hand for maintenance and replacements.

The urgent desire of the energetic Mr Fane to get the Cambridge branch open as soon as possible was met with annoying technical difficulties for the junction with ECR at Cambridge. In the parliamentary plans, the curve at the junction was shown with a radius of 20 chains but it was found necessary to create a deviation that altered the radius of the curve to 8 chains. For this, the consent of the Commissioners of Railways was required and was applied for in July 1851. However, the Company's compulsory powers of acquiring land had expired so the Commissioners refused to approve the deviation without the consents of the owners and occupiers of the land affected. Mr Fane believed it would save time to get the deviation approved first and then obtain the consents of the landowners. On 30th July 1851, Fane wrote to Captain Simmons, R.E., of the Railway Commissioners' Office, the following pathetic note:

'Wednesday 30th 4 before 10

'Dear Sir,

'As it will be impossible that the Company should make the curve without the consent of the owners of the land, no possible evil can arise from the Commissioners considering the curve first. If therefore, they could be induced to approve or disapprove the curve first, it would be the greatest possible convenience to me personally.

'Every day's delay is a question of £50 at least and the difficulty I have to deal with is enormous. The land I have to negotiate for is vested in 2 Trustees – one in Derbyshire and one in Yorkshire – in trust for a wife, nearly out of her mind, her 2 children, and afterwards for her husband, who will not see or speak to her.

'I am off for Lincoln this moment to see one of the Trustees; and to labour to get 5 or 6 consents to the sale. And then to get written consents to the curve again, would be more than one's life is worth.

'Pray help me, if you possibly can.

'Yours truly,
'C. Fane.'

But the Commissioners were not to be touched by any such human appeal; it was very much more important to them that the correct protocols of procedure should be preserved so they rendered the following reply:

'Office of Commissioners of Railways
Whitehall
August 1st 1851

'Sir,

'I have been directed by the Commissioners of Railways to acknowledge the receipt of your letter of 30th ultimo and to inform you that they cannot enter into a consideration of the propriety of sanctioning the proposed deviations in the curve therein alluded to until they are satisfied that the consents required, before their authority can be given, have been obtained.

'I have, etc.,

'Douglas Calton,
'Assistant Secretary
To: C. Fane, Esq.'

Mr Commissioner Fane, however, was not to be out-done by red tape of the finest quality. He even succeeded in infusing some of his abounding energy into a Civil Service Department. On 7 October 1851, he got the Commissioners of Railways' approval of the new 8 chains radius curve and approval of the line by the Inspecting Engineer – the fencing and the Cambridge Station junction having been completed. On 8 October 1851, he obtained the formal consent to the line being opened for the purposes of public traffic.

The line was opened from Cambridge Station to Six Mile Bottom, and thence to Newmarket on 9 October 1851. Immediately the Cambridge line was opened, the Chesterford line closed to passenger traffic. The distance from London to Newmarket was increased by about seven-and-a-half miles.

There were to be two stations between Six Mile Bottom and Cambridge, one at Fulbourn, and the other at Cherry Hinton. However, these stations were not ready for the opening of the line in October 1851 and do not appear in Bradshaw until August 1852.

At Cherry Hinton level crossing, a building similar to the old station at Fulbourn still exists but the Station closed by 1854.

The line from Cambridge to Newmarket was not especially prosperous but, as the ECR timetable in **Fig. 19** shows, the ECR was interested in the link to Cambridge because it offered connections which generated passenger and goods traffic. One missing link was eastwards from Newmarket to Bury St Edmunds. That continued with horse-drawn coaches until 1878 when, under GER management, trains could continue from Newmarket to Bury, Haughley Junction and thence southwards to Stowmarket, Ipswich, Colchester, Chelmsford and London.

At Cambridge Station the 8-chain radius curve bringing the Newmarket branch into a Station platform created operational difficulties that were not resolved until

NEWMARKET RAILWAY.

Fig. 19

Junction with Main Line at Cambridge, see pages 6 and 8.

Reference to Branch Trains.	DOWN TRAINS.	WEEK DAYS.		
		Parl. 1 2 3 Class.	Mail. 1 2 Class.	1 2 Class.
Page	FROM	morn.	morn	morn.	even.
9	LONDON	7. 0	8. 0	11.30	5. 0
16	PETERBORO'		7.20	11.40	3. 0
13	WISBEACH		7 30	12. 0	3.15
8	YARMOUTH		7. 0	9.45	..
19	LOWESTOFT		6.45	9 30	..
8	NORWICH		7.45	11. 0	..
	CAMBRIDGE		10.10	1 40	6.35
	Cherry Hinton		13.15	1.45	6.40
	Fulbourn		10.20	1.50	6.45
	Six Mile Bottom		10.25	1.55	6.50
	Dullingham		10.32	2. 7	6.57
	NEWMARKET ....arrival		10.45	2 15	7.10

from EASTERN COUNTIES RAILWAY timetable 1853

Reference to Branch Trains.	UP TRAINS.	WEEK DAYS.		
		1 2 Class.	1 2 Class.	1 2 Class.
Page	FROM	morn.	even.	even.	
	NEWMARKET	8.40	11.45	4.15	..
	Dullingham	8.47	11.52	4.22	..
	Six Mile Bottom	8.53	11.57	4.23	..
	Fulbourn	8.58	1. 2	4.33	..
	Cherry Hinton	9. 3	1. 7	4.38	..
18	CAMBRIDGE ...... arrival	9.15	1.20	4.50	..
13	WISBEACH do.	12. 0	3.30	8.15	..
6	PETERBORO' do.	11.15	7.55		..
19	NORWICH do.	11. 0	4. 0	8.15	..
8	LOWESTOFT do.	12.20	5.30	9.20	..
8	YARMOUTH do.	12.10	5.10	9. 5	..
	LONDON do.	11. 0	3.40	7.10	..

BURY.—Coaches leave Newmarket for Bury on arrival of the 8.0 and 11.30 a.m. and 5.0 p.m. Trains from London; and Bury for Newmarket at 7.0 and 11. 0 a.m. and 2.30 p.m., in connexion with the 8.40 a.m., 12 45 and 4.15 p.m. Trains from thence.

CHERRY HINTON, FULBOURN, SIX MILE BOTTOM, AND DULLINGHAM.— The Trains, although noted in the Tables to call, will not do so except when there are Passengers to take up or set down.—Passengers wishing to alight are requested to intimate the same to the Guard at the preceding Station.

the new Coldham Junction connection to Newmarket was completed in 1896.

As **Fig. 20** (circa 1890) shows, the Newmarket line cut across all the carriage sidings and the goods up and down through roads and conflicted with the down Platform 4 at which a train is waiting. By this date, the main platform

Fig. 20

at Cambridge had been lengthened north (down) and south (up) improving the station for most services but rendering the Newmarket line services even more difficult. Previously Platform 4 was shorter and the Newmarket line came onto this platform and into the down bay to Platform 5 as **Fig. 21** illustrates.

A minor accident in 1883 reveals details of the working of the Newmarket line at that date and the subsequent Board of Trade Accident Enquiry, 1884, provides the plan in **Fig. 21** illustrating the trackwork. Any railway accident at that time had to be reported to the Board of Trade and the account below is edited

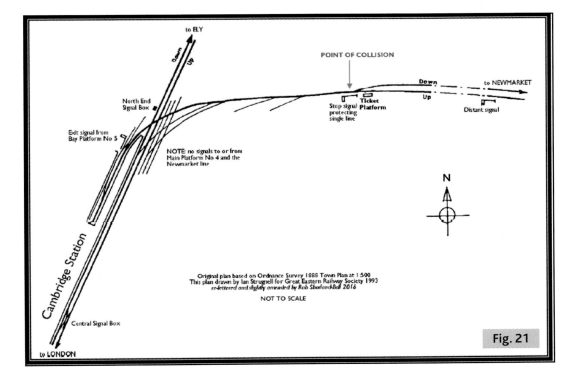

to ELY

POINT OF COLLISION

Down   to NEWMARKET

North End
Signal Box

Ticket
Stop signal **Platform**
protecting
single line

Up

Distant signal

Exit signal from
Bay Platform No 5

NOTE: no signals to or from
Main Platform No 4 and the
Newmarket line

N

Cambridge Station

Original plan based on Ordnance Survey 1888 Town Plan at 1:500
This plan drawn by Ian Strugnell for Great Eastern Railway Society 1993
re-lettered and slightly amended by Rob Shorland-Ball 2016

NOT TO SCALE

Central Signal Box

to LONDON

Fig. 21

from the BoT Enquiry that was led by Inspecting Officer Major-General C S Hutchinson[7].

'Late October racing at Newmarket required some special up and down trains. On the afternoon of 23rd October 1883 a collision occurred between two passenger trains at the point illustrated on the plan [**Fig. 21**] a short distance along the Newmarket branch.

'The 3.00pm down special passenger train from Tottenham to Newmarket had just passed onto the branch when it was run into by the engine of the 3.55pm up special passenger train from Newmarket to Cambridge.

'No passengers in either train were injured (there were only four in the down special) but the fireman of the down train broke a bone in his leg when he jumped from the engine just before the collision. The leading four vehicles of the down train were derailed and slightly damaged as were both the engines.

'At the time of the accident the Newmarket branch was mostly double track but it became single at a ticket platform 200 yards from Cambridge Station. After the ticket platform the single line passed several sidings before crossing the goods and main lines to make a junction with the platform line.

'Between Cambridge Station and the ticket platform was North End Signal Box, which worked a stop signal from bay platform 5 and another at the ticket platform so controlling each end of the short stretch of single line. North End Box also controlled an up branch distant signal (half-a-mile from the Box).'

Not relevant to this Accident Report, so not included on the plan, are home signals leading to and from the bay platforms 5 and 6 which were also controlled by the North End Box. There were no fixed signals for trains passing between the main platform lines and the branch.

'All trains passing over the single line to and from the ticket platform were accompanied by a pilot-man who also worked the points at the junction of the up and down Newmarket lines next to that platform. There was block telegraph working between the North End Signal Box and Fulbourn but there was no interlocking of points or signals for the single line section of the Newmarket branch.'

Dramatis personae for what follows were:

▸ Reuben Jaggard: signalman North End Box with 11 years experience, all at that Box.

▸ George Simpson: pilotman.

▸ Cornelius Humm: driver of the down special. 19 years in service; $6\frac{1}{2}$ as a driver.

▸ *A N Other*: fireman of the down train. He jumped off his footplate just before the collision and broke a leg-bone.

▸ James Rausley: guard of the down train; 5 years in service; $3\frac{1}{2}$ as a guard.

▸ Frederic Edwards: rostered front guard of the up special who was replaced at Newmarket Station by –

▸ Robert Godfrey: Traffic Inspector. He had been at Newmarket on the day of the accident and had to return to London that afternoon. On hearing this the Newmarket Station Master had, at about 3.30pm, ordered him to act as the front guard of the 3.55pm up special train to Cambridge so that Guard Edwards could be kept back to work a later train.

▸ Underwood Dyer: driver of the up special. 35 years in service; 20 years as a driver

▸ James Stately: fireman of the up special

'The Accident: Driver Humm tells the Enquiry that his down train, from Tottenham to Newmarket via Cambridge, is 14 minutes late at Cambridge Station. He has clear signals along the main platform down line and pauses to pick up Pilotman Simpson. He sees a flag-signalled 'All Clear' from the Cambridge Station Master (*note no signals for turning off onto the Newmarket branch from main Platform No 4*) and crosses over the main lines towards the Newmarket line ticket platform at – he states – 4 to 5 MPH.

'Pilotman Simpson, on Driver Humm's footplate, sees the up train slowly approaching the Newmarket end of the ticket platform and preparing, as he thought, to stop at the signal guarding the beginning of the single line.

'Driver Humm also saw the up train and, in his judgement, it was travelling too fast to stop at the ticket platform signal. Humm claimed that he and Pilotman Simpson concluded at the same time that the up train could not stop so he opened his regulator to speed into the 'safety' of the down line on the double-track section.

'Unfortunately, maintained Humm, he was not fast enough and the up train engine caught the footplate steps of his engine then the corner of his engine's tender and finally the first three vehicles of his train.'

It must be remembered that this is the spoken evidence of one of the drivers concerned in the accident so it is likely that they will put as favourable a gloss as possible on their evidence. Guard Rausley's evidence – he was the down train guard – supported Humm's estimate of speed of 4 to 5mph and thought that the up train had slowed to 2 or 3mph.

It is clear, however, that if the up train engine caught the footplate steps of Humm's engine there was no prospect of accelerating the whole train onto the down line before the up train had reached the point of collision. Guard Rausley was in the sixth vehicle of the down train, which we can assume was the last vehicle, so it was not a long train but too long to clear the junction.

The evidence from the crew of the up train – 3.55pm Newmarket to Cambridge – was a little different from the story told by the down train Driver and Guard:

'Driver Dyer had a train of 20 vehicles and he left Newmarket 6 minutes late, at 16.01pm. The train had run fast but they found the North End distant against them, implying that the road was not clear into Cambridge Station.

'Traffic Inspector Godfrey, acting as front guard, said Driver Dyer had shut off steam a good ½-mile from the distant signal, which had been passed at about 30mph.

'Driver Dyer admitted that he left Newmarket without learning from Traffic Inspector/Front Guard Godfrey about the train's brake power. However, the relieved Front Guard Edwards told the Enquiry that before he left the train he had told Rear Guard Moore, *and Driver Dyer*, [author's italics] that there twenty vehicles on the train but only three were connected to the locomotive's Westinghouse air brake.

'Driver Dyer denied that he had any information about the train so only when he applied the brake at the distant signal did he discover that he could not easily stop. He said that he then pulled over the reversing lever, opened the regulator 'to give her back steam,' opened the sand valves and whistled for Rear Guard Moore to apply his brakes. However, the rails were greasy and his train collided at low speed with the down train.

'Driver Dyer's mate, Fireman Stately, told the Enquiry that his Driver only discovered the lack of brake power at the Newmarket end of the short Ticket Platform, only gave back steam half-way along that platform and, Stately said, "I did not hear any whistle for the Rear Guard's brakes."

'Inspecting Officer's Findings: Major-General Hutchinson concluded that the principal blame for the accident lay with Driver Dyer.

Underwood Dyer: failed to ascertain his available brake power before leaving Newmarket; approached the Ticket Platform too fast to be able to halt his train at the stop signal; had been slow in reversing the locomotive and applying back steam.

'Hutchinson also commented that Driver Humm had not been judicious in trying to accelerate his train clear when he saw that a collision was imminent.

He would have done much better, Hutchinson said, to have allowed the engines to meet head-on at low speed rather than risk the carriages of his train being derailed or stove-in.'

Very relevant to this book about Cambridge Station is Major-General Hutchinson's concluding remark. He said that when the second line of rails between Cambridge and Six Mile Bottom had been examined by Captain Tyler, on behalf of the BoT in 1875, the arrangements at the Cambridge end had been stated to be of a temporary character.

'Captain Tyler had approved the layout on the understanding that improvements would shortly be carried out but nothing had been done in the 8 years between his inspection and the recent accident.

The problem, as we shall see, is that the proposed new junction for the Newmarket Railway on a sweeping curve across Coldham Common took several years to agree because the land-owner – Jesus College again – was reluctant to sell.

Chapter 6

GER'S BRANCH LINES TO AND FROM CAMBRIDGE

Branch lines often constituted what was once called the 'Country Railway' or perhaps more recently the 'Social Railway'. The late David St. John Thomas, author and publisher, sums up the importance of branch lines in his last book, published by Francis Lincoln in 2013, *Farewell to Trains*.

'[The country railway] was a business, a commercial venture that often failed in narrow financial terms but proved of enormous benefit to the community. Nearly all country stations, at least those handling freight as well as passengers, were the most important trading posts for miles around. The business they handled revolutionised local life and attitudes.'

The map in **Fig. 22** illustrates Cambridge at the centre of a web of railway lines. Some, like those to London King's Cross and London Liverpool Street might be termed 'main lines' and certainly so to early railway promoters who were building lines from London to 'revolutionise' local life. The map indicates links beyond Newmarket to Bury St Edmunds and Ipswich – deep into Suffolk.

To the north of Cambridge, Ely and Kettering are not of themselves major towns but they offered important links with other expanding railway companies – the Midland at Kettering and the Great Northern from Ely.

Remember the 'disgruntled shareholder' in Chapter 2? Here he is again!

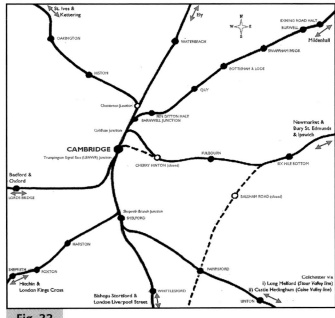

Fig. 22

'Cambridge is sufficiently near to Ely to be described as at the centre of our system. It is the object, of course, of every Railway Company to convey to and from the centre of its system to the points which are the furthest extremities thereof.'

So Ely was, and is, another important link to Peterborough NNW and to Kings Lynn NNE.

'Branch lines' in the nineteenth century meant lines to link with other railway companies and both the ECR and, more successfully, the GER were keen to establish such links and to create Joint lines by agreements and running rights over sections of the partner companies' railways. The line from Bedford and Oxford was a penetration into GER territory by the London & North Western Railway (L&NWR).

The reference on the map to 'Shepreth Branch Junction' is a reminder of ECR / GER interest in a link with the powerful GNR who were equally interested in a link which would give them access to Cambridge. The GNR received parliamentary authority to build a line from Hitchin to Shepreth in 1848 but an extension to Cambridge was not permitted. Eventually, and with effect from 1866, a GER 'branch' from Shelford – but note from the map that Shelford Station is not on this branch – to Shepreth was worked jointly with the GNR. Shepreth Branch Junction is an end-on meeting point of the two railway companies and not a junction when one line joins, or leaves, another.

The real 'country railway' branch lines were those shown on the map to the east and south of Cambridge. The Mildenhall line branched off the Ely line at Barnwell Junction, shown in **Fig. 23**, which only had platforms on the Mildenhall branch. The branch meandered north-eastwards as a single line to Fordham Junction and then north-east again to Mildenhall – 20 miles 62 chains from Cambridge Station.

The stations shown on the map may

Fig. 23

well have been 'the most important trading points for miles around' but by the time I knew the line in the late 1950s it carried few passengers and there was little sign of goods activity at most of the stations. The Halts, – Fen Ditton, Exning Road and Worlington Golf Links – were permissive stops because passengers dismounting had to inform the Guard when they joined the train so that a set of extendable steps in the brake 3rd could be lowered to the rail-level clinker 'platform'. All three halts were conveniently near a road over-bridge to provide passenger shelter from inclement weather.

Just south of Shelford Station, on the GER line to London Liverpool Street, was an extensive system of branches that took the intending passenger into an area served by small independent railway companies (see Fig.14 on page 31). The Colne Valley and Halstead Railway was completed from Haverhill Station to Chappel and Wakes Colne Station in 1859 and the Colchester, Stour Valley, Sudbury & Halstead Railway opened a separate route to Haverhill North – and thence via the GER to Cambridge – in 1865. This line was amalgamated with the GER by an Act of 1 July 1898. The Colne Valley line remained independent until the Grouping in 1923 when, like the Stour Valley line, it became an LNER branch.

And finally, the Newmarket branch again which, once it had a route across Coldham Common, was a busy double-track line. It carried freight and passenger traffic, both illustrated in **Fig. 24**, showing an LNER 4-6-0, Class B12 hauling an up passenger train in the 1950s passing the Norman Cement Works near Cherry Hinton. The Works supplied some railway traffic but this railway still carried a lot of Newmarket Racecourse business – for spectators, and for racehorses in quite lengthy trains of horseboxes.

Fig. 24

Chapter 7

CAMBRIDGE STATION AS AN ENTREPÔT

T his map illustrates Cambridge's marginal position in relation to principal routes from London into East Anglia in 1834 so I have relettered Cambridge in red capitals for the purposes of this book. It must be remembered that the map was drawn to illustrate a book about stage coach routes in the 'Eastern Counties' which generally means Norfolk, Suffolk and Essex so Cambridge is necessarily on the margin. But viewing Cambridge as an 'entrepôt' means a *tour d'horizon* around Cambridge.

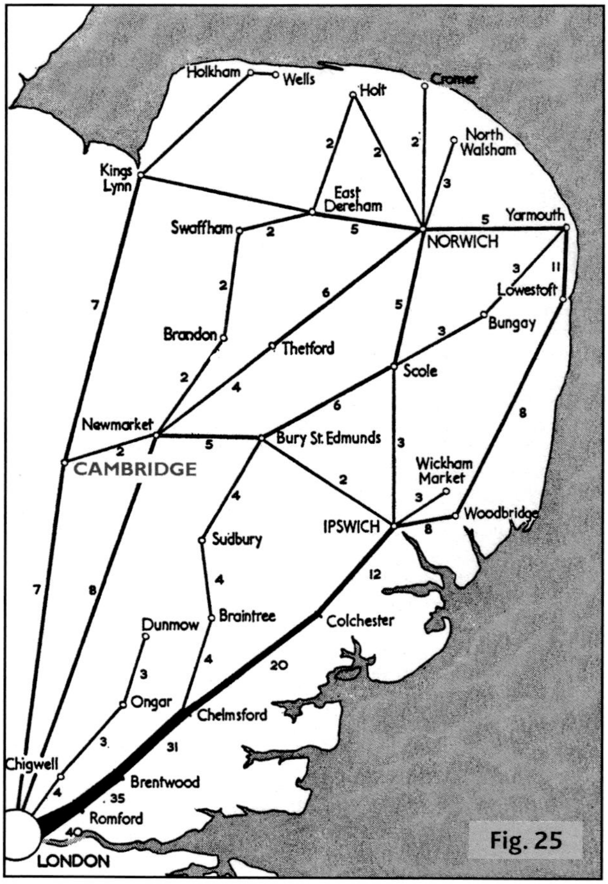

One of the stagecoach operators was a partnership run by Isaac Marsh and William Swan. They owned stables, warehouses, granaries, a smithy/farriery and a wheel-wright shop. An advertisement for the company still survives in Ely (**Fig. 26**) and offers transport in vans, a fly and stage wagons so they were carrying goods as well as passengers.

In 1803 the *Annals of Cambridge* indicated that:

> '… the London, Cambridge and Norwich carriers, offered to furnish Government in case of invasion with 100 horses, 12 broad-wheel waggons and 24 men to drive and guard the same …'

They were a flourishing business.

I have started this chapter with reference to carriers other than the

Fig. 25

Fig. 25: shows the number of licensed stage coaches running between principal centres in East Anglia in 1834, eleven years before the railway arrived in Cambridge.

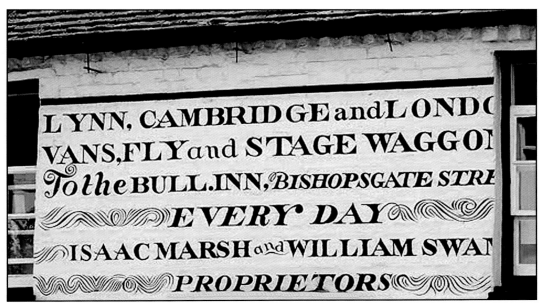

Fig. 26: Remains of a painted sign advertising Marsh & Swan services on a house front in Market St. Ely, Cambridgeshire.

railway to illustrate that Cambridge was a busy entrepôt before the railway came. 'Entrepôt' is an economic geography term meaning a commercial centre to which goods are brought for import and export, and for collection and distribution. The railway brought about changes to Cambridge, including the end of water-transport on the Cam and Messrs Marsh & Swan's horse-drawn traffic. If passengers may be regarded as a form of 'goods' – which, for railway companies, they are –

the Cambridge Station was soon busy with passengers and a variety of other goods. The station was, and for passengers still is, an important entrepôt for itself, for the town of Cambridge and for the hinterland it serves which **Figs. 2, 14 and 27** all illustrate.

Marsh & Swan's wagons and stage coaches were busy in the early nineteenth century and we have already learned from the ECR Prospectus that, once the railway was established, thousands of passengers and tons of goods were providing profitable traffic so Cambridge was a busy traffic node. In the following chapters, we shall see how Cambridge Station operated as a busy entrepôt and still does so today.

Chapter 8

'FOUR RAILWAY COMPANIES IN A TANGLE OF MUTUAL INCONVENIENCE'

Cambridge Station was never an easy station to operate and the details of developing track layouts, platforms, Goods Sheds, Good Yards and the Motive Power Depots are explained and illustrated in Chapter 9.

The memorably robust phrase which is the title for this chapter is from: *Express Trains, English and Foreign*. E Foxwell and T. C. Farrer, republished as a facsimile by Kessinger Publishing in 2010. To illustrate the phrase I cannot improve on the map – **Fig. 27** – from Geoffrey Skelsey's two-part article about Cambridge Station in *BackTrack*, August 2005.[2]

The tangled history of the different railway companies which embraced Cambridge in their route plans have been detailed in several studies, including those by Cecil J Allen and D. I. Gordon but Cambridge Station's development as an entrepôt can be briefly summarised here. The 'via' references are to stations marked on the **Fig. 27** map:

01 ECR / GER from London via Bishop's Stortford and onwards to Ely, Norwich, Yarmouth

02 Cambridge branch of Newmarket Railway via Fulbourn and Cherry Hinton

03 GNR, jointly with ECR / GER from London via Hitchin

04 ECR / GER to St Ives and Huntingdon via Histon

05 L&NWR to Bedford, Bletchley (and Oxford) via Lords Bridge

06 ECR / GER to Haverhill Sudbury, Marks Tey and Ipswich via Shelford and Pampisford

07 GER to Mildenhall via Barnwell Junction and Fordham

Good proof readers, or mathematicians, may have worked out that, unless the Eastern Counties Railway (ECR) and the successor Great Eastern Railway (GER) can be counted as two railway companies, there is only one more company listed in 05 above – the London & North Western Railway (L&NWR) so GER + GNR + L&NWR = three. The 'missing' fourth company, shown on the map only as 'MR Mill Road Goods', is the Midland Railway (MR) which had agreed running rights with GER:

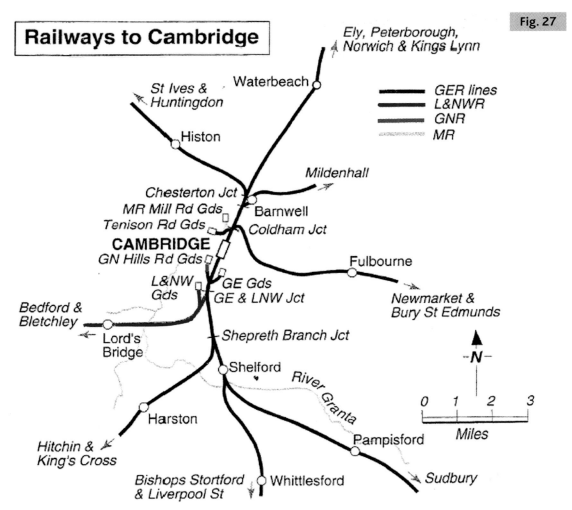

Railways to Cambridge

Fig. 27

Ely, Peterborough, Norwich & Kings Lynn

Waterbeach

St Ives & Huntingdon

GER lines
L&NWR
GNR
MR

Histon

Mildenhall

Chesterton Jct
MR Mill Rd Gds
Tenison Rd Gds
CAMBRIDGE
GN Hills Rd Gds

Barnwell
Coldham Jct

Fulbourne

L&NW
Gds
GE Gds
GE & LNW Jct

Newmarket &
Bury St Edmunds

Bedford &
Bletchley

Lord's
Bridge

Shepreth Branch Jct

Shelford

River Granta

-N-

Harston

Hitchin &
King's Cross

Pampisford

0 1 2 3

Miles

Bishops Stortford
& Liverpool St

Whittlesford

Sudbury

Map from: *Of Great Public Advantage – Aspects of Cambridge and its railways 1845 – 2005.* Geoffrey Skelsey LVO. *BackTrack* July & August 2005.. (*Pendragon Publishing*)

Fig. 28 is a 1916 MR plan which shows the position of Mill Road Goods Station, adjoining Mill Road over-bridge that I have added to this plan. The MR had running rights over GER tracks from St. Ives to Cambridge Station. The MR goods trains could work through to the Company's own Goods Station and to the GER Goods Station east of Cambridge Passenger Station. However, as the plan shows, MR locomotives were not permitted access to the 'G E Engine Sheds'.

Operating such a tangled station was never easy and the number of separate railway company goods yards and sheds illustrates the potential for disagreements.

The working of passenger trains by different companies was simplified when it was decided that the two principal companies, GER and GNR, would share one station. However, Cambridge was originally a single-platform station and even after the bays were added it was still, essentially, one very long principal

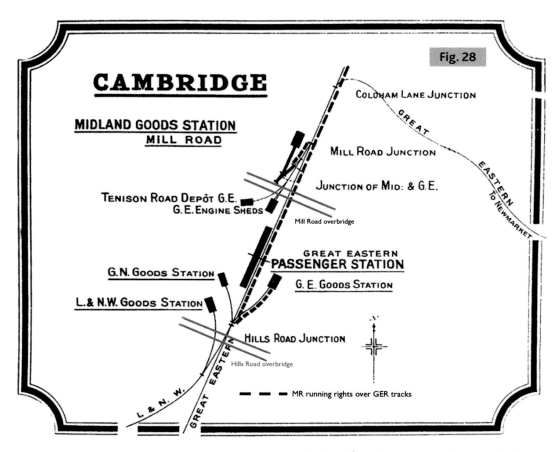

Fig. 28: A diagrammatic plan: MR running rights over GER tracks, Cambridge. (*Midland Railway Study Centre*)

platform served by one track. **Fig. 29** is a useful illustration of the complexities of working the station.

A useful reminder of double-track running in the UK is that – facing forward in the direction of travel – Up lines are on the left-hand side so Down lines are on the right-hand side. It was decided at Cambridge, from the beginning of passenger train operation, that trains to London, that is Up trains, would use the southern or London end of the long platform. Down trains which were travelling north of the Station would use the northern or Country end.

Before the scissors crossing was built at the centre of the long platform, an Up train approaching Cambridge from the North had to be crossed to the Down line for wrong-line-working when approaching the platform. The train usually worked to the London end of the long platform and, when departing, had to be crossed over again to the Up line. Meanwhile a Down train approaching Cambridge had to be held at the London end of the station layout until the Up train had departed, and crossed over, before the Down train could work to the country end of the long platform.

A significant addition to the station track-work during the 1863 re-modelling was the insertion of a scissors crossing at the centre of the single platform. This

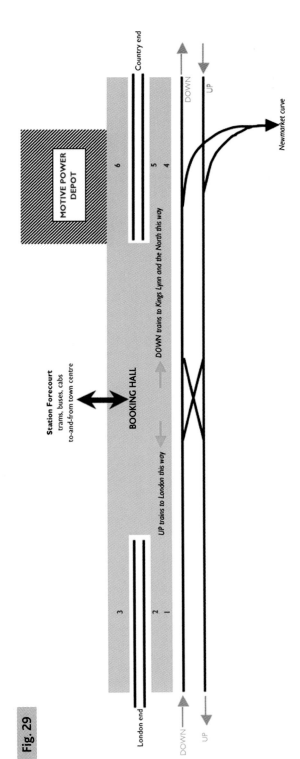

Fig. 29: Diagrammatic plan of Cambridge Station: track layout for platforms and Newmarket branch. (*Author's collection*)

enabled a more space- and time-efficient working of the long platform so that Up trains worked over the scissors to Platform 1 and Down trains to Platform 4.

Passengers still faced a long walk but those familiar with the station knew in which direction to walk from the central booking hall and platform entrance. 'Turn right for London; turn left for Kings Lynn,' was the sort of direction passengers received from the central entrance ticket inspectors. The blue arrow on **Fig. 29** marks the point of decision!

A track-work problem which was only finally resolved in 1896 was the Newmarket Railway branch which arrived in Cambridge from the Chesterford-Newmarket Railway in 1851. It approached Cambridge Station almost at a right angle and was sharply turned across all the running lines and sidings in an 8-chain radius curve to the Down end of the Station platform.

Surviving records show that GER was working to secure a deviation of the Newmarket branch approach but negotiations were long and slow. The intention, as shown on the *BackTrack* 'Railways to Cambridge' map – **Fig. 27** – was to go north from the station to a new junction at Coldham Common and then across the Common to re-join the branch west of Cherry Hinton station. Jesus College owned much of the land required and were party to the negotiations but the GER's first recourse to parliament for a deviation was rejected and it was only in 1896 that the company were successful. The original curve, as shown in **Fig. 21** and then in **Fig. 29**, was retained as a long siding for at least ten years after the new junction was opened.

At either end of the station were bay platforms as shown on **Fig. 29**. Platforms 2 and 3 served London King's Cross and Oxford trains at the London end. Platforms 5 and 6 served GER branches, including after 1896 the Newmarket line, at the country end.

Cecil Allen provided a sketch plan with his 1908 *Railway Magazine* article – which is reproduced as **Fig. 30**. He labels the platforms by the railway company which used them most and the GNR Offices beside Platform 3. This is a reminder that the GNR had their own entrance to Cambridge Station onto Platform 3 and their own offices. There was also a GNR Station Master as well as a GER Station Master but, fortunately, they seemed to work together quite well.

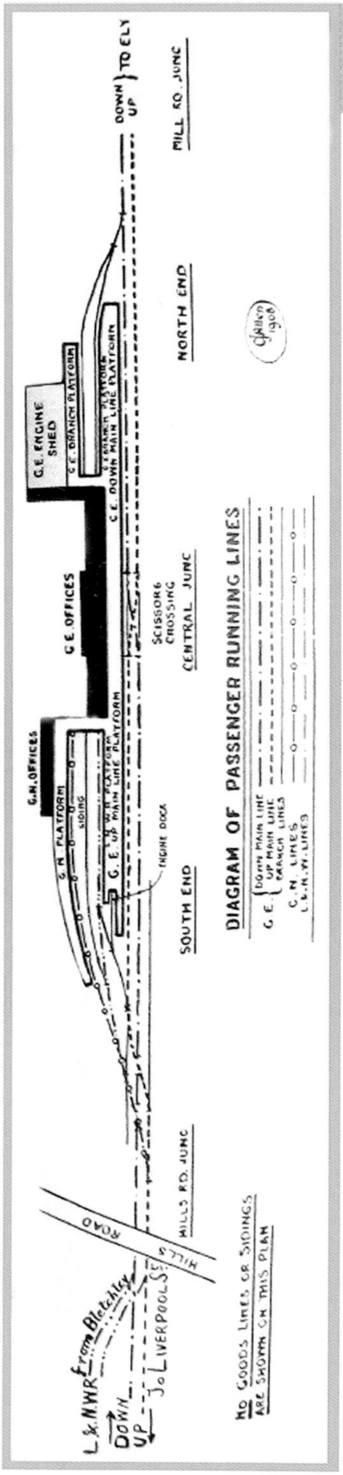

Fig. 30: Diagram of Passenger Running Lines, Cambridge Station 1908. Cecil Allen. *Railway Magazine* 1908

Chapter 9

HOW THE STATION WAS OPERATED: 1845-1990S

Track layouts, platforms and passengers

Fig. **10**, (page 26), from the *Illustrated London News* is an artist's impression of the new Cambridge Station published on 2 August 1845 but, as I have indicated earlier, the artist was less accurate than we would wish. The Station building, and a nearby Engine Shed, are shown as attractive structures but the track-work is a little wayward. The engraving below, **Fig. 31**, must be of similar date because, although Hills Road bridge is the main feature, Cambridge Station building completed

in 1845 is shown beyond the bridge. **Fig 31** is therefore an early view of the new works and is a little more accurate than **Fig 10** in showing the single track to the long single platform. The design of the principal building only allowed for a single track to pass through the track-side train shed so the platform, especially

Fig. 31: Engraving from around 1845, of original Hills Road bridge looking north and Up end of 1845 Station building. =

Fig. 31

inside the building, was narrow and did not extend much outside the central building.

In the 1840s, trains were still relatively short and usually composed of 4-wheel carriages drawn by quite small engines like the 2-2-2 in the *Illustrated London News*. But Cambridge Station opened in the heart of the 'Railway Mania' when speculation was rife and railways were news. As the ECR told its shareholders in the 1851 *Illustrated Guide* already quoted, railways gave '… heretofore unprecedented facilities [for] locomotion [and] have induced nearly all classes to travel'.

Cambridge Station was very soon inadequate for the passenger traffic it attracted and operating up and down trains from a single short platform was potentially dangerous and very slow. Quite soon a second parallel track was added outside the colonnade and it may be that track which is in the earlier *Illustrated London News* **Fig. 10** illustration. To add to our confusion, however, or perhaps as a warning that contemporary accounts in journals like the *Illustrated London News* may not always be wholly accurate, the article accompanying the picture in **Fig. 10**, states:

> 'In our view, the front, and one of the ends, or sides are seen. The rail outside, and through the arch, are also depicted.'

That seems to be proof that there was a line 'through the arch' but the artist has omitted it, and blocked its path with a water column.

Fig. 32: The site of carriage lamp room at Cambridge Station.

Fig. 32

The Royal Commission on Historic Monuments in England (*City of Cambridge: a survey and inventory* Volumes I & II. HMSO 1959) reports that during 1848, a wooden island platform was constructed for up trains at a cost of £273 18s 6d. To gain access to this platform, passengers apparently had to climb down onto the line and cross the track. Perhaps the steps leading down from the short platform in the *Illustrated London News* illustration were used for that purpose?

Access to the island platform was considered to be dangerous particularly at busy times, for example when undergraduates with large amounts of luggage were using the station at the beginning and end of University terms. In 1849 an ECR Report referred to the island platform as 'now removed' but public complaints and the increasing difficulty of operating more trains required its restoration in 1850. We know it was joined to the main platform by a steep footbridge and luggage was moved to it by porterage through a narrow, low, and rather noisome subway.

No pictures have survived of this island platform, or the footbridge, but when I worked as a goods porter at the station, one of my extra jobs was up end carriage-tail-lamp-man. The carriage lamps, and the paraffin for refilling them, was kept in a small timber-built lamp-room with a sloping roof against the wall at the end of bay platforms 3 and 4. I enquired about the sloping roof and was assured by several long-serving porters, 'That is where the old footbridge was.' On a field-work visit to Cambridge Station in 2015, I was not surprised to find the lamp-room gone but delighted to find a pitch-painted black wall still partly visible behind twenty-first century additions. - **Fig. 32**.

I am always cautious about oral history 'evidence' but I enquired separately and of several older men who all gave me the same answer so perhaps the sloping roof of the lamp-room recaptures a little past history. The orange arrow indicates the black-painted slope on the station wall but subsequent research suggests that the 'old footbridge' can never have been to an island platform. We know that the train shed wall enclosing the single track was not removed until 1863, so the footbridge must have been built against the southern end-wall of the main station building. That end-wall, where it has survived, will be hidden by subsequent building extensions and the wall shown was not built until the 1870s.

However, a helpful comment to me from Graham Berry, a train dispatcher at Cambridge Station, suggests that the 'old footbridge' did exist and was part of the GNR/GER story:

'Photographs (dated from the 1930s to the 1960s) taken of the main station building from the south end of Platform 1 show a wooden structure behind and above the stops at the end of Platforms 2 and 3 obscuring the brick face of the end of the main building at first floor level. The steelwork which supported this structure is still in place [but hidden because it] now supports a lightweight roof ... steelwork which seems far too substantial for that simple purpose.

'I would suggest that the [black painted slope] was actually the outline of former steps to this building which I imagine was a GN enginemen's mess or GN control office, being above the old GN platforms. The gates nearby are still to this day referred to as "the GN gates".'

Graham's helpful memory has taken me a little beyond this chapter's progressive chronology but **Fig 33** is very pertinent. This photograph probably dates from the late 1920s and shows the 'GN gates' leading directly from the station forecourt onto Platform 3. Inside on the right were the GNR Offices, including a booking office downstairs for GN passengers. Perhaps the first floor shown to the left of the GN gates is the building which the old footbridge served. An awning was installed over the door and sometimes taxis waited outside for wealthy passengers.

Research for this book took me on several occasions to Jesus College Archives in Cambridge because most of the railway station and goods yards development in Cambridge was on land purchased from the College. I believe several of the images which follow have never been published before. They show how the ECR's Engineer's Office, and the Head Offices at Shoreditch Station, London, were exploring, and pursuing, the purchase of station area lands and then considering various track and building layouts.

Fig. 9 on page 25 is the Plan accompanying the Jesus College

Agreement to sell over eleven acres of College agricultural land to the ECR. A hand-written superscription reads:

> 'This is the Plan referred to in the Agreement made between the Reverend William French DD Master of Jesus College Cambridge and Thomas Smith Woolley on behalf of the Eastern Counties Railway Company and which Agreement bears date the 10th day of February 1846'

The Agreement document is also in the College Archive detailing the lessees of some of the land, the relevant acreages and the parish of St Andrews in which 6 acres lay. I have superimposed two helpful notes on the Plan to relate it to later developments. We must remember, however, that Cambridge Station opened on 29 July 1845 so the Agreement is to formalise the arrangements which Dr French had already concluded with the ECR. A 'paper trail' was essential for legal

Fig. 33

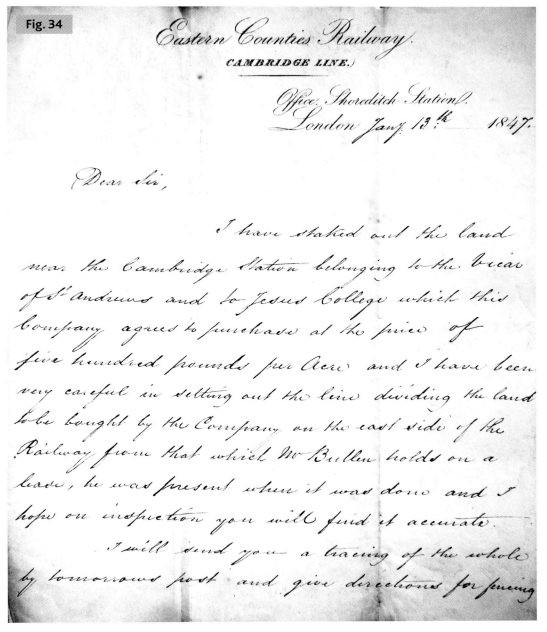

Fig. 34

Eastern Counties Railway.
CAMBRIDGE LINE.)

Office, Shoreditch Station
London Jany. 13th 1847.

Dear Sir,

I have staked out the land near the Cambridge Station belonging to the bicas of St Andrews and to Jesus College which this Company agrees to purchase at the price of five hundred pounds per Acre and I have been very careful in setting out the line dividing the land to be bought by the Company on the east side of the Railway from that which Mr Bullen holds on a lease, he was present when it was done and I hope on inspection you will find it accurate.

I will send you a tracing of the whole by tomorrows post and give directions for fencing

completeness but, in the days before the IT devices we can use today, everything was hand-drawn and hand-written. Due process took time!

Fig. 34 is the first page of a letter dated January 13 1847 from the ECR Head Office to Jesus College. It advises that the

Railway surveyors have 'staked-out' land near the Station which the College has agreed to sell at £500 per acre. It can be seen from **Figs. 9** and **35** that the originals from which these have been scanned had been stained, folded, crumpled and torn. This is not a reflection on the skills of Jesus

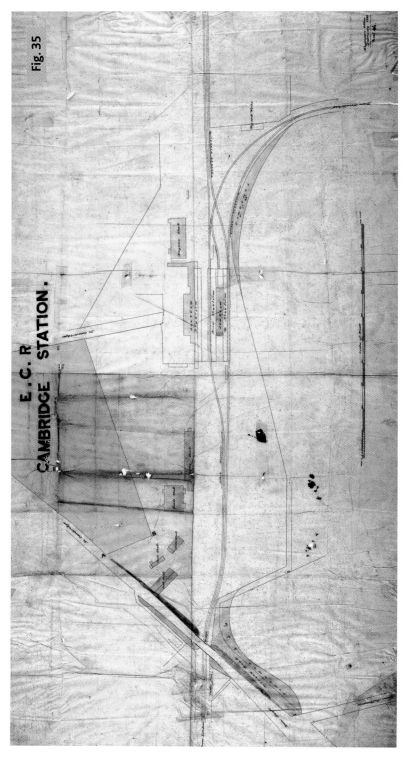

Fig. 35: Plan from ECR Engineer's Office of site of Cambridge Station including some track and buildings and indications of additional land to be purchased from Jesus College Cambridge. Handwritten dating, February 1861 then March 1862.

College archivists but shows that these were working documents. The next find that the archivists showed me is, or was, especially so.

Fig. 36 is the original document, dated February 1861 then March 1862 and from the ECR Engineer's Office. Extensive and very careful Adobe Photoshop treatment to preserve the integrity of all the details in the Station area produces **Fig. 36** which I believe to be a very valuable resource. It is the only known plan which shows the details of the second and more substantial island platform that was installed in 1850. The footbridge and subway which were the means of access from the main station building are not indicated and the original single line through the station train shed is also omitted. Indeed, the main Station building and platform is incomplete but we know that from 1851 the Newmarket branch joined it over an 8 chain radius curve.

My judgement is that this was a working and discussion document, probably for the ECR Board to consider, because by 1861 the island platform was very unpopular with passengers and staff. What is particularly interesting is that the plan shows how the island platform was worked, with labelled Up and Down platforms, links to up and down lines with the Newmarket branch and three Ticket Platforms. **Fig. 37** is an enlargement of the Station area of **Fig. 36** to show the labelling and two of the Ticket Platforms.

These long, narrow structures were devised for ticket inspections before trains arrived at the island platform when a rush to the exit would prevent inspection. These passenger trains were all non-corridor stock and generally 4-wheeled carriages as shown in **Fig. 10** on page 26. Inspectors, standing on the narrow ticket platforms could reach into carriages through open windows and since the platform was on one side

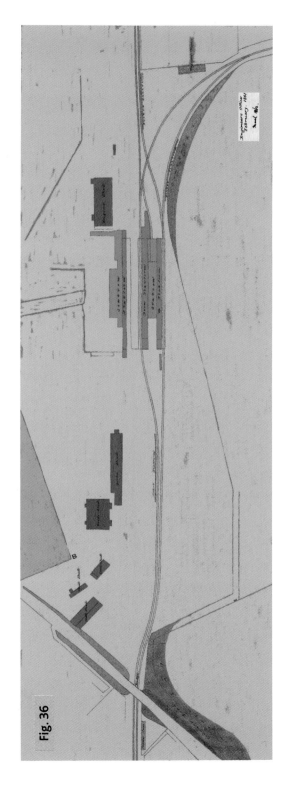

Fig. 36

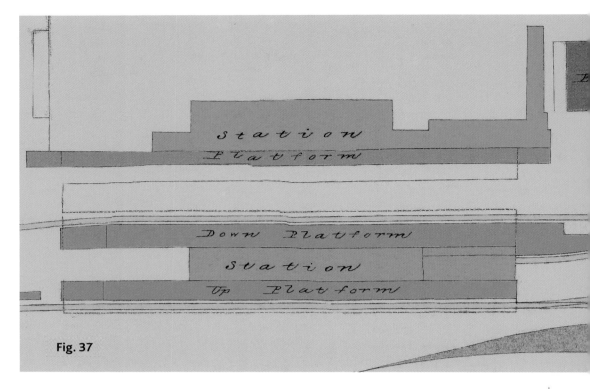

Station

Platform

Down   Platform

Station

Up   Platform

Fig. 37

Fig. 38

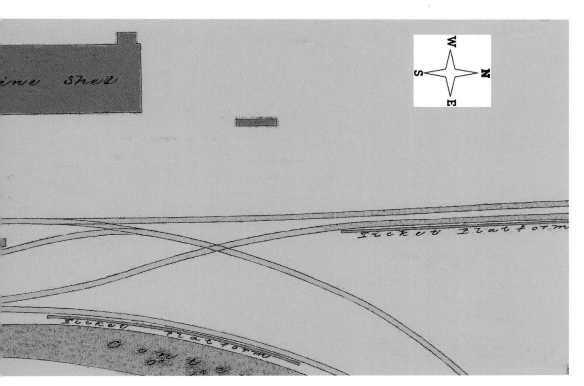

of the waiting train they could see one another and signal to the guard when their inspection was complete. This procedure meant that every train had to stop at the ticket platform and perhaps wait for five minutes before moving to the main station platform.

Fig 38 is an early twentieth century picture (1912) of a surviving Ticket Platform at the GNR Spalding Station, perhaps retained for carriage cleaning. Imagine the inspectors' job on such a platform at Cambridge Station on a cold, wet day; the timber platform slippery underfoot, in an East Anglian wind 'lazy and straight from the Urals', numbing their fingers.

A hand-written note (on **Figs. 35 and 36**) reads: '[ECR] Engineer's Office. February 1861. March 1862.' We know that by 1862 ECR and its constituent companies had morphed into the GER. In 1863 the GER undertook a major re-building of

the Station, removing the island platform and the eastern train shed colonnade of the Station building; lengthening and widening the original single platform; adding north and south bay platforms; and installing a scissors crossing in the middle of the long platform.

Fig. 39 is an interesting and slightly puzzling plan from Jesus College Archives, dated 1860 in the Archives List but without a date, or title, on the Plan itself except for the nicely ambiguous 'Plan marked B'. It shows some track and a number of labelled buildings and a useful indicator is the presence of the Newmarket line, curving into the main single platform, which opened on 9 October 1851.

I suspect that the purpose of the 'Plan marked B' was to record land belonging to the College and recording land-sale negotiations for the Cattle Market east of Hills Road bridge and an extensive area between Hills Road and Station Road

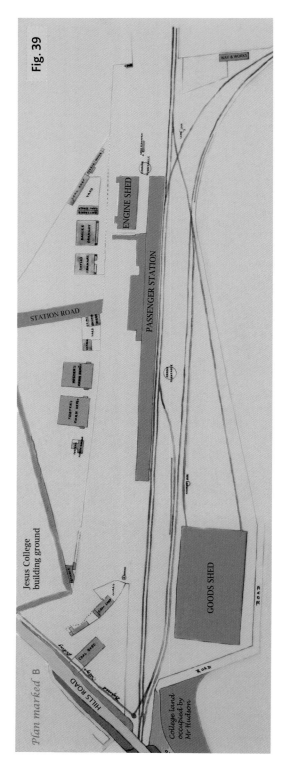

Fig. 39

WAY & WORKS

ENGINE SHED

PASSENGER STATION

STATION ROAD

GOODS SHED

ROAD

ROAD

Jesus College building ground

HILLS ROAD

College land occupied by Mr Hudson

Plan marked B

which became the Great Northern Goods Yard. It corresponds to the B which is just visible on **Fig. 35** and I have retained on the southern corner of the light brown coloured triangular area near the top middle left of the plan on **Fig. 36**.

On **Fig. 39** the track layout is curiously incomplete because two 'Engine Turntables' are shown, one near the 'Engine Shed' which may be correct but another shown in the centre of the station area, which seems unlikely. Both turntables have no rail connections so this and the other peculiarities suggest to me that this may have been an incomplete base-map used for marking-in land purchase negotiations indicated by red shading and a note – 'Jesus College building ground' – which is area B and was subsequently purchased from the College for an extensive Goods Yard.

The next Plan – **Fig. 40** – is dated 1873 and indicates progress with that purchase and records the absorbing of the ECR by the GER, which was accomplished in 1862. This Plan shows the southern bay platforms and labels Platform 3 'Great Northern Railway Passenger Station' whereas the southern end of the long main platform is simply 'Cambridge Station' and Great Eastern Railway is only named on the railway lines. Although the GNR and the GER seemed to have worked together relatively amicably, the GNR had aspirations to have its own station and for several years GNR passengers entered by a door leading directly to Platform 3 – **Fig. 33**. Here was a GNR Booking Office but no other facilities, so the main station was already shared.

By the early 1870s, common sense and more effective passenger service created a Booking Hall in the centre entrance of the Station with separate ticket offices to left and right of the Hall.

Fig. 41 is that Booking Hall in the 1920s after 'the Grouping' of individual Railway

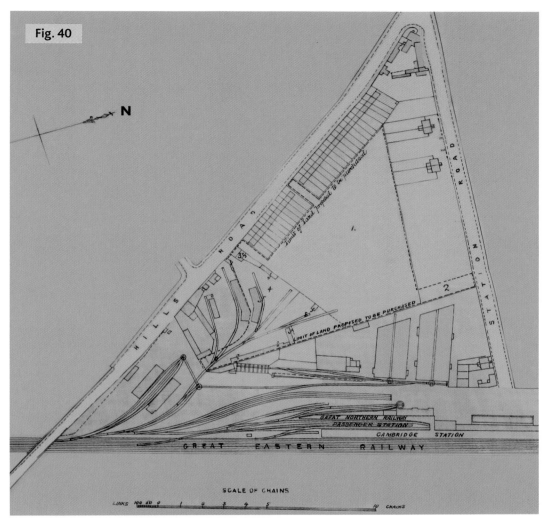

Fig. 40

Companies into larger Companies like the LNER – which subsumed the GER and the GNR. Because Cambridge Station was still served by several Railway Companies, the left and right division of the Booking Hall has been retained, LNER to the left and LMS to the right.

Jesus College Archives has two more important map resources. **Fig. 42** is a GNR & GER Station Plan dated 1874 which illustrates further ambitions for purchase of land from Jesus College. This land will become the Tennison Fields sidings and will also allow the growth of the Motive

Power Depot as Cambridge Station becomes the entrepôt already described.

The Plan is useful, too, because it includes some GER labelling on the long main platform. The GNR Station is labelled on platform 3 and the main Station is now called 'GER Station.' Although the scissors crossing, installed in 1863, is not marked in the track-work, the labelling of 'Up platform' on the London end and 'Down platform' on the country end confirms the working arrangement which allowed Cambridge to retain its long single platform until the twentieth

Fig. 41

century. Starting work in 2009, Network Rail added a twenty-first century island platform, to separate up and down trains when necessary, as a permanent feature. Passengers still complain (as they did in the 1850s) about the footbridge steps they must climb and descend but there are now lifts, too, in the footbridge structure.

Fig. 42 is also useful because the various buildings around the station site tell us something about how railways operated in the late nineteenth century. There is a great deal of track-work not shown on this plan, probably again because its main purpose was for land-purchase negotiations. The large goods shed which was shown on **Fig. 38** as rail-connected is still present but a new building near it is marked 'Stables'. This is a reminder of the importance of horses for cartage – to and from the goods shed – and for shunting in some of the goods yards. Shunting horses were useful because they could easily move from siding to siding between hauling single wagons whereas shunting engines sometimes needed signalman's clearance for moves and always needed

to move to the head-end of the siding, over a set of points and then set back into another siding.

Beyond the goods shed and stables is a 'coke stage' which is characteristic of steam–engine working in the nineteenth century. Coke was the most reliable fuel for locomotive boilers to avoid clinkering, or excessive smoke, until harder coals – like Welsh steam coal – became available.

At the northern end of the **Fig. 42** plan, the single-building 'Way & Works' has now become an extensive group of buildings. They are now called Way & Works Shops and indicate the growing need for civil engineering and track maintenance as the ECR/GER network expanded. There is another line of unspecified 'workshops' and 'shops' alongside a dotted line which is the 'Limit of Land proposed to be purchased'. These workshops are probably for locomotive repairs and maintenance because the relatively small engine shed may be equipped for heavier work but the smaller workshops were necessary for precision metal-work – like turning and grinding

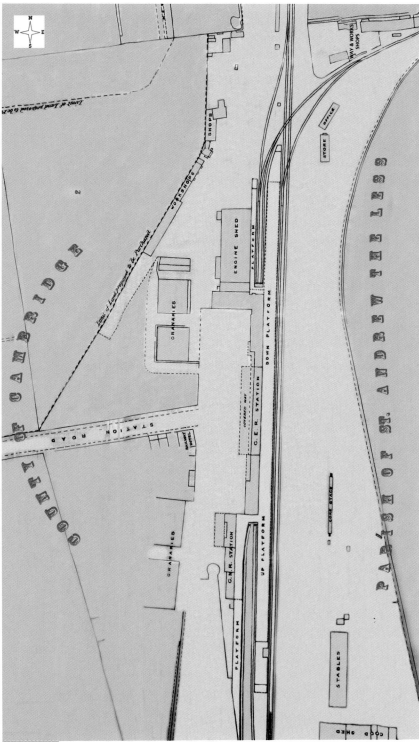

Fig. 42 - Land purchase negotiations and record plan between Jesus College, Cambridge and GER/GNR; undated, so probably 1870s. Edited and Adobe Photo shopped crop from larger plan.

Fig. 42

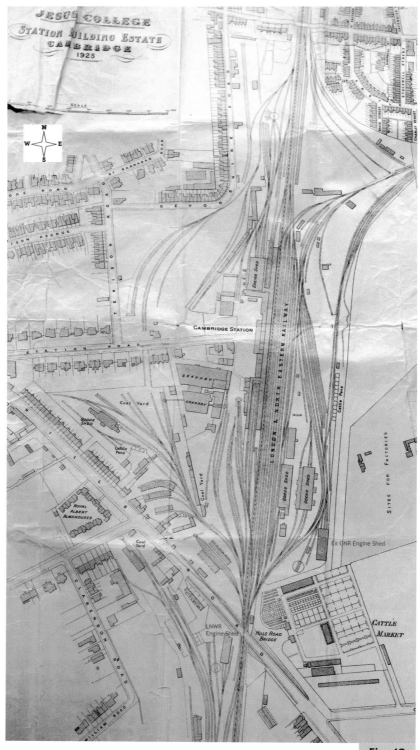

Fig. 43

– and some woodwork for rolling-stock repairs.

Finally, the reference to the Parish of St Andrew the Less will be a geographical indication of the extent of that parish but also, as another document at Jesus College Archives showed, the parish was failing to pay tithes to the College but was 'excused' because some parish land was now railway land.

The final Plan from the Jesus College Archives – **Fig. 43**– is: 'Jesus College Station Building Estate Cambridge 1925'. It is based on Ordnance Survey maps and carries a note:

> 'This Plan is based on the Ordnance Survey Map with the sanction of the Controller of HM Stationery Office.'

The Plan was prepared for Jesus College by Cook Hammond & Kell Ltd, based in Whitehall, and specialising in 'lithographing plans of estates not only for auctioneers but for land agents and owners'. The company remained in London – the address on this plan is 47 & 49 Tothill Street, Westminster – until a final closure in September 2011.

Unfortunately, this Plan shows signs of heavy use – or misuse sometimes; it is torn and discoloured but the railway details are generally clear and take our story through to the Grouping in 1923. London and North Eastern Railway is over-printed in small bold capitals. Cambridge Station buildings and much of the track-work, including the Goods Yards and carriage sidings, is shown so it is an appropriate Plan to end this chapter.

Chapter 10

HOW THE STATION WAS OPERATED: 1845 TO THE 1990S

Changing the station track layout – Signalling

hapter **9** illustrates the growth of Cambridge Station and **Fig 43** shows the increasingly complex track layout which had been developed by 1925. We are familiar with the Highway Code and the rules which govern vehicles and pedestrians on British roads. The nearest way in which road traffic management systems approach railway traffic management systems is traffic lights at road junctions or where one traffic stream must cross or join another traffic stream. Traffic lights use the same colours as colour light signals on the railway – red for stop; yellow or amber for caution and green for go.

The fundamental difference between railways and roads is that vehicles on roads are steered by a driver who can choose where to go. Railway vehicles are steered, or guided, by the rail tracks and railway drivers do not steer but start or stop a locomotive/train in accordance with the instructions they receive from signals. Railways are integrated machines where the signalling system, the trains and the tracks work together to achieve safe movements for the rolling stock on the railway and safe journeys for passengers and goods.

So the use of the track layout at Cambridge Station must be managed by a signalling system.

The essence of a signalling system is simple – like the messages from traffic lights to road users – and the detailed complexities of railway signalling need not concern this book. The Select Bibliography lists some excellent railway signalling books. I have used them to underpin this basic explanation of how changes in railway signalling technology have affected the Cambridge Station site.

The earliest form of signalling was manual, by hand signals to locomotive drivers. A C19th signalman, often called 'Policeman' because he policed or managed the railway traffic, was indicating GO if his arm was extended horizontally – **Fig. 44**.

If he raised one arm, as in **Fig 45**, that indicated caution and warned the driver that at, or possibly before, reaching the next signalman the driver may need to stop.

If the next signal man required the driver to stop, he held up both his arms – **Fig 46** – in a gesture which is still

GO   **CAUTION**   **STOP**

Fig. 44   Fig. 45   Fig. 46

recognizable today though no longer used for railway signalling except, perhaps for shunting movements.

At first, train management other than by the hand signals illustrated here, was on a sight or time-interval system which was soon proved to be very hazardous, especially when visibility was poor. By 1846, when Cambridge Station had opened, signalling was becoming mechanical so it will be helpful to summarise in chronological order from I to VI below how signalling has progressed:

I   Manual by hand signals

II   Mechanical, initially using simple signals and, from the 1860s, with the

signals shown in **Fig. 48** and **Fig. 49**. They were operated from Signal Boxes, connected to the signals and points by wire and rodding and operated by levers in the Signal Box. Cambridge Station was controlled by five mechanical Signal Boxes

III   Interlocking was introduced, mechanically and subsequently electrically, so that Signal Boxes became integrated mechanisms to ensure safe working of the railway machine. Sometimes mechanisms failed but most accidents were the results of human errors and misjudgements.

IV   Electro-Mechanical using electric

CAMBRIDGE MECHANICAL SIGNAL BOXES
Chesterton Junction Box

Barnwell Junction Box (on Mildenhall Branch)

Coldham Junction Box (for Newmarket branch)

Mill Road Junction Box

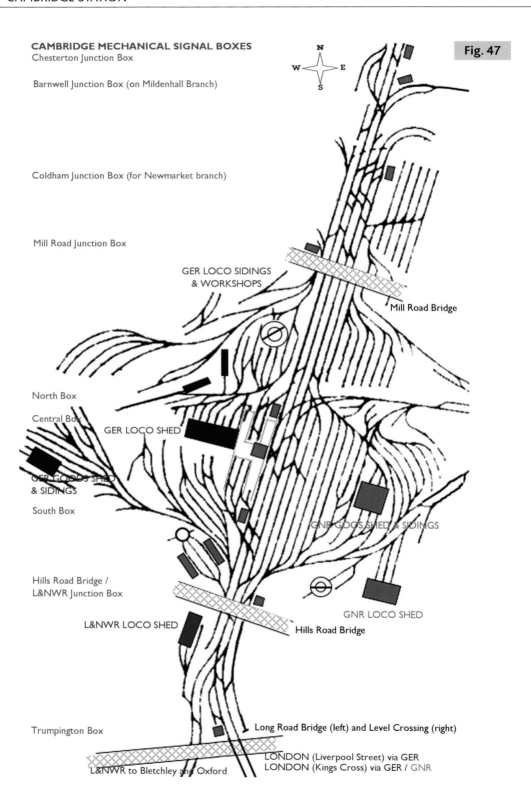

Fig. 47

N
W   E
S

GER LOCO SIDINGS
& WORKSHOPS

Mill Road Bridge

North Box

Central Box

GER LOCO SHED

GER GOODS SHED
& SIDINGS

South Box

GNR GOODS SHED & SIDINGS

Hills Road Bridge /
L&NWR Junction Box

GNR LOCO SHED

L&NWR LOCO SHED

Hills Road Bridge

Trumpington Box

Long Road Bridge (left) and Level Crossing (right)

LONDON (Liverpool Street) via GER
LONDON (Kings Cross) via GER / GNR

L&NWR to Bletchley and Oxford

motors to operate points and some signals distant from the Signal Box. Electric currents – track circuits – detected the whereabouts of trains and displayed that information to signal men. Signal levers in Signal Boxes were usually re-designed to operate as switches. Interlocking was achieved by electro-mechanical relays housed in large rooms under the lever-floors where the signalmen worked. After 1936 Cambridge Station was controlled by 2 electro-mechanical Signal Boxes.

V Digital interlocking, using microprocessors; VDU displays, and the automation of functions like routesetting, led to Power Boxes replacing several electro-mechanical Signal Boxes with one building. The acronym for such a Power Box was IECC – Integrated Electronic Control Centre. From 17 October 1982 Cambridge Station was controlled by one Power Box.

VI Regional Operating Centres (ROCs) are now replacing IECCs. Cambridge Power Box will be supplanted by Romford ROC.

At Cambridge Station, a complex track layout required five signal boxes and additional hand levers – often called ground frames – to operate points in sidings and in bay platforms 2 and 3. A middle road was provided to release the locomotive which brought a train into the dead end of the bay.

I have created **Fig. 47** from the GER's Diagrammatic Map of the System which was drawn by B C Dix of the Operating Department at Liverpool Street Station in 1919. The map shows the complete track layout of the whole station area, including goods yards, sidings and loco sheds. All the text on the map, the coloured buildings and the three road bridges are my additions. Most relevant to this Chapter are the nine mechanical signal boxes shown as red rectangles and named in red text. Five of these boxes were necessary to control railway traffic in and out of Cambridge Station.

Fig 48 is a clear and sharp photograph showing the principal types of semaphore signals which drivers approaching the south end of Cambridge Station on a down train in the early 1920s would see.

Not all the signals in the **Fig 48**

Fig. 48

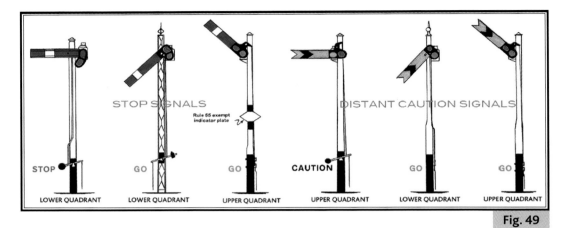

STOP SIGNALS

Rule 55 exempt
indicator plate

DISTANT CAUTION SIGNALS

STOP   GO   GO   CAUTION   GO   GO

LOWER QUADRANT   LOWER QUADRANT   UPPER QUADRANT   UPPER QUADRANT   LOWER QUADRANT   UPPER QUADRANT

Fig. 49

photograph are the same as those illustrated in **Fig. 49** but that reflects the way different railway companies designed their infrastructures. The principles of all the signals did not significantly differ from railway to railway in the 1920s and were laid down by the Board of Trade to ensure country-wide consistency. For Cambridge Station, however, a significant signalling change came about in 1926 when a new electro-mechanical system was installed. It was reported in *The Engineer* 10 December 1926 and below is a much condensed and edited account.

I have shortened and re-drawn the track and signalling plan, **Fig. 50**, from *The Engineer* article, omitting all the signals drawn onto the original plan because they obscure the detail we need to understand the working of the station.

'Cambridge Station, which is the property of the London & North Eastern Railway Company, is singular among the big railway stations in this country. There is perpetuated here one long platform to serve both Up and Down trains which was, in the past, very much favoured, in particular by the GWR as at Reading, Didcot and Gloucester.

'The platform at Cambridge is 600 yards [1,800ft] and as seen in the diagram it is served by a platform road which is common to both Up and Down trains.

'Down trains pass along the Through

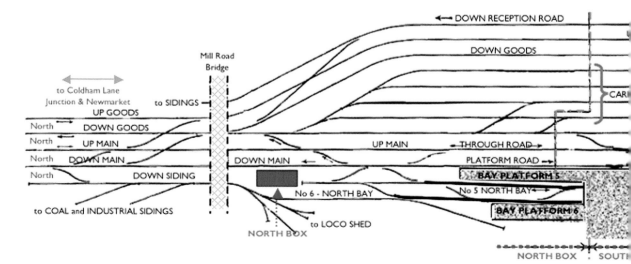

Road (which is also the Down Main and the Up Main), just south of the South Box, then across the scissors crossover onto the Platform Road (which is the Down Main) to the northern end of the long platform. Down trains then continue north on the Down Main.

'Up trains can enter the platform road by the crossover road just south of the North Box or, and more usually, they continue south on the Through Road (which is also the up Main and the Down Main) then across the scissors crossover onto the Platform Road at the southern end of the long platform. Up trains depart onto the Through Road just south of South Box and enter what becomes the Up main line.

'Paralleling the Platform Road is the Through Road which is a continuation of the Up main line. It, like the Platform Road, is common to Up and Down movements from the double slips, near the South Box, to the crossover road near the North Box.'

This is an early example of what today is termed bi-directional working. In the 1920s it was called 'reversible working' but the principle is the same. The new signalling system, and the potential for bi-directional working, made the long platform more practical as the explanation

of the uses of the scissors crossing illustrates –

'In addition, there is a scissors crossover at the centre of the long platform which allows:

01 a Down train that has been standing at the south end of the long platform to use the scissors crossover onto the Through Road and thus pass a train standing at the north end

02 a Down train to pass along the Through Road in front of the South Box and thence by the scissors crossover to the north end of the platform

03 an Up train that has been standing at the north end of the long platform to use the scissors crossover onto the Through Road and thus pass a train standing at the south end

04 an Up train to pass along the Through Road and thence by the scissors crossover to the south end of the platform.

'There are also two bay lines at each end of the station serving Platforms 2 and 3 at the south end and Platforms 5 and 6 at the north end. All these bay

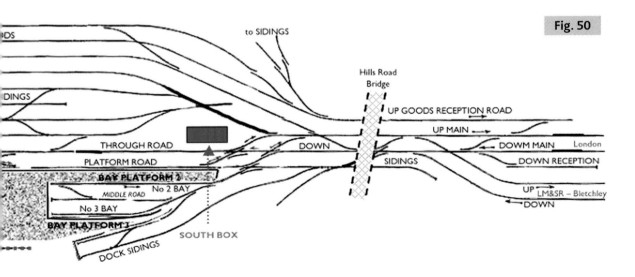

Fig. 50

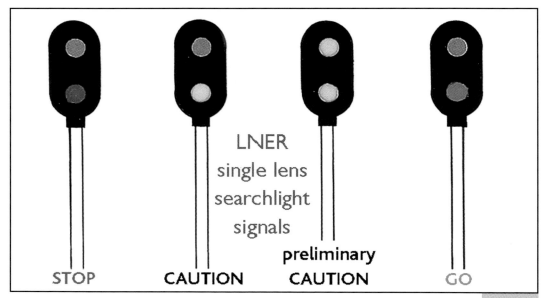

LNER
single lens
searchlight
signals

STOP   CAUTION   preliminary CAUTION   GO

Fig. 51

platform roads are signalled for both arrival and departure.

'Before re-signalling was put in hand in 1926, movements through the station required two mechanical signal-boxes at the south end; a centre signal box to work the scissors crossover – **Fig. 52**; two boxes at the north end – five boxes in all as shown on **Fig. 47**.

'These have now been replaced by one box at the south and one at the north end, Both are operated by power on the all-electric system associated with the British Power Railway Signal Company, Ltd., of Caxton House, Westminster, SW1.

'The South Box contains a frame of 128 levers, of which 17 are spare and the North Box has a frame of 72 levers, of which 13 are spare.

Another significant signalling change was the introduction of colour light signals as shown in **Fig. 51**:

Finally, North and South boxes were closed in 1982 when the new Cambridge Power Box opened. It controlled lines north to Ely, as far south as Stansted, and to Dullingham on the Newmarket and Bury St Edmunds line.

By 2018 Romford ROC will control the whole of the Anglian rail network.

Fig .52: Central Signal box and some of the semaphore signals it controlled for the scissors crossover.

Fig. 52

Fig. 53

Fig.53: Cambridge Station colonnade in the mid-1920s with an unattractive awning along the centre bays and the LNER advertising its presence on the former ECR/GNR/GER Station.

Fig 54: LNER continued to operate branch lines, often with elderly steam locomotives and rolling stock. E4 2-4-0 2790 (built Stratford works, September 1900) on 10.28am to Mildenhall 30 March 1948.

Fig. 54

Chapter 11

HOW THE STATION WAS OPERATED: 1845 TO THE 1990S

Goods Sheds, Goods Yards and goods by rail

Figs. 55 and 56 are OS map extracts which illustrate the 1927 complexity of goods sheds and sidings which the LNER sustained and operated around the passenger Station. Because the whole site is so extensive the maps are divided into a south side – **Fig. 55** – and a north side – **Fig. 56**. The whole layout is not significantly different from the GER/GNR 1919 layout in **Fig. 47** on page 74 and all the maps show the importance of goods traffic to Railway Companies in the mid-twentieth century.

Both maps show the extensive range of sidings north, north west, south west and east of the station as well as the layout of tracks in **Fig. 56** which serve the large engine shed adjoining Platform 6. The lines east of the station include a number of carriage sidings and, to the east of them, goods sidings and in **Fig. 55** two goods sheds and a small engine shed.

A plan of the Cambridge Station area today shows that the engine sheds, associated track work, and the large areas of goods yards have all gone. It is reasonable to ask what was happening before around Cambridge Station to require these facilities.

The *Great Eastern Railway Magazine* in 1919 contains the notes from a lecture by R.A. Newman from the Company's Commercial Superintendent's Office which explains that:

'Goods are accepted for conveyance at Goods Stations, Wharves or Sidings, or in the case of smalls, traffic is collected from traders by the Company's vans, or by Cartage Agents employed by the Company.'

Mr Newman did not explain that the parliamentary legislation which governed the operation of railways made it explicit that a railway was a 'Common Carrier'. In simple terms this meant that, for instance, if a circus proprietor called at a railway station and asked for an elephant to be moved to another show site, the railway could not refuse the request. It may be that the elephant could not immediately be transported but go it must. If a road transport operator was approached, however, the answer would almost certainly be, 'No; we do not move elephants' and the circus proprietor could not quote any legislation to support his request. The railways' common carrier obligations were understandable when there was no other means of swiftly

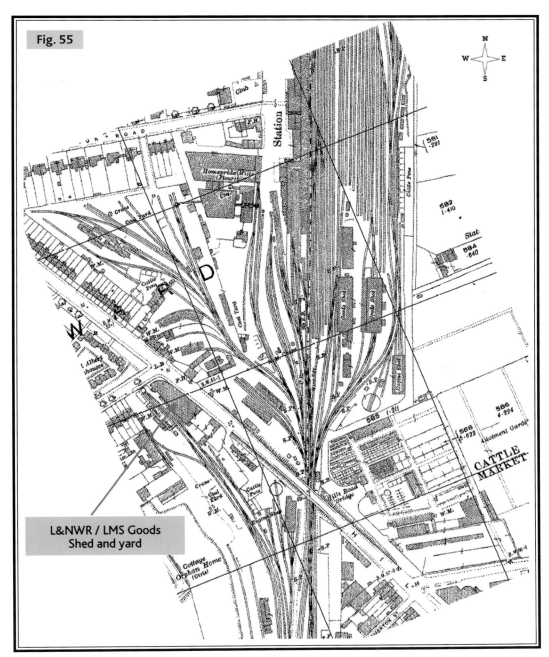

Fig. 55

L&NWR / LMS Goods
Shed and yard

moving goods about the country. But, as road transport companies developed, the railway companies – which had to maintain their own permanent way and civil engineering infrastructure – were economically disadvantaged until the 1962 Transport Act finally released them from common carrier requirements.

Mr Newman did explain that the railway companies could negotiate terms for some traffic but national

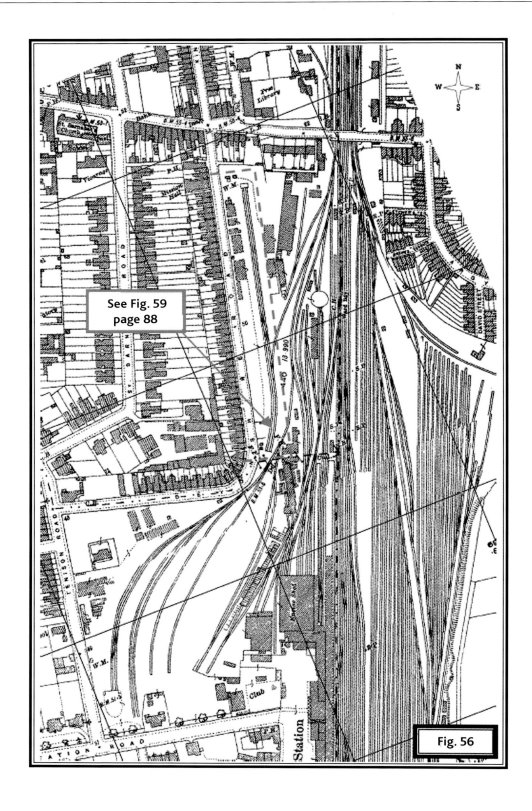

See Fig. 59
page 88

Fig. 56

emergencies or military requirements could not be evaded:

'… the railway companies were not compelled to carry dangerous goods or inflammable substances but were at liberty to make their own terms. There is, however, one exception to this rule. All companies are bound to carry munitions of war for the Army and Navy, not only in times of war but also in times of peace.'

He did not comment on this sort of anomaly but he did give a helpful list of the sort of traffic which passed through Cambridge:

'The Railway Company caters for nearly all kinds of traffic:

> East Anglia: Barley, Oats, Wheat, other Cereals; Flour mills including Cambridge; roots – especially mangolds, potatoes in the Fen district

> Fruit from the Cambridge and Wisbech areas – Strawberries, Raspberries, Gooseberries, Currants. Plums and Apples

> Broxbourne, Cheshunt, Lea Valley stations, Long Stanton, Waltham: cut-flowers, grapes, cucumbers, tomatoes raised under glass.

> Neighbourhood of Colchester, Fordham, Kelvedon, Norwich, Witham: seed farms

> Norfolk and Suffolk stations: Dairy, poultry

> Live Stock to and from the chief Cattle Markets: Bury St Edmunds, Cambridge, Chelmsford, Colchester, Ipswich, King's Lynn, Norwich, St. Ives – and Tufnell Park for the Metropolitan Cattle Market,

> Bramford, Stowmarket, King's Lynn: Chemical Manures

> Bury St- Edmund's, Cambridge, Colchester, Ipswich Lowestoft, Norwich, Romford, Yarmouth: Breweries

> Fish traffic:

>> Herrings and Trawl Fish from Lowestoft, Yarmouth

>> Oysters from Brightlingsea, Wivenhoe

>> Sprats from Aldeburgh.

>> Shrimps from Harwich

>> Crabs from Cromer

>> Mussels, Cockles, Whelks from Kings Lynn and Wells

> Machinery from Bury St Edmunds, Chelmsford, Colchester Ipswich, Leiston, Maldon Norwich Thetford

> Ely, Histon, Silvertown, Tiptree: Jams, marmalades and preserves

> Norwich (from Coleman & Co): Mustard, Starch, and Wincarnis Tonic Wine [originally marketed as Liebig's Extract of Meat and Malt Wine.]

> Cambridge, Churchbury, Edmonton, Harold Wood, Rayleigh, Rochford, Shenfield, Stansted Sudbury Whittlesea: Bricks, tiles and cement.'

Much of the railway business for a hub like Cambridge is shunting wagons into different trains from those they arrived in, then redistributing the contents of some wagons into other wagons to forward them; loading or unloading goods brought into the goods yards by railway cartage or by the consignors or recipients so although Cambridge is not specifically mentioned often in this list, its place is implied.

Another side of the generic 'goods' title in this chapter is railway sundries and parcels traffic. The most cost-effective goods traffic for railways was 'Wagon load traffic'. Many items in Mr Newman's list – like the last item: bricks, tiles and cement – would be bulk transport in wagons or, even better, in train loads. However, railways also carried many single items, or groups of several small items, which would not constitute a wagon load and were categorised as 'smalls,' or 'sundries' and/or 'parcels'. The differences between these two categories were size/weight and urgency. Any item weighing more than about 50lb (22.5kg) and measuring more than about 6ft (2m) in length was a 'sundry' and would be handled in the goods sheds at Cambridge.

Railway parcels were generally more urgent than sundries, sometimes of higher value and would be carried in the guard's brake of a passenger train or in special trains of parcels vans which were usually bogie vehicles like the passenger carriages.

At Cambridge Station, railway parcels were handled for many years in a large Parcels Office on Platform 3. When I worked at the Station in the 1950s, the chief parcels clerk and the man expertly in charge of the Parcels Office was Harry Plumb. He knew railway geography like the back of his hand because many parcels, like passengers but entirely inert, had to make quite complex journeys from Cambridge to, say, South Molton or Barnstaple in Devon; Pitlochry in Perth & Kinross, Scotland; Corris in Gwyneth, Wales. Harry knew the way, often the changes the parcel would need and certainly the train time and platform for the parcel's departure from Cambridge.

The foregoing maps in this book, Mr Newman's list and this brief summary of Cambridge as a goods hub illustrates the complexity of railway goods services. The mechanical operation of goods trains, the shunting of wagons and re-marshalling into new trains, and the loading/unloading of goods, sundries and parcels were the most visible aspects of railway good services.

Relatively unseen was the clerical administration and my researches have uncovered an article entitled *Invoices and Other Documents* by A.C. Chauncy in an 1899 *Railway Magazine*. I have culled some relevant passages and it is instructive to read them in the light our knowledge of twenty-first century digital office procedures:

> 'The public does not concern itself much about the transit of its precious merchandize. The goods are sent off, and they are received, or if they are not received, or received in bad order, the public wants to know the reason why. But it may repay us to look behind the scenes, and see some of the few things that really go on when goods are sent by rail.
>
> 'The sender … makes out a Consignment Note [for the Railway Goods Office]. When this Note is made out in the sender's office by one of his clerks, well and good; it is generally legible … The Consignment Note is the evidence of the contract between the public and the carriers. It may be smart and regular, done in ink and a big round hand, or it may be scrawled in pencil on greasy paper. In either form it is legal evidence of the contract.'

As Mr Chauncy explains, the Consignment Note is stage 1 of the clerical process – what we now speak of as 'the paper trail' (though it may be digital) which underpins the contract implicit in the Consignment Note. Stage 2, for the railways, is the Invoice:

> 'The Invoice is started on the journey through life by the Invoice Clerk, seated on a high stool and working under a flaring globe-less gas jet.
>
> 'In most cases the goods are brought in at the last moment, all together, and

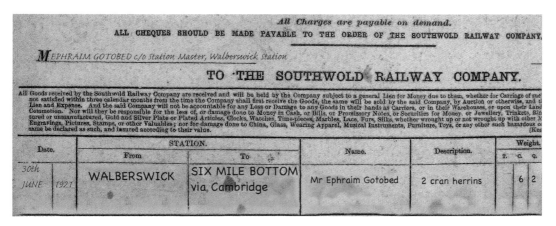

All Charges are payable on demand.

ALL CHEQUES SHOULD BE MADE PAYABLE TO THE ORDER OF THE SOUTHWOLD RAILWAY COMPANY.

Mr EPHRAIM GOTOBED c/o Station Master, Walberswick Station

TO ·THE SOUTHWOLD RAILWAY COMPANY.

All Goods received by the Southwold Railway Company are received and will be held by the Company subject to a general Lien for Money due to them, whether for Carriage of such
not satisfied within three calendar months from the time the Company shall first receive the Goods, the same will be sold by the said Company, by Auction or otherwise, and t
Lien and Expense. And the said Company will not be accountable for any Loss or Damage to any Goods in their hands as Carriers, or in their Warehouses, or upon their Land
Commotion. Nor will they be responsible for the loss of, or damage done to Money in Cash, or Bills, or Promissory Notes, or Securities for Money, or Jewellery, Trinkets, Rin
tured or unmanufactured, Gold and Silver Plate or Plated Articles, Clocks, Watches, Time-pieces, Marbles, Lace, Furs, Silks, whether wrought up or not wrought up with other M
Engravings, Pictures, Stamps, or other Valuables; nor for damage done to China, Glass, Wearing Apparel, Musical Instruments, Furniture, Toys, or any other such hazardous or
same be declared as such, and insured according to their value.   [Kn

| Date. | STATION. | | Name. | Description. | Weight. | | |
	From	To			T.	C.	Q.
30th JUNE 1921	WALBERSWICK	SIX MILE BOTTOM via. Cambridge	Mr Ephraim Gotobed	2 cran herrins		6	2

Fig. 57: A contrived example of a typically pretentious Invoice from the eight and a half mile long narrow gauge Southwold Railway.

the Invoice Clerk has any time, from an hour to ten minutes, in which to make out his daily quota of invoices. [He must, for example, calculate the appropriate rate for the goods in question], say, 13 cwt. 2 qrs. 25 lbs. @ 13s. 4d. per ton … These Invoices, when made out, are passed through the tissue copying book, where the copies, which when dry are fairly distinct, are left until they are abstracted.

'The Invoices, as a general rule, travel with the traffic. They are still in many cases nailed to the side of the wagon by the office youth with hammer and tin-tacks; though most … up-to-date wagons are fitted with invoice clips.

The goods are entered from the Invoice on a clean Carman's Delivery Sheet, which goes out with the Carman and comes back covered with signatures and various specimens of dirt, grease, and micro-organisms too numerous to mention [however] a 'clean signature' (the dirt on the Delivery Sheet excepted) is held as evidence of completion of the contract.'

Meanwhile, in the Railway Goods Office –

'Then comes the abstracting of the invoices. There are, of course, 2 sets of invoices to be abstracted: the "outwards" and the "inwards".… The invoices that are "outwards" at the sending station are "inwards" at the receiving station.

'The outwards invoices are abstracted from the tissue copying book by a clerk with a pen laden with copying ink in one hand, and a red chalk pencil in the other. Given ordinary luck and fairly distinct tissues to work from, quite a respectable number of invoices can be abstracted in one day.

'[All the outwards and inwards] Invoices [are given] a progressive number, known commonly as the 'pro,' placed on the top right hand corner. Then they are pasted in a book in the order of their 'pro' numbers. And a motley collection they make. As a rule, the smaller the railway company the larger and more pretentious the invoice.

One might suppose that there was little more to do to the Invoices, now neatly numbered, pasted into a book, their details and charges entered into Accounts Ledgers, and filed for reference. Not so says Mr Chauncy:

'After all the worry, anxiety and stationery that has been spent upon a consignment of traffic, a grateful public, one would think, will pay the charges cheerfully and with a good grace.

'But, alas! it is not so.'

We must refer, therefore, to yet another piece of railway stationery – the Overcharge Sheet. Experience showed that overcharges on Invoices were far more numerous than undercharges. And it was much easier to refund an overcharge than to collect an undercharge. Mr Chauncy explains:

'The public may not agree with this, but it is the sad experience of one who has tried. The long experience [of the Invoice Clerk] tends to make him err, when err he does, on the right side. [i.e. on the Railway Company's side.]

'Overcharge sheets are of two kinds, local and foreign. The former are soon dealt with. The agents or stationmasters at both ends sign them, and the cash is refunded.

'The foreign overcharge sheets, however, have a longer and more varied existence. They have to go through the Goods Managers' offices of the various [railway and cartage] companies interested … Sometimes they do not return until the overcharge is "forgiven" [rarely] and "forgotten." [never].'

Mr Chauncy concludes his paper with an entertaining comparison of the 'inert' goods and the 'active passenger:'

'A consignment of goods, as we have seen, takes a great deal more looking after than does a passenger.

'The latter takes his ticket and jumps in. Thus he consigns and invoices himself. As a rule, too, he knows where he wants to go to; "tranships" himself at the proper junction, and is 'not carted' – at any rate by the railway company – at his destination. It is a ready money transaction too, which is not always the case with goods traffic.

'There is no necessity to label a good, steady, sober passenger and, if the carriage wherein he travels is labelled, the name of the destination is shown on a neatly painted board. But a choice collection of labels are kept for decorating goods wagons …

'We stand often on a platform and see the fast express, with a shriek and a whirl, dash through the station at lightning speed. Here is the showy side of railway work.

'To-day you have been with me for a while in the prosy, grim, [gas-lit] and grubby Goods Office. Here you have seen the dull matter-of-fact side of railway goods work. The public does not often see it.'

The public does not often see the work of the Goods Sheds and Goods Offices because they are usually – as at Cambridge – in areas of railway property, sidings and Goods Yards which are not open to the public except on railway business. **Fig. 58** is an exemplar of the warnings which Railway Companies liberally displayed:

Glimpses of the Parcels Office at Cambridge Station, Platform 3, would be available to passengers catching a train from that platform, or just to the curious wanderer looking around the station while awaiting a train. It was a busy scene, often

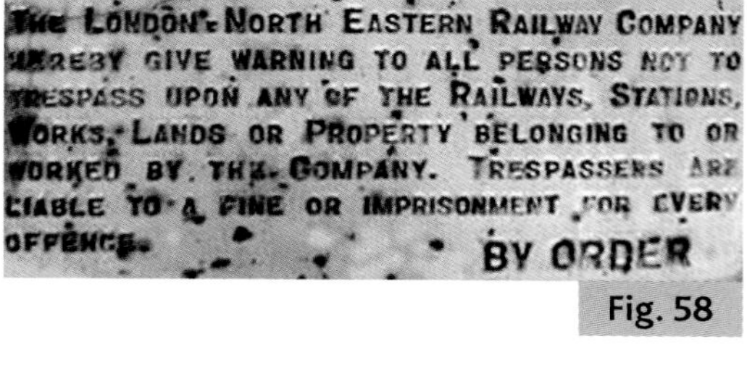

Fig. 58

with many varied sizes of parcels, large platform scales beside the office doorway, and several clerks with clipboards recording details of parcels or sticking on labels and parcel stamps.

Mr Newman, whose lecture on Goods traffic has been quoted above, gave a similar lecture on The Parcels Office (*Great Eastern Railway Magazine* 1920) and sections from it are a useful complement:

'Railway companies are not compelled to carry all kinds of goods by passenger trains but most, if not all, are bound by a private Act to afford reasonable facilities for the conveyance of perishables such as milk, fruit, fish, meat, etc, and the rates are accordingly fixed. For non-perishables by passenger train we have the right to make our own charges.

'Railway companies are not common carriers of dogs, horses, cattle and other animals, live poultry and birds and their liability to charge specific sums is limited, unless the value is declared at the time of booking, and a percentage is paid for the extra risk taken.

'All ordinary parcels are charged upon a mileage scale. Certain articles can be carried at a reduced scale provided the sender signs an owner's risk note.

'Parcels by passenger train are categorised in the same terms as for goods train traffic:

S-to-S rate: station to station only – no cartage performed at either end

C-and-D rate: which includes collection and delivery (or in some instances it might be D only)

Passenger train parcels traffic, like the goods train traffic, has a large number of special or exceptional rates for specific traffics, such as:

> newspapers
> milk

> fish
> fruit
> flowers
> carriages
> boats
> bicycles
> mail-carts
> wild and domestic animals
> and many other things

'Parcel charges by passenger train can be paid at the Parcels Office on the S-to-S rate and, as with the Post Office, railways use parcel stamps at values which relate to mileage charges.

Let us assume that a parcel is brought into Cambridge Station Parcels Office, weighed, found to be less than 50lb, and charged for carriage to Bishop's Stortford, a distance of 30 miles and 27 chains. The distance is just over 30 miles but under 50 miles so the charge would be 1s.11d.

'The Clerk would collect that amount from the sender and draw stamps of 1s. and 11d. value and affix them to the parcel. He would then enter the particulars upon his Outwards Counter Sheet. The booking is then completed … and the parcel can be passed out ready for a porter to place it in the next train. The Outwards Counter Sheets constitute the record of sending stations' transactions with the public. At the close of the day the money column is cast up and the total figure is entered into an Abstract book.

'The Stamp Issue Book shows the commencing number and closing number for the day, the total number issued and the amount; much the same as the Booking Clerk with his [Edmundson] passenger tickets. The total for the day should agree with the total of the Outwards Counter Sheet. The money in the till, subject to refunds or other credits, should also agree, and the figure is then recorded in the Daily

Fig. 59

Cash Settlement Book and the amount paid over to the Station Master.

'The idea of the Counter Sheet having to agree with the daily record of stamps issued is to enable each day's debit to be fixed against the Parcels Clerk.

'Because all parcels traffic by passenger train is forwarded carriage-paid the Parcels Clerk at the receiving station should have no charges to raise or to record on his Inwards Counter Sheet.

Most of us have memories of passenger travel on the railways, some of us may remember railway parcels services but, except perhaps for business people, railway goods traffic is a long-forgotten story.

Fig. 59 is another long-forgotten story for many of us. It shows the Devonshire Road sidings, indicated on the **Fig. 56** map by an orange dashed line. At this time, coal was still the principal source of energy for both domestic heating and industrial power. For example, all the houses along Devonshire Road have chimneys and there are many tons of coal in the yard. The piles of coal are divided by timber walls (made mainly from redundant railway sleepers) into a number of pens owned and managed by the coal merchants. There were at least ten coal merchants operating from the various railway yards at Cambridge Station all distributing coal to Cambridge customers.

The Goods Offices for Cambridge appeared to be welcoming profitable train load business in coal but the number of coal merchants and the separate and scattered wagons in **Fig. 59** suggest otherwise. Train load traffic should be like the merry-go-round trains that deliver coal to major customers such as coal-burning power stations. But where were these customers in Cambridge, and did they have private sidings serving their needs?

No, they did not and, as all the principal railway companies which served Cambridge – ECR; GER; L&NWR; LMS; LNER – knew to their cost, East Anglia had no coal, few other minerals and Cambridge had no major industries. But as Barbara Freese in *Coal – A human history*, published by Arrow Books in 2006 has suggested, 'With Coal we have light, strength, power, wealth and civilisation; without Coal we have darkness, poverty and barbarism.'

There was a very large market for domestic coal, for heating and cooking. Large institutions like the Colleges which make up the University of Cambridge all had residential accommodation to heat and the University embraced many large buildings like lecture theatres and laboratories, for instance, the Cavendish Laboratories, where the first controlled nuclear disintegrations were achieved and the double-helix structure of the DNA molecule was determined by Francis Crick and James Watson.

Ironically, from a railway perspective, a large market for coking coal was Cambridge Gas Works but although it had a private siding near Coldham Junction the coal had then to be transhipped by road to the gasworks site adjoining the River Cam.

As **Fig. 59** shows, railway goods traffic in Cambridge often meant extensive shunting to break up goods trains arriving in the Reception Sidings and to move wagons to whichever Goods Yard/Goods Shed their contents were expected. In the Coal Yard illustrated, the open wagon at the buffer stop has been unloaded of

building materials which are at present on the ground beside the wagon. Perhaps they are intended for internal railway use, or for one of the coal merchants, or perhaps there was nowhere else to put them. The next nearest wagon, on the adjoining track, appears to contain gravel or sand but because it is next to coal pens it must probably be moved again before unloading is practicable.

Coal from the next two wagons has been unloaded onto the ground so must be moved again, perhaps into a specific merchant's pen which was not accessible when the wagons arrived. It may be the wagons had to be unloaded because they are 'foreigners' – belonging to another railway company – or private owner wagons belonging to the colliery which mined the coal. In either case their owners would want them back swiftly and if they were delayed because of slow handling at Cambridge the owner could charge demurrage. Remembering Mr Newman's lecture on Invoices:

'This demurrage charge against the home station – Cambridge – would be an entry on the Foreign Overcharge Sheet and would eventually have to be justified to the LNE Railway Audit Office. This Office, and the senior officers administering the railway, wanted to see speedy unloading and return of empties to improve utilisation of rolling stock.'

Fig. 60 shows the Hills Road bridge and brings the Cambridge goods story a little

Fig. 60

more up to date, probably to the mid-1960s. There is a fixed crane on the left; the jib of a mobile crane on the right; a Class 04 0-6-0 diesel shunter in the background; and 2 containers.

In the image of Hills Road bridge sidings, the cranes speak for themselves about the need to have lifting capacity available in the Goods Yards. The containers are a solution to the development of cost-effective wagon load traffic. The contents of the container, unlike the wagon, did not have to be filled or emptied on railway premises but could be filled by a consignor; delivered by road to a goods yard; craned onto a flat wagon and travel by rail to a goods yard nearest to its ultimate destination; craned off onto a flat lorry then finally delivered to a consignee.

The diesel shunter reflects the gradual elimination of steam locomotives from British Railways. Subsequent chapters discuss this development so it seems appropriate to end this chapter by looking back once more. Lyn Brooks in *Great Eastern Journal* No 5 reflects on shunters which preceded the diesel shunter:

'GER 1hp SHUNTING ENGINE – CLASS GG

'Amongst the many diverse loco types inherited by the GER in 1862 were several hundred of these units, of basically similar design … All were from 'Outside Suppliers', as was the great majority of GER motive-power at that time …. The design did not change much over the history of the GER, and even James Holden did not try to standardise them.

'[In 1911] the Class total was 1,750 units; the bulk of them worked in the London Area and the rest were distributed all over the GER system. All were numbered, the number being engraved on small brass plates. They all had names.

'There were 3 distinct types under the one classification depending on the unit's weight in full working order:

> Light Parcels: 12-13cwt
> Single Vans & Trolleys: 14-15cwt
> Shunters: 15cwt and over

'Heaviest of the lot was the Bishop's Stortford shunter at 1 ton 3/4 cwt. One diagram issued for a 17cwt shunter showed the weight distribution as 9cwt 2qtrs on the front end and 7cwt 2qtrs on the rear.

'One very important aspect of the engines was their ability to be worked in multiple, many years before this was possible with modern locomotives. To each GG was allocated a driver, and in many cases one driver had two units under his charge.

'The LNER continued to buy more of the Class, although compared with more conventional motive-power their life expectancy was short – six years at the most. The LNER also separated the Class into two Class parts - GG/M and GG/F, the two parts referring to slight differences in undercarriage details. BR also continued to purchase replacement units, and the last of the Class was 'Charlie' of Newmarket, withdrawn in 1967.

'There was no standard livery for the Class, and they usually appeared in varying shades of black, brown, grey, white and attractive two-tone schemes … it is said that BR withdrew them from service because of difficulty applying yellow warning panels.

'[Finally] whereas the disposal of residual ash and clinker on other locos was a problem, on this Class the fuel residual was a great help in the Annual Station Gardens Competition. Country Station gardens have never been quite the same since the last of the Class disappeared.'

We may enjoy a chuckle at Mr Brooks' entertaining memory of some of the working horses – the shunting horses – in GER, LNER and BR times on the railway in East Anglia but we must remember that they gave very useful service. A number of other memories of working shunting horses were prompted in subsequent issues of *Great Eastern Journal* by Mr Brooks' article but unfortunately none mentioned Cambridge. I remember watching a shunting horse working in the Hills Road – Station Road Goods Yard in the 1950s and 1960s but I did not record anything at the time. Fortunately, a description of one horse working at Gidea Park Goods Yard in 1957 has been published in the *GE Journal* and it shows why the horse was especially useful working a network of sidings:

'[The horse's] main duties [were] to pull wagons in and out of the various installations [in the Yard] and to form a train in the late afternoon.

'[For instance], the shunter unhooked [a wagon] from a train. The horse

was then positioned alongside and to the front, a lead from the collar being hooked into the 'W' iron of the leading pair of wheels of the wagon on the same side as the horse was standing. On a word of command, the horse would move slowly off until the lead became taut; when this happened, an extra exertion was made and the wagon would begin to roll. Once rolling, of course, very little effort was required to keep it moving and so long as the lead was kept tight, it continued to move. If the wagon needed to change tracks, the shunter either preset the points or alternatively, where this could not be done, the horse would be called upon to stop whilst the wagon was braked, the points were changed, and the above procedure repeated.

'If a change of direction of travel for the wagon was required, i.e., setting back into another siding after passing over a set of points, the horse was unhooked from the wagon and re-attached to the other end to pull it back into the siding.

'When forming a train, the horse

Fig.61: Boxer the horse shunting at Cambridge in January 1957. The GNR Goods Shed is on the left and the GER Goods Shed on the right. The horse driver is Sidney Arthur Plumb and the picture is recording Boxer's retirement from railway work.

Fig. 61

knew by experience exactly what effort was needed to move a wagon and when to stop pulling, thus letting it roll to a stop. In most cases, the wagon would slow to a stop with either the buffers slightly apart or just touching the buffers of the wagon in front. It was then a simple matter for the shunter to couple up. Consequently, very little noise was made during shunting as the wagons never rolled with any real force into each other. This lack of noise was the most noticeable thing about the whole procedure when using horses for shunting.'

I suspect, from my own experience with driving a heavy horse on agricultural tasks, that Mr Plumb used to talk to Boxer when he was having his 'bait' and Boxer his nosebag. If they talked of local railway

matters and shunting I am sure that Whitemoor Marshalling Yard at March would have been mentioned. It was an enormous hump-shunting yard, opened 3 March 1929 with 43 sorting sidings and space for 4,000 wagons to be sorted by shunting to up to 350 destinations. Developments and enlargements meant that by the start of the Second World War, 8,000 wagons could be sorted each day. At the time, it was a state-of-the art LNER development. Instead of shunters pushing down a wagon brake lever, as Sidney Plumb is doing in **Fig. 61**, it was the first hump shunting yard in the UK to use pneumatically operated retarders, or wagon brakes, to slow the wagons as they ran down from the hump and into the sidings for marshalling into trains.

At Whitemoor, all the coal and goods

Fig. 62: The view south from the hump at Whitemoor showing the retarders and the Control Tower at the North End of the Yard. Coal wagons, which constituted much of the railway traffic into East Anglia, are being divided into the various sidings for onward transit.

Fig. 62

traffic intended for the Eastern Section of the LNER from places north, east and west of Doncaster, via Peterborough and from collieries and yards in Nottinghamshire Derbyshire and South Yorkshire via Lincoln, was received, sorted and marshalled for forward transit.

All the sidings were numbered and, initially, the wagons shunted into the centre groups of sidings were through loads to other sorting and delivery yards on the GER/LNER lines in East Anglia – and south to London – including Norwich, Spitalfields, Ilford, Angel Road, and Cambridge. Sidney Plumb would have known that many of the wagons he shunted with Boxer would have come through Whitemoor, or be bound for it.

I remember seeing Boxer and Mr Plumb at work in the Cambridge Goods Yards and, though I never spoke to him, I learned of Whitemoor in my railway work when I was a cut-flower clerk at Long Stanton on the St. Ives branch. A quick check-back to Mr Newman's list of railway goods traffic (page 83) shows Long Stanton and cut flowers. Each afternoon hundreds of boxes of cut flowers were delivered to Long Stanton station by growers, or brought in by railway cartage. They were labelled to markets – Covent Garden for instance, or Liverpool, Birmingham, Bristol, Cardiff, Edinburgh

– so all over the country. A goods pick-up from Cambridge arrived at Long Stanton about 4.30pm and every day took on to Whitemoor more than twenty VanFits (goods closed vans with fitted brakes) for night express goods trains which guaranteed the growers an early-morning delivery to their chosen market.

This chapter has concentrated on the Goods facilities which were formerly GER and GNR but another major railway company had an interest in Cambridge as a potentially profitable entrepôt. L&NWR, subsequently to become LMS, came to Cambridge in a south westerly direction from Bletchley and Oxford. The company built a Loco Shed at Cambridge which is marked on the **Fig. 47** map on page 74 but the position of the shed – and the absence of an L&NWR Goods Shed confirms that the company was not successful breaking into the GER / GNR developments.

However, and not to be outdone, the L&NWR bought land north west of their Loco Shed and built an enormous and superficially very impressive Good Shed on the junction of Brooklands Avenue with Hills Road. I have labelled this substantial development on **Fig. 55** map (page 81) which also shows cattle pens, a coal yard and a yard crane. **Fig. 63** illustrates the road side façade in the 1930s

Fig. 63: The L&NWR then LMS Goods Station on the Hills Road/Brooklands Avenue corner, and boldly labelled London Midland & Scottish Railway, in around 1935.

Fig. 63

when LMS was the operating company. The picture shows that, like the LNER on the front of Cambridge Station (page 79), the LMS were good at advertising their Railway.

I remember the building in the 1960s when it no longer carried a railway name. I suspect it was no longer in railway ownership but it was still an important warehouse and distribution centre for E. Pordage & Co, a long-established vegetable and fruit wholesalers. Their name is just visible in **Fig. 63** and more so in **Fig. 64**.

This goods shed was a splendid building, now replaced by a large office block. I recall seeing steam-heated banana vans being shunted along the siding behind the building in the 1960s. Cambridge Goods Sheds and Yards were part of the busy entrepôt that this chapter has illustrated.

'Coal! Coal! Coal! Received from GNR, MR, L&NWR. It pours through March

Fig. 64

[before Whitemoor] in a never-ending stream. To … London, Norwich, Parkeston, East Anglia in general. Travel from London on the Cambridge line and see how many long trains … you will pass. Some 90% ….are coal and goods trains.' *Great Eastern Railway Magazine*. 1913

We have seen something of the Cambridge coal business but the railway itself was a major consumer – not least for the steam locomotives that hauled the trains!

Chapter 12

HOW THE STATION WAS OPERATED: 1845 TO THE 1990S

Cambridge Motive Power Depots

To write of Motive Power Depots, or MPDs, rather than Engine Sheds indicates that this chapter is a cusp in the generally progressive chronological story of the operation of Cambridge Station. All the map illustrations thus far have labelled engine sheds, or loco sheds, but change is coming.

Sydney Plumb and Boxer in the last chapter, and my experiences at Long Stanton and Cambridge stations, were in the 1950s and 1960s. At this time, steam locomotives were being replaced by diesel-powered locomotives and multiple units. The term Engine Shed was rightly seen as inappropriate for the clean, well-equipped and relatively sophisticated facilities needed for servicing and repairing diesel stock. Fortunately, the term Motive Power Depot – MPD – could at first be all-embracing. It had to be in early diesel days, when the only spaces and the only workshops were in steam Engine Sheds.

Beginning at the beginning the first illustration we have of Cambridge Station is that from the *Illustrated London News* of the 'new' Station (**Fig. 10**, page 26) and beside it appears to be a rather

rudimentary Engine Shed. As with the railway line which should have served the platform at the Station the artist omitted any lines into or out of the Engine Shed although a hazy image of a locomotive is seen through the Shed.

Map evidence, and plans/diagrams of the Station area tell us a little more about the need for more than one Engine Shed at Cambridge because at least four railway companies were working to and from Cambridge.

Fig. 30, page 56, signed off by C J Allen – who worked for the GER – in 1908 is a Diagram of Passenger Running Lines and shows the GE Engine Shed at the country end of the Station and adjoining Platform 6.

Earlier evidence, and with the Engine Shed in the same place, is an ECR Plan, from Jesus College Archives, dated 1861 and 1862 – **Figs 35, 36, 37** pages 62, 63 and 64–65. **Fig. 42**, page 69 is another Plan from the same Archive but now a GNR & GER Station Plan of 1874 and the same, quite large Engine Shed is shown. Although the GNR and the GER apparently worked together relatively harmoniously, this Engine Shed is a GER Shed, as Cecil Allen's diagram shows, because the GER owned and managed the whole Station.

One more piece of useful map evidence is **Fig. 43**, page 70, which is the Jesus College Station Building Estate 1925 and by this date the LNER has taken over the station site. To allow more equitable management of 'foreign' locomotives there are two more Engine Sheds shown, each with a turntable as has the main GER/ LNER Shed. The other sheds are not even named as 'Engine Shed' but the turntable helps to identify them and I have added a red railway company name near each one.

Near the Cattle Market is the former GNR Shed and just south west of Hills Road bridge is the former L&NWR Shed which was created to serve the Bletchley and Oxford line.

A final piece of evidence is the Midland Railway's running rights over GER lines and illustrated in **Fig. 28**, page 54 but MR did not have running rights access to any of the Cambridge Engine Sheds.

An excellent and detailed illustrated description of Cambridge Engine Sheds is *Great Eastern Railway Engine Sheds, Vol II.* The Shed is described as:

'Principal Shed of a main GE District [with] over 100 locomotives. GER was not an especially prosperous railway company so, at the Grouping, the LNER inherited … a series of (often partly derelict) buildings [around the main Shed] ranging from stores and a machine-shop [to] smiths and carpenters premises strung out in a long line of hovels merging with what was grandly termed the "Locomotive Shops".

'These premises had originated long years before as a small timber shack containing the shear-legs and by 1923 engines were being repaired at the rate of 75 a year; an astonishing and most praise worthy figure carried out to high standards …'

The LNER put in hand a number of improvements, including a coaling plant to replace the extensive coal banks where men worked without any roof in all sorts of weather. A new north-light roof was built over the Engine Shed and overall capacity was 130 locomotives, though only one third of that number could be accommodated in the roofed Shed. **Fig. 65** shows the north-facing front of the shed and illustrates the draughty and dark atmosphere characteristic of most steam locomotive sheds.

Cambridge Engine Shed was responsible for a variety of locomotive types and ages, from mainline passenger express locos to many goods 2-4-0s and 0-6-0s including several   0-6-0Ts for

Fig. 65

Fig. 66

shunting the extensive goods yards. Because Sandringham House was a fairly frequent royal destination, via Kings Lynn and Wolferton, the Shed maintained several 'Royal' locomotives including LNER Nigel Gresley-designed Class B2 4-6-0 No 61671 *Royal Sovereign* which received an almost unique level of attention.

I recall seeing the locomotive, at Cambridge, gleaming even when not on a royal duty. An illustration in *Great Eastern Railway Engine Sheds* shows eight cleaners working on *Royal Sovereign* with a driver, fireman and another man in the cab, presumably also cleaning, and preparing for a journey because the blower is on.

The dirty, sometimes dangerous, and very laborious work necessary to clean, maintain and operate steam locomotives is rarely described. I am relying on my own experience of working steam locomotives at the National Railway Museum and my observations whilst working at Cambridge Station to tell the story of Cambridge loco sheds. I am also drawing on *The Railway Workers 1840-1970* by Frank McKenna, published by Faber and Faber in 1980. McKenna began working as an engine cleaner in 1946 at Kingmoor Shed. By 1949, he was a fireman at Willesden Shed

and then engine driver at Kentish Town Shed. He was an ASLEF lay official from 1956 to 1969 so his book is a little coloured by his justifiable concern to illustrate the hardships and low pay that were the unhappy lot of some hard-working engine shed staff. **Fig. 66**, from the ash pits beside Cambridge Loco Shed in the 1950s, illustrates the background to some of that work.

The picture shows the loco disposal area and ash pits at Cambridge, adjoining and immediately west of the principal engine shed. 'Disposal' in the context of a steam loco shed means carrying out the necessary tasks on a locomotive which has completed a turn of duty and is 'On Shed' until its next turn. Unless the loco is scheduled for immediate duty it will be moved, while it is still in steam, over an ash pit so that the fire and the contents of the ash-pan under the firebox can be disposed of. The loco will then have to be moved for more coal and water to be added in the tender ready for the next turn.

It is quite likely, when the loco is handed over to the shed staff by the driver and fireman who worked its last turn, that the fire and steam pressure will be low. Most locos can move gently until steam pressure is down to about 50psi but once the fire is out any other necessary moves, perhaps into the roofed-over shed, must be made fairly promptly. If the loco needs coal it will be moved under the Cambridge coaling tower which dates from 1932 and is shown in **Fig. 69**. I remember going to watch this impressive machine working, hoisting a 16 ton mineral wagon full of coal and tipping the contents into the tower and thence into a loco tender. **Fig. 67** shows a similar coaling tower working at King's Cross; it was noisy, dusty but impressive engineering and it saved the manual shovelling of tons of coal from coal banks in the Loco Shed yard into the tenders of locomotives alongside the coal bank.

Once coaled the loco was driven to the ash pits, or 'dust holes' in railway-speak. The last steam locomotives were replaced at Cambridge Shed in the early 1960s so, though they are still to be seen working on preserved railways, I am writing about experiences of more than sixty years ago.

In **Fig. 68** I have included an ash pit under the loco and an outline image of a Shed engine-man in the pit. I have called him Man 2 in the account which follows and his mate, not shown here, will be in the loco cab working with him and can be Man 1. Engine Sheds were

Fig. 67

generally predominantly male working environments, partly because the work was physically very demanding. However, during the two world wars women worked in Loco Sheds and did very well.

The loco in **Fig. 68** can be assumed to have been coaled and watered and will probably have a fairly low fire and much

Fig. 68: A sectioned 4-4-0 steam locomotive and tender illustrating the basic working principles of a steam locomotive and the work of disposal which is explained in the text.

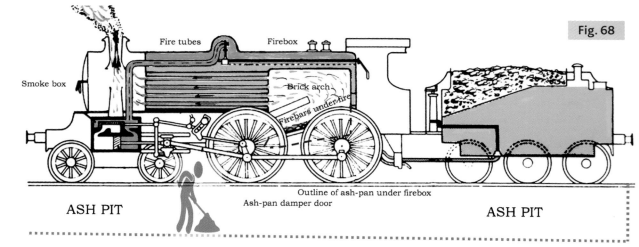

Fig. 68

Fire tubes   Firebox

Smoke box

Brick arch

Firebars under fire

Outline of ash-pan under firebox
Ash-pan damper door

ASH PIT   ASH PIT

reduced steam pressure. Man 1, in the cab, opens the firebox door and if he judges there is a largish fire remaining he needs a clinker shovel – one of the very long-handled shovels in **Fig. 66** – to dig out the remaining fire and tip each shovel-full over the cabside onto the ground. Imagine using a 9ft-long shovel in the restricted space of a loco cab, digging out red-hot coal and clinker through a smallish firebox door, then turning sideways, holding the shovel-handle which will be hot, and trying to avoid the dust and hot fumes which are all around Man 1.

Once the central section of the fire has been cleared, the firebars should be visible. Firebars are a larger version of a household grate but formed of a number of heavy cast-iron bars, parallel to each other and supported fore and aft on the bottom of the firebox.

'Should be visible' is a phrase which is a little economical with the true situation facing Man 1. He must bend double, approach as near as heat and dust allows to the firebox door and insert a heavy pair of long-handled tongs to grasp firmly one of the 'visible' firebars. Then, with a heave and a twist, he dislodges the bar and pulls it out of the firebox onto the cab floor. He repeats the process three or four times to remove enough firebars to enable him to shovel the rest of the fire down into the ash-pan below the firebox.

Meanwhile, his mate, Man 2, climbs down into the ash pit and walks under the loco with a 10ft long ash-pan rake. Man 1 opens the ash-pan damper door from the cab and the raker-out, Man 2, begins to draw clinker, probably some red-hot coal and quantities of ash towards him and into the ash pit.

Imagine, for a moment, his job. He will have put on an old pair of overalls, a cap, a pair of goggles, a scarf or old handkerchief tied round his mouth, and a pair of leather gloves. He has limited clearance under the locomotive – for instance he will have to bend down to get under the bogie at the front of the loco – and once he is underneath he is splashed with drips of very hot oil, and boiling water. There may also be slight steam leaks from the cylinder drain cocks, or from any inside cylinders over his head.

Once he begins raking-out, all the ash, dust, soot and remains of the fire is coming towards him so the long rake is essential but dust, ash and heat are all around him in the restricted space where he is working.

When ash pits were introduced, in the late nineteenth century, the ash was raked onto the ash pit floor then subsequently shovelled out onto the trackside. In the twentieth century, most ash pits at larger Engine Sheds like Cambridge were equipped with metal skips, running on rails on the ash pit floor, which could be pushed under the loco ahead of Man 2 then subsequently emptied.

Fine; progress, but there is more dirty work to do. The smokebox, at the front of the locomotive, is a collecting-point of more black ash, soot and other small debris that has been drawn through the fire tubes by the blast of exhausting steam. Another Shed man – Man 3 – or sometimes the fireman from the locomotive's last turn – has to climb onto the front end of the loco above the buffer beam, swing open the heavy smokebox door then, partly choked by swirling dust and soot, shovel out the dirt.

Ash pit and smokebox work done, the locomotive, if it still has sufficient steam pressure, is moved to wherever the Shed Master, or a senior Shed Foreman, has decided to 'stable' it until its next turn. If the steam pressure is now too low to move the loco blame will fall on Man 1 and Man 2 for: 'Wasting time and not getting your job done quickly enough; it should only take a few minutes.' The complainant's concern is understandable because the 'dead' engine is blocking an ash pit road and, in a large and busy shed like Cambridge, locomotives are coming on shed for attention frequently. Like an industrial production line the shed is receiving locos but also preparing and despatching them for new turns. Any delays are inimical to the whole railway division which the shed serves.

Supposing, however, that all is well and the loco is driven to another part of the shed, but there is still work to do. The loco's fire tubes are cleaned by Man 4, an engine tuber or tube sweeper. More dirt, but if tubes are not cleaned the loco will not steam well. If it can be established in any subsequent delay enquiry that the tubes were not swept then blame can be attributed to Man 4 – and to Shed supervision.

Man 5 is the boiler washout man who can only work when the boiler is dead because he unscrews several washout plugs in the bottom of the firebox sides

and drains off all the boiler water and any small debris which comes out with it. Then he refills the boiler from a hose attached to a nearby hydrant and checks the level in the water gauges in the cab.

Men 6, 7 and possibly 8 are fitters and oilers who visually check the working parts of the locomotive and fill the oil reservoirs. A specialist (Man 9) is the firebox brick-arch repair-man who crawls into the firebox – which will still be hot – to check and repair, if necessary, the brick arch. Men 10 + + + are the engine cleaners whose job is apparent from their name but they are also, if they choose, on the first railway hierarchical steps to fireman and driver.

Once the engine we have followed from the ash pit is in the hands of the cleaners it is beginning preparation for its next working turn; the next Man to visit is the fire-raiser. With wood kindling and other flammable scraps – like oil-soaked overalls and cleaners' rags – he lights a fire in the firebox and re-visits it periodically to put

Fig. 69: The ash pits, coaling tower and extensive sidings beside the Cambridge Loco Shed.

Fig. 69

on coal. He is succeeded by the rostered fireman for the engine's next turn who continues to build up the fire, oils round the engine and watches the steam pressure gradually rising.

I recall, while part of the Steam Team at the National Railway Museum, coming in at 04.00 on a coldish morning to be fire-raiser on BR Standard Class 9F 92220 *Evening Star* which was scheduled for a main-line run. This, for me, was an exciting and enjoyable experience but, as my account of Cambridge engine shed work has shown, it was not something I wanted to do every day. I remember learning as a child in the 1940s:

'When I grow up to be a man,
I'm going to drive a train,
From somewhere to somewhere,
And all the way back again.'

I achieved something of that but I learned, too, that the 'Steam Age' on the railway was not a romantic enthusiast's play time!

Chapter 13

INDUSTRIAL SIDINGS IN THE CAMBRIDGE STATION AREA

Cambridge Station was surrounded by sidings as several of the maps illustrate. A useful historical guide to the sidings and craneage capacity of Railway Stations was the Railway Clearing House *Official Handbook of Stations* including junctions, sidings, collieries, works etc..

Fig. 70 is the Cambridge entry in 1938 and is part of one page from the 1938 edition – 654 page – Price Full Cloth

STATION ACCOMMODATION.						CRANE POWER.		STATIONS, &c.	COUNTY.	COMPANY.	POSITION.
						Tons	Cwts				
G	P	F	L	H	C	10	0	CAMBRIDGE—		L. N. E. (G. E.).............	} Bishops Stortford and Ely.
.	P	.	.	H	C	.	.	(Station, L. N. E., G. E.)	Cambs......	L. N. E. (G. N.).............	
.	P	F	.	H	C	.	.			L. M. S. (L. N. W.)	Over L.N.E. from Cambridge Junc.
G	P	F	L	H	C	10	0			L. M. S. (Mid.)	Over L.N.E. from St. Ives Junction.
.	.	.	.	.	.	.	.	Anglo-American Oil Co.'s Sid.	Cambs	L. M. S. (L. N. W.).........	Cambridge.
.	.	.	.	.	.	.	.	Artificial Stone Co. (L.N.E.)	Cambs......	L. N. E. (G.E.)–L. M. S. (Mid.)	Cambridge Corporation Siding.
.	.	.	.	.	.	.	.	Beales, P., & Co.'s Siding (L. N. E., G. N.)	Cambs......	L. N. E. (G N.–G. E.)	Cambridge Station.
.	.	.	.	.	.	.	.	Cambridge & District Co-operative Society's Siding (L. N. E.)..................	Cambs......	L.N.E.(G.E.)–L.M.S.(Mid)	Cambridge and Waterbeach.
.	.	.	.	.	.	.	.	Cambridge Brick Co.'s Siding (L. N. E.)	Cambs......	L. N. E. (G. E.)–L. M. S. (L. N. W.–Mid.)	Cambridge and Barnwell Junction.
.	.	.	.	.	.	.	.	Cambridge Corporation Siding (L. N. E.).........	Cambs......	L. N. E. (G. E.)–L. M. S. (Mid.)	Cambridge, L. N. E. Yard.
.	.	.	.	.	.	.	.	Cambridge Gas Co.'s Siding (L. N. E.).............	Cambs......	L. N. E. (G. E.)–L.M.S (Mid.)	Cambridge and Barnwell Junction.
.	.	.	.	.	.	.	.	Coldham Lane Siding (L.N.E.)......................	Cambs......	L. N. E. (G. E.)–L.M.S. (Mid.)	Cambridge and Waterbeach. .
.	.	.	.	.	.	.	.	Coote & Warren's Sid.(LNE)	Cambs......	L. N. E. (G. E.)–L. M. S. (Mid.)	Cambridge and Barnwell Junction.
.	.	.	.	.	.	.	.	Coulson & Sons, Ltd. (L. N. E.)	Cambs......	L. N. E. (G.E.)–L. M. S. (L. N. W.–Mid.)	Watts & Son's Siding.
.	.	.	.	.	.	.	.	Foster Mills Siding	Cambs:.....	L. N. E. (G. N.)	Cambridge, Upper Yard.
.	.	.	.	.	.	.	.	Foster Mills Siding (L. N. E.)	Cambs......	L. N. E. (G. E.)–L. M. S. (L. N. W.–Mid.)	Cambridge Station.
G	.	F	L	.	.	10	0	Hallack & Bond's Siding...	Cambs......	L. M. S. (L. N. W.).........	Cambridge and Lords Bridge.
.	.	.	.	.	.	.	.	Hills Road	Cambs......	L. M. S. (L. N. W.).........	Bch.—Lords Bridge & Cambridge Jn.
.	.	.	.	.	.	.	.	Junction	Cambs......	L. M. S. (L. N. W.)– L. N. E. (G. E.)	Cambridge Pass. and Lords Bridge.
G	.	.	.	.	.	.	.	Mill Road Wharf	Cambs......	L. M. S. (Mid.)...............	Over L.N.E. from St. Ives Junc.
.	.	.	.	.	.	.	.	Ridgeon, C., & Sons' Siding (L. N. E.)......................	Cambs......	L.N.E.(G.E.)–L.M.S.(Mid)	Cambridge and Waterbeach.
.	.	.	.	.	.	.	.	Tenison Road Siding (L. N. E.)......................	Cambs......	L. N. E. (G. E.)–L. M. S. (Mid.)	Cambridge.
G	.	F	L	.	.	10	0	Upper Yard	Cambs......	L. N. E. (G. N.)	Branch near Cambridge, Pass.
.	.	.	.	.	.	.	.	Vinter, J. O., & Son's Siding (L. N. E., G. N.).............	Cambs......	L. N. E. (G. N.–G. E.)	Cambridge, Upper Yard.
.	.	.	.	.	.	.	.	Watts & Son's Siding (L.N.E.)......................	Cambs......	L. N. E. (G.E.)–L.M.S. (L. N. W.–Mid.)	Cambridge and Barnwell Junction.

Fig. 70

10s.6d. carriage paid. It is a measure of the continuing Company-based and regional loyalties fourteen years after the grouping created four large 'umbrella' companies – including LNER – that there is a column in the Handbook for 'Company'. The various Railway Companies that served Cambridge 'in a tangle of mutual inconvenience' are still reference names for identifying sidings.

I have starred three sidings to explain and illustrate in a little more detail. Foster Mills Sidings are closest to Cambridge Station (see **Fig. 55**, page 81) and serve the large roller flour mill developed and owned by the Foster family – who were bankers in Cambridge – and taken over by Spillers in 1947. In **Fig. 55** the site is called 'Homepride Mills (flour)' which was a Spillers brand name for a self-raising flour. I remember in the 1960s and 1970s that it was still called 'Foster's Mill' by long-term Cambridge folk; so old names die hard!

Another star is for a siding best illustrated in **Fig. 71** with an extract from a 1926-1927 1:2:500 OS map. It is the Corporation (Cambridge City) Siding near Mill Road bridge.

The area around the Corporation Depot yard – marked in the centre of the map – was surrounded to the west by tightly-packed 'railway' houses and to the east by a coal depot and the main lines leading north from Cambridge Station. Road approach was off Hooper Street and the RCH Handbook notes that the yard also contained access to the Artificial Stone Company.

For a time, the siding was used – perhaps leased to – Richard Duce, a well-known Cambridge Scrap Metal dealer. A close view of **Fig. 72** photograph shows a Kitson (Leeds, 1932) 0-6-0ST used at Fisons Fertiliser Works in Burwell, off the Mildenhall branch. Chalked on the boiler is: TO / R DUCE HOOPER ST SIDING CAMBRIDGE.

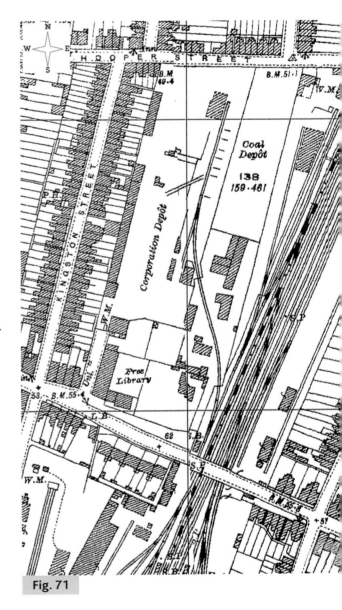

Fig. 71

The engine is partially dismantled and is at Hooper Street because the very large Duce Scrapyard alongside Coldham Lane bridge had no rail connection. Cambridge City Council still owns the Hooper Street site, though the rail siding was removed in the early 1960s. The extensive yard is now the base for the City's Fleet and Transport Department. As a sign of changing social

Fig. 72

times in the twenty-first century, the Free Library shown on the 1927 OS map was opened by the City Council in 1897, closed in 1996 and is now the Bharat Bavan Hindu community centre and shrine.

The third star is for the Cambridge Gas Company's siding near Coldham Lane bridge and shown on another section of the 1926-1927 1:2,500 OS map – **Fig. 73**.

Cambridge Gas Works initially made gas from coal brought to Cambridge via the River Cam in lighters from Kings Lynn, a sea-harbour, so coals from Newcastle and other NE ports arrived in sea-going coasters. These ships discharged their coal into river-going lighters which could navigate the Cam as far as Cambridge. Once the railway arrived sidings were provided in St Matthew's Ward, named on the map. Unfortunately, as the map and the aerial view in **Fig. 74** shows, the sidings stopped well short of the Gas Works which was north of the sidings in Abbey Ward.

The sidings opened in 1869 and were shunted by the gas company's own horses.

In 1929, a Sentinel steam locomotive was purchased after locomotives hired from LNER had been tried to shunt the considerable tonnages of coal that the gasworks needed. Because the very large gasworks never had direct rail connection, coal arriving at the sidings was unloaded into steam, and later motor, lorries for a short journey. I remember, during the Suez crisis in 1956, that fuel rationing was introduced so the gasworks brought back into service a Sentinel steam lorry to move the coal. A little unkindly, the local *Cambridge Daily News* commented that the steam lorry was burning more coal than it moved but that was not the case.

Much local interest was shown in the 1929 Sentinel steam locomotive – **Fig. 75** – which could be watched at work from Coldham Lane. It was very different from the main-line railway locomotives, was nicknamed 'Gasbag,' and was an 0-6-0, chain-driven by a vertical 2-cylinder double-acting 80HP steam engine. The vertical boiler was in the cab and the chimney in the cab roof. What appears

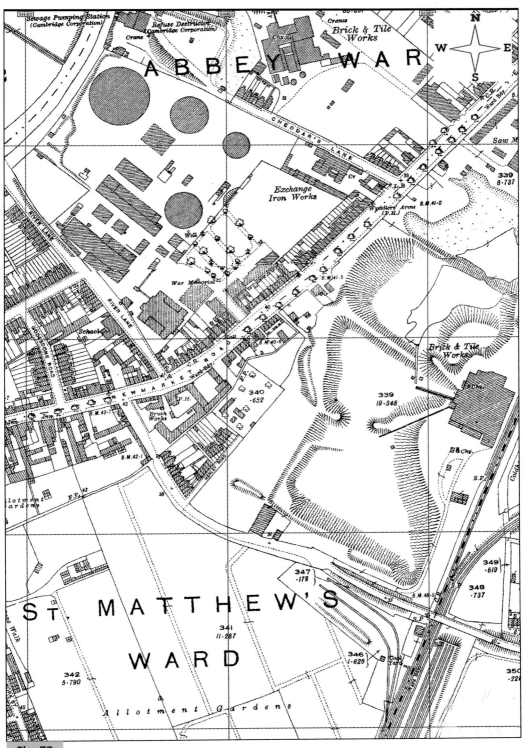

Fig. 73

site of Duce's
scrap metal yard
from 1940s

Gas Company
sidings

(for a conventional 0-6-0 tank engine) to be the boiler is the water supply tank and the 'smokebox' is a casing over the engine.

The makers claimed 'Gasbag' could move 120 tons on the level from a standing start.

Fig. 75

Chapter 14

THE ROYAL SHOW IN CAMBRIDGE

1840; 1894; 1922; 1951; 1960 & 1961

The Royal Show was an agricultural show initiated, and subsequently managed, by the Agricultural Society of England which received a Royal Charter in 1840. The Society (RASE) came about because of agricultural problems precipitated by the end of the Napoleonic War in 1815. Very large numbers of demobbed soldiers found little employment when they returned home from the war. On the land, the progressive introduction of machinery to replace manual labour provoked protests and in some cases the breaking-up of new threshing machines.

Agricultural progress was checked but by the 1830s a growing population was needing more food than the land was currently producing. In 1838 a body of concerned people, especially land-owners, met to explore a way forward and the RASE was one response to a national problem.

The first Agricultural Show – in itself a new concept – was held in Oxford in 1839. Both Oxford and Cambridge Universities were anxious to encourage agricultural research and development so the first Royal Show was in Cambridge the following year. The Royal Show was a moveable feast which reflected, and celebrated, the national importance of the agricultural industry. The Show illustrated all aspects of farming: the production of food; the richness and variety of rural life; the best of livestock, displayed and gaining highly regarded prizes; agricultural machinery and buildings. There were over 1,000 stands and much to attract general visitors as well as farmers, so attendances each year were more than 100,000.

By 1922, when the Royal Show came to Cambridge for the third time, it was a very large-scale event. The elaborate logistics that created the Show before it opened to visitors, sustained it on its site, delivered animals, machines and people to that site, and took them away again afterwards were expensive for the RASE. Good railway and road links to the Showground were necessary but rail connections were not always achievable. It is not surprising that, after 1968, the Show found a permanent home at Stoneleigh in Warwickshire.

The 1894 Royal Show ran in Cambridge from 23 to 29 June including get-in and get-out times This Show was held on Midsummer Common and Jesus Green, occupying 64 acres. The GER laid sidings in Tennison Field, just north of Mill Road bridge in 1893 and a special platform nearby to handle the anticipated crowds of visitors.

The Show attracted 110,000 people of whom 76,000 arrived by train. As well as some 180 passenger trains either arriving or departing, there were 57 Cheap Day Trips run by GER and GNR, all arriving at Cambridge Station, or at the Mill Road Bridge Show platform, between 9.30 and 11.30am and corresponding returns later in the day. Neither Cambridge Station nor the Mill Road Bridge Show platform were conveniently near Midsummer Common or Jesus Green and the horse-drawn tramways did not serve either.

The 1922 Royal Show in Cambridge was open from 4 July to 8 July plus unloading time from 25 May and clearing after the Show. It is a measure of the increasing size of Royal Shows that the show site in 1894 required 64 acres. In 1922 the Show Ground was 125 acres and the nearest available site was to the east of the city near Trumpington.

The table illustrates the number of items which needed to be moved to and from the Show Ground. 12,000 items of machinery would be likely to be heavy and large; 369 rabbits might not be too difficult. However, 713 horses, 1,547 cattle and 1,614 pigs would require special wagons, fodder and bedding and the wagons would need to be thoroughly cleaned after each load.

Items began to arrive for unloading on 25 May. Cartage to the Show Ground required 1,564 loads, representing 1,732 tons carted or trailed by GER teams. In order to deal with the traffic, GER built a temporary station adjacent to the Show Ground on a piece of land hired from Trinity College between the GER Main Line and the L&NWR Line – **Fig. 77**.

This Show Station was near the level crossing gates on Long Road and beside Trumpington Signal Box marked as SB on the plan. An island platform was constructed of sleepers, 500ft x 45ft on the Down side of the line, and another, narrower, platform on the Up side, 500ft x 27ft. From west to east the three platform faces were labelled A, B and C. In addition, two end-on loading docks were built on the west side of these platforms, connected with the siding leading to the Down Goods Reception Line and thence to the Cambridge Station site.

I have slightly edited and enhanced the plan of this temporary station which was first published in the *Railway Gazette* of 14 July 1922. The labelling is a helpful guide to the provisions necessary to handle all the traffic and to provide for the staff working on the Station and, especially for cartage, on the Show Ground. The *Gazette* article is also helpful in explaining the special arrangements the GER had to make to manage all the additional goods traffic generated before and after the Show and the relevant paragraphs are quoted here:

'To facilitate the working of trains temporary block telegraph signal-boxes were provided. One was about midway between Shepreth Branch Junction and Trumpington and another about midway between Chesterton Junction and Waterbeach Station. Fixed signals were not provided at these boxes but men were stationed there with hand

Fig. 76: Table showing the principal categories of entries for the 1894 and 1922 Cambridge Royal Shows.

Year	Machinery	Horses	Cattle	Sheep	Pigs	Rabbits	Poultry	Goats	Horticulture	Produce	Total No of Entries
1894	6,032	617	659	588	—	—	769	—	—	540	9,204
1922	12,191	713	1,547	715	1,614	369	1,205	61	46	247	18,258

Fig. 76

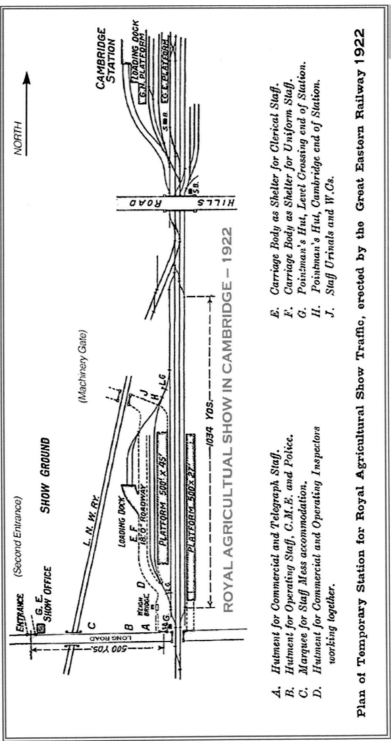

Fig. 77

ROYAL AGRICULTURAL SHOW IN CAMBRIDGE – 1922

A. Hutment for Commercial and Telegraph Staff.
B. Hutment for Operating Staff, C.M.E. and Police.
C. Marquee for Staff Mess accommodation.
D. Hutment for Commercial and Operating Inspectors working together.
E. Carriage Body as Shelter for Clerical Staff.
F. Carriage Body as Shelter for Uniform Staff.
G. Pointman's Hut, Level Crossing end of Station.
H. Pointman's Hut, Cambridge end of Station.
J. Staff Urinals and W.Cs.

Plan of Temporary Station for Royal Agricultural Show Traffic, erected by the Great Eastern Railway 1922

and detonating signals, detonators being placed on each line until the signalman gave instructions for them to be removed and permission to give trainmen a green flag or green light signal.

'All trains approaching Cambridge were required to proceed with special care and to be prepared for hand or detonating signals at these temporary cabins, when passing the Show Station, or elsewhere.

'In connection with the working of special trains general instructions were issued that certain lines or branches might have to be kept open beyond the ordinary times to provide for the running of special trains and that signal-boxes might have to be switched-in at times when they would ordinarily not be in use.

'Between 5 June and 10 July restrictions were placed upon the loading of GER cattle vehicles to foreign lines and from Friday 30 June to Sunday 9 July a number of special instructions applied to communications with the stock controller at Cambridge Station in order that a sufficient number of vehicles should be available to meet all requirements and that none of them should be used for other traffic except by special permission. All movements of live-stock special trains approaching Cambridge had to be telegraphed from various centres. In view of the limited storage accommodation in the immediate vicinity the empty vehicles of live-stock trains were, as a rule, worked away to [Gidea] Park [stabling sidings], Whittlesea or Crown Point (Norwich).

'A number [of vehicles] received from the L&SWR Company were returned to that line for storage. In order to facilitate return arrangements the general rule was that labels attached to vehicles of arriving live-stock trains were allowed to remain thereon until replaced by new labels, the same vehicles being, as far as possible, used for taking away the loads they had brought. Live-stock vehicles were cleaned and disinfected at Trumpington before leaving.

'A difficult part of the work was that of arranging the duties of guards and enginemen, and for relief. In order to avoid congestion a number of alterations in ordinary goods train working, and occasionally in regard to passenger trains, had to be made involving, in some instances, the special routing of goods trains to reach the Colchester main line, whereas ordinarily they would pass through Cambridge.'

It is very helpful for this book to have an account of Show traffic which includes goods trains not usually seen by the general public or by Show visitors. Even visitors who were taken by special passenger trains to the Show Station would probably have been unaware of the preparation and dismantling work the Show generated. The fact, too, that the livestock wagons were stabled well away from Cambridge would have enhanced the Show Station site. Many of us of my generation may remember railway cattle wagons, leaking droppings and giving off what my CofE vicar uncle used to describe, tongue-in-cheek as '… a wonderfully rich country smell'.

The Railway Gazette on passenger workings is another informative quote:

'During the days immediately preceding the Show many trains serving Cambridge were given reliefs and throughout the actual Show period a liberal train service was provided on all routes converging on Cambridge. For London-Cambridge traffic, the principal additions calling for comment were the 8.37am restaurant car express from Liverpool Street behind the ordinary 8.30am train, due at the Show Station at 10.05am and the 9.50am relief to the 10.50am.

'These ran on each day except Monday and Saturday. On Monday there were trains at 11.40am, 2.39pm, 4.50pm and 5.40pm, respectively, relieving the 11.50am, 2.34pm, 4.45pm and 5.49pm trains, The 8.37am and 9.50am additional trains called at the Show Station, the ordinary train serving Cambridge main station as usual.

'On Saturday, 8 July reliefs were provided to the 11.50am and 2.34pm trains from Liverpool Street. In the opposite direction corresponding additions were made.

'A special booklet was issued by GER Company combining in alphabetical tables the entire train facilities to and from Cambridge throughout the Show period, including excursions from all directions and from other railways in connection.

'On Tuesday, Wednesday, Thursday, Friday and Saturday, 4, 5 , 6, 7 and 8 July respectively, day-return tickets at single fares were issued from stations within a radius of 60 miles and at single fare+3d from stations more distant and available on July 4, 7 and 8 by any train arriving at Cambridge not later than 4.30pm and on July 5 and 6 by any train. Special day-excursions were also run from certain stations to Cambridge on July 5, 6, 7 and 8.

'On Wednesday and Thursday 5 and 6 July there were illuminated fêtes in the grounds of Trinity College and St. John's College, including a river pageant, water sports, flower shows, etc. Special trains were run between 10.50pm and 11.20pm for stations within 20 miles or so of Cambridge in

all directions. There were also late trains on various routes on the Friday and Saturday between 8.30pm and 10.10pm where the ordinary services terminated earlier.

'Besides GER trains there were additional and excursion trains worked by L&NWR, MR and GNR Companies, in several instances from relatively distant places, while other railways arranged through-services to Cambridge, handing over their trains to GER as convenient. For example, the GCR provided a day-excursion train from Manchester, etc, to Cambridge on which a dining car was run; the train was handed over to GER at Lincoln.'

On Friday 30 June a meeting was called by the Commercial Superintendent, Mr T.W. Watts, attended by all grades concerned. Mr R.A. Newman, Chief Outdoor Assistant, explained the methods to be adopted. Mr Watts and Lt-Col Mauldin followed with a few words asking for full co-operation and that all should endeavour to uphold the best traditions of the GER Company.

This request was fully responded to and the *Railway Gazette* was asked to record that:

'… too much credit cannot be attached to the splendid team work put in by everyone, including those out on the line and elsewhere on the system who had to deal with the marshalling and working of the traffic, often of a complicated and generally of a heavy and difficult character.'

In some respects, work at the Trumpington Show Station was facilitated because trains could be received and despatched in both directions without reversing and without interference, the Station being a 'through' one. But the large numbers of entries, particularly in the cattle and pig sections, entailed an abnormal amount of cartage.

A special point was made that catering for the staff should be of the best quality and ample in quantity. No intoxicants were served but tea and coffee could be had as often as desired without tickets and the meals were substantial and good. They were supplied under the direction of the GER's Hotel and Refreshment Rooms Department.

Unfortunately, the numbers visiting the Show did not fulfil expectations, mainly because of the weather. On every day, cold showers were experienced which had an adverse effect on the RASE's Gate and on the GER passenger takings. The admissions to the Show Ground were –

Tuesday	3,338
Wednesday	21,880
Thursday	31,903
Friday	21,408
Saturday	13,739
Total	**92,268**

– which, considering the inclement weather prevailing throughout the Show, may be considered satisfactory, although comparing unfavourably with the last occasion on which Cambridge was the venue.

Despite the poor weather experienced in 1922, the Show came to Cambridge again in 1951 and for two successive years in 1960 and 1961. But there were no more temporary Show Stations. A new 'Show Ground' was developed on land between Shelford Road and the Cambridge-Bedford-Oxford railway line.

William Parker, a retired senior BR officer, has kindly helped me for this book with memories of his service on the Great Eastern Line, Cambridge District. William, 'Bill' to me, was General Assistant to the Cambridge District Traffic Manager, Alan Suddaby. He recalls:

'One event I remember very well was when I was called into Alan's office and asked what I knew about the movement of animals and farm machinery? My answer was that I had virtually no experience except for the occasional horse box, a few pigeons at Mexborough …

'Alan then told me that he wanted me to be his personal representative at the Royal Show, which was to be held in Cambridge, and take charge of all the associated railway arrangements.

'In the event it was rather good fun, especially having with me as my assistant Geoff Herbert who had just completed his traffic apprentice training and had been appointed into this work as 'Supernumerary Assistant - Royal Show'. We 'managed' the vast amount of farm machinery and animals transported by rail into and out of Cambridge Goods Depot.

'We had most successful (and most enjoyable) times with the Show officials, the exhibitors – with their very valuable machinery, display items and VIP four-legged charges – and the land owner of the Showground field off the Shelford Road in the Trumpington area [**Fig. 78**].

'One particular job was the delivery of hundreds of railway sleepers for roadways in the Showground, purchased from our civil engineers.

'Geoff did an exceptionally good job – as did everyone in all the departments concerned – and, particularly, the goods agent. Everything worked exceptionally well; truly a great team effort but I was pleased I didn't have to do it again elsewhere in my railway life!'

So another railway success and, as I remember, the 1951 and 1960/1961 Shows were very successful. I was involved in the 1960/1961 Show, not for the railway but as a short-term (five days!) assistant to Harry, the Stores Manager for the Show catering contractor. This contractor also

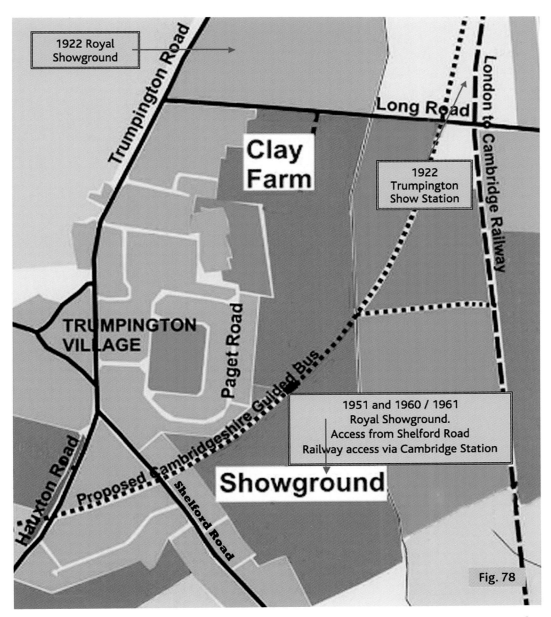

Fig. 78: An edited twenty-first century planning proposals map where the 'Showground' is still marked, as part of Clay Farm land, nearly 60 years after the last Royal Show!

managed the small-sales kiosks dotted around the Showground and Harry – who was a chain smoker – made an interesting mistake in asking me to run a kiosk on the first day of the Show when he was very short-staffed.

A 'mistake' because I was a non-smoker and, as soon as I opened the kiosk, I discovered that packets of cigarettes were much in demand. I sold them at the price on a rather battered price list which was in the kiosk and did not query the very low price. The 'bargains' I was innocently selling were soon the talk of the Showground and I quickly sold out so sent a message back to Harry for more supplies. They came, with Harry, who was 'astonished' that I did not know 'the price of a pack o'fags'. Unlike Bill's 'Supernumerary Assistant' I did not do an exceptionally good job that day but Harry kept me on, and employed me again for the 1961 Show so all was well.

There were rumours in the 1960s that the itinerant Royal Show was losing money so, in 1968 the RASE set up a permanent Showground at Stoneleigh Park (previously known as the National Agricultural Centre) in Warwickshire. The first Show at Stoneleigh Park was for four days and attracted 111, 196 visitors. But, although – and perhaps because – the annual County Shows continued to flourish the RASE National Show did less well as this article from the *Independent* of 7 July 2009 shows:

> 'Yesterday the gates opened for the 160th, and last time, on the Royal Show [at Stoneleigh Park].
>
> 'Since the beginning of Queen Victoria's reign, it has been one of the biggest events in the rural calendar, but

it no longer attracts the visitors that it used to.

> 'It has been losing money for years, lately more than £200,000 a year, and the Royal Agricultural Society of England announced last April that it is not financially viable and cannot continue in its present form.
>
> 'In its heyday in the 1980s, the Royal Show could count on 130,000 visitors. Last year there were around 100,000.'

I have spent some time on the Royal Show story in Cambridge because the success in 1922, and the changes in 1951, 1960/1961, epitomise the changes in rail and road transport and their effect on the railways.

In the 1920s, the railway was still an effective mover of freight, partly because the road system we have today was undeveloped. A railway company, such as the GER, could effectively mount a major logistics exercise like their success for the 1922 Royal Show. By 1951, motor transport was much more developed and the railways were losing traffic and income.

The black dotted line labelled 'Proposed Cambridgeshire guided bus' [route] on the **Fig. 78** plan is another sign of changes to come for some of the railway branches around Cambridge Station.

Chapter 15

CAMBRIDGE UNIVERSITY RAILWAY CLUB - CURC

Cambridge Station Traffic Survey
06.00 to 00.00 Friday 27 October 1961

have already acknowledged Anthony Kirby, graduate of Gonville & Caius College, but the contents of this chapter were, for me, a real treasure. Tony, a member of CURC when it was still a flourishing and busy Club, lent me his complete copy of the 1961 Traffic Survey and otained permission from the twenty first century remnant of the Club to use its findings in the book.

Although Tony was an active member

of the Club in the 1960s his time at Cambridge post-dated the Survey and what he lent me was forty four typewritten foolscap pages. The author is anonymous and his acknowledgements only mention: the observers who watched and recorded the trains, the collators and editors who prepared the copy,

Fig. 79: The south end of Cambridge Station looking north from Hills Road bridge..

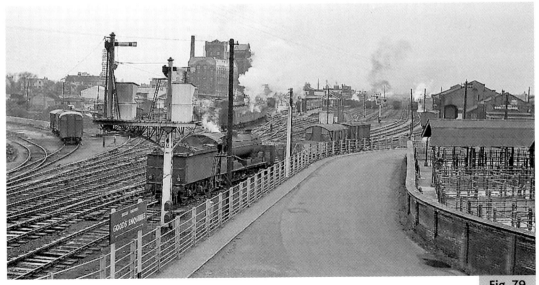

Fig. 79

Christopher Turner, formerly of the CURC and author of a smaller 1960 Survey which inspired this one, and Mr Crosthwaite, BR District Operating Superintendent. This chapter draws extensively from the 1961 Survey but, because the original is so long and wordy I have summarised rather than attempted lengthy direct quotes.

Traffic Surveying is an esoteric art (or science). The 1960 survey in Cambridge was a magnum opus and its author, Christopher Turner, had analysed every fact in sight with his usual meticulous accuracy and had spiced its text with his inimitable style and sense of humour.

Thus inspired, a few members of the Club decided on a large-scale survey for Friday 27 October 1961. From the multitudinous records of our observers this Report has since been compiled in the long winter evenings in Cambridge, causing its editors much agonised discussion and occasional fits of despair. We hope that we have not laboured in vain.

The method adopted was similar to that of the previous survey. Observers were stationed at eight points from soon after 06.00 to as near to 00.00 as possible:

> Shepreth Branch Junction

> Long Road bridge (near Trumpington Box)

> Cattle Market (near the South Box)

> Station South [Up end]

> Station North [Down end]

> Mill Road bridge (near the North Box)

> Chesterton Junction

> and, to provide a check on freight operating –

> March South Junction.'

All observers recorded as many details as possible of time-keeping, line occupation and train formation. The analysis which

follows has been developed from these records in order to show the methods of operating and the types of traffic in Cambridge. The map – **Fig. 22**, page 47 – of Cambridge as a centre of a web of railway lines is a useful background to what follows:

The axis of lines in the area is the Cambridge main line of the Great Eastern (GE) Line, from Liverpool Street via Bishop's Stortford to Ely – dividing there to Kings Lynn and Norwich – and carrying an express service to and from Lynn and Cambridge. London commuter trains serve the latter and Diesel Multiple Units (DMUs), or locomotive-hauled carriages, provide local and connectional services.

The other main line route from London, though not as direct as the GE Line, is the Great Northern's (GN) line from King's Cross via Hitchin which joins the GE main line at Shepreth Branch Junction 2¾ miles south of Cambridge Station. It is served by the Cambridge Buffet Expresses and various semi-fast and local trains. The network of branch lines is:

> Colchester via Sudbury and Haverhill where the Colne Valley line from Marks Tey joins.

> Oxford via Bletchley and Bedford

> Newmarket, Bury St Edmunds and Ipswich

> Mildenhall

> St Ives, March and thence Wisbech and Peterborough

The GE main line is an important freight route between London, particularly Temple Mills Yard near Stratford, and Whitemoor Yard situated just north of March station. Several other lines carry important through freight services. For instance, the St. Ives route to March relieves the main line via Ely to a considerable extent and there are various feeder and local services centred on Cambridge. There is also increasing traffic to and from the Permanent Way Engineer's Depot which is situated in the 'V' at Chesterton Junction.

The GE main line is double-track throughout. At Cambridge Station it becomes two reversibly-worked lines. The western track serves the single 1,650ft platform now unique in Great Britain: it is operated in two halves by virtue of a central scissors-crossover aptly known as the Rubicon. The idiom 'Crossing the Rubicon' means to pass a point of no return, and refers to Julius Caesar's army's crossing the Rubicon river in 49 BC. Julius Caesar uttered the famous phrase *'alea iacta est'* – the die is cast – as his army marched through the shallow river. The southern half of the long platform is Platform 1, the northern half Platform 4. The long platform has 2 bay platforms: at the south Up end Platforms 2 and 3, with a siding between them, and at the north Down end Platforms 5 and 6. **Figs. 30 and 50**. pages 56 and 77 show the Station track layout

Approaching Cambridge Station from the south, there are Up and Down loops, extending from Trumpington Box, one mile south of the station, to Cambridge South Junction Box which also controls the junction with the Bletchley line and with the Down and Up goods lines. These goods lines run to the east of the station and then parallel the main lines as far as Coldham Lane Junction becoming then, in effect, the Newmarket line, with crossovers providing for exchange between the 2 pairs of lines. **Fig. 22**, page 47 is a useful general guide and **Fig. 47**, 74 a more specific guide to the previous paragraphs and to those which follow.

Similarly, by means of crossovers at Cambridge North Junction Box, freights can transfer to the main line and, by the

establishment of absolute block working, Newmarket passenger trains to the goods lines, which also provide access to the Diesel Depot at Coldham Lane.

The North and South Boxes share control of access to the double-ended carriage sidings, lying between the through lines and the goods lines, and to the Up and Down yards, situated to the east of the goods lines. The North Box also controls the Motive Power Depot, lying behind the northern bay Platforms 5 and 6; the Gas Siding near Coldhan Lane bridge, in effect a Down loop; and the 4 reception loops off the Up goods line.

Both pairs of bays have shunt spurs not conflicting with the main lines, the southern Up one also serving a small freight yard behind the bay Platforms 2 and 3. One of the Up goods loops at the north Down end serves as a shunting neck for the Down yard, and the Up loop at the south end for the Up yard.

Finally there is the LNWR Yard on the Down side of the Bletchley line, controlled by Hills Road Bridge/L&NWR Junction Box.

Tables in the survey record the locomotives working the services: 29 steam locomotives – exactly half the number recorded during the June 1960 survey – 72 diesel locomotives and 33 DMUs plus one German Railbus. The diesel locomotives and the DMUs were the principal form of motive power throughout the GE Lines. Steam locomotives were no longer working any through passenger or freight trains and very few local passenger trains. Steam was still used for some parcels trains and most local and branch freight trains.

The principal conclusion of the 8 June 1960 and 27 October 1961 Surveys is that the standard of performance was high.

The two Surveys each produced a 'typical' exception. In 1960, one train was an exception to normal working.

It was a Deepdene working which is a railway telegraph code term used to alert all railway staff along the route that this was a Royal train but with the lowest security for such a train. The train was therefore carrying members of the Royal family but not the monarch, her consort or her immediate successors; the code for their train would be Grove. The locomotive would carry two headlamps (if the Monarch was aboard there would be four headlamps) and signalmen must use the 4-4-4 bell code. The train could be worked under standard block rules but the shunting of any other trains within contact of the train's route must cease five minutes before the passage of the Royal Train. Any public crossings – level crossing or over and underbridges – must be closed to traffic ten minutes before the Royal Train. The several exceptions in the 1961 Survey was for a Race Meeting at Newmarket which required several Refreshment Car Excursion trains from London through to Newmarket via Cambridge and much Horse Box traffic.

However, the basic fabric of GE Cambridge Line and associated branch passenger services – although still recognisable after the Survey – has undergone a fairly substantial change, as from 21 November 1960, with the NE London electrification. Kings Lynn and Cambridge expresses must now work to a rigorous interval timetable and locals stopping trains to Liverpool Street are now confined to the peaks. The Kings Cross services are basically unaltered but Cambridge Platform 2 has lost its monopoly for Kings Cross express services.

The Mildenhall branch line, with BR's timeless regard for economic reality, continues with little-used passenger trains and weekday freight services

Handling of parcels traffic by passenger trains corresponds closely to the established forms, although certain additional Main-line freight services south of Cambridge now carry parcels traffic because the DMUs replacing loco hauled carriage stock have less space for parcels.

The complete Survey summarises the observations of passenger and freight train workings in a number of Tables; two examples in this summary illustrate the complexity of railway working. **Fig. 80** is one day's passenger trains between Bletchley [BLY] and Cambridge [CAM] and shows the booked and actual arrival and departure times. Good time-keeping is still the essence of successful railway working not least because each train has a timetable 'path' which ensures that it makes its journey without interference from, or interference with, any other trains. Unlike a road vehicle which is able to overtake other vehicles a train is contained by the rails and can only overtake if points and an alternative track is available, and permissable. If a train looses its path, Control, which has an overview of the railway, must decide whether to instruct signal men to delay other trains and pass the late-running train or to devise a new timetable path and subsequent late running to destination. In **Fig. 81**, for a day of freight trains starting from Cambridge, the timetabled and actual departure times indicate how much more work Control had to undertake to thread the freight trains through and amongst the passenger trains. Some freight trains left a little early, some a little late and one, already very late, is a cross country freight to Cardiff via the Severn Tunnel.

The change in the relative use of steam and diesel locomotives is a further pointer to the 'rationalisation' of GE motive power. Carriage workings have undergone great changes which is all to the good if the amount of under-utilised capital invested in coaching vehicles is

TABLE 4G: Bletchley Line Passenger Trains (BLY & CAM) – DOWN and UP

		DOWN trains				UP trains	
Loco	Set	BLY Depart	CAM Arrival Booked	CAM Arrival Actual	Platform	CAM departure Booked	CAM departure Actual
75037	D	—	—	—	3	07.37	07.38½
DMU	5	07.14	08.41	08.42½	3	10.12	10.13
DMU	7	0.925	10.51	10.53	2 (1)	11.22	11.24
DMU	5	12.00	13.29	13.29½	3	14.12	14.15
DMU	6	13.08	14.38	14.41½	3	16.47	16.48
DMU	8	15.53*	17.21	17.21	3	18.18	18.22
DMU	4	17.11	18.55	19.02	2	19.15	19.17½
D5018	D	20.45*	22.13	22.21	2 (1)	—	—
NOTES*	15.53 OXF-CAM: 14.46 ex OXF						
	20.45 BLY-CAM: conveyed Oxfit						

Fig. 80

to be reduced to a tolerable level. DMUs performed well and reliably.

The evidence presented in the Survey demonstrates that the processes of reorganisation and consolidation have developed and that they are still unfolding. The question of the final extent and pattern of lines and services in East

UP starting freights from CAM

Description		Loco	CAM.SJ Actual	LINE TO TRU	Class & Load	Notes including traffic carried
07.20	CAM-GC	65532	07.17	UM	K 9	6 vans and 3 opens
10.25	CAM-CLARE	43149	09.20	UR	K 21	Mainly coal. 3 for Linton; 12 HAV; 6 CLARE
09.25	CAM-FOX	61287	09.28	UR	K 33	2 Presflos, coal and sheeted opens – all for Barrington Cement Works
11.58	CAM-FORD.SDG	61378	12.44	LNW	K 10	
12.25	CAM-FRM.PRK	—	—	—	D	Runs when required, probably for movement of empty vans
15.05	CAM-BLY	48534	14.56	LNW	K 15	
15.20	CAM-TM	D5626	15.35	UR	K 23	
16.26	CAM-HITCH	D8026	16.08	UM	K 38	Including vans for fertilizer traffic
19.24	IPS-CDF	61801	22.35	LNW	D 33 D 49	For arrival see 04Jv below. Booked departure 22.05 German vans; vans; containers; 19 for CDF, 1 to Severn Tunnel Junction, 29 Bristol
23.25	CAM-SPIT	D5659	23.46	UM	C 30	Mainly vans
23.55	CAM-TM	D5620	00.35	—	E 51	

NOTE. The times given in the description column are the YD departure times, 2 or 3 minutes earlier than the booked time at SJ.

Fig. 81

Anglia is still a matter for speculation; the ultimate supply of rail transport must very largely depend upon the demands made upon it.

The BLY (Bletchley) line typifies the dilemma of many cross-country routes today. It has become a popular byword for poor timetabling, although the product of an outcry over a closure proposal, now shelved, was predominant, but for journeys to many places in the Midlands and North the latter is limited by the practicability of good connections to only one train in each direction.

Generally speaking on this line there are two types of traffic; local journeys to Bedford and Oxford and exchange traffic at Bletchley to and from the LMS main line to the Midlands, Rugby, Crewe and the north west. The former is at present predominant, but for journeys to many places in the Midlands and North the latter is limited by the practicability of good connections.

The complete Survey details all the freight workings observed in 12 hours. **Fig. 81** is only a sample but it shows that Cambridge was handling a lot of varied freight in 1961:The freight side of the Cambridge railway scene is of particular interest for several reasons. The London via Cambridge to March Whitemoor marshalling yard service is the first intensive long-distance freight service on BR to be exclusively diesel-worked There are expanding sources of traffic in Essex and there is heavy seasonal agricultural activity and the list below is some of the commodities that regularly pass through Cambridge in large quantities:

Bricks: From the many works north of Cambriddge for re-sorting.

Cables: Some of the express freight trains from London and particularly 'The Lea Valley Enterprise' convey Enfield cables from Brimsdown.

Cars: New Ford cars from Dagenham travel on two trains: the 14.10 to Whitemoor, carrying traffic for the Manchester area, and the 20.32 to Niddrie (Edinburgh).

Cement: A good deal of cement traffic passes through Cambridge everyday from the local factories and the many works on Thames-side. Most of the latter is for Scottish destinations and, conveyed in Presflos, normally forms the greater part of the load of the 11.26 Ripple Lane inter-modal freight depot – Dringhouses Sidings (York) and often, also, of the preceeding Ripple Lane to Whitemoor. The Foxton trip (freight train dropping off and picking up wagons) consists mainly of traffic for the Barrington Cement Works. The Norman Works on the Cambridge to Ipswich line is served by the Mildenhall branch goods.

Chemicals: Many chemicals are conveyed to and from the Tilbury Line. Among these is ammonium nitrate solution for Fison's fertilizers at Bramford near Ipswich, carried in a block load of special tanks between Stanford-le-Hope and Immingham. This train, one of the very few steam-hauled main-line freights through Cambridge, does not run during the hours of the survey. There is also traffic in soda-ash, various types of tar, and special oils.

Coal: Cambridge coal traffic is normally carried by the 08.35, 10.30 and 21.50 Whitemoor to Cambridge trains. The chief returning empties service is the 13.16 Cambridge to Whitemoor, which is booked to convey wagons from the Cambridge MPD and coal merchants on that side of the line, but often starts from the Cambridge Up and Down yards. A chief purposes of the marshalling yard at Whitemoor is to collect traffic from Yorkshire and

Midland collieries for despatch via Cambridge to north east London. Most of the Up through trains consisting entirely of coal are block loads for the Lea Valley generating stations at Brimsdown, Broxbourne or Lea Bridge, or for the gas works at Angel Road, Enfield, London.

Grain: Various types of grain are conveyed in season, much of it in Bulk Grain Vans, from local stations in the area. Some goes to Foster Mills, Cambridge.

Oil: Various petroleum products are sent out on the Ripple Lane trains from Thames-side. There are also block workings from Thames Haven to Royston and Hethersett, supplying the distribution centres at these points.

Sugar: Harvesting of sugar beet takes place during the autumn, and there is considerable traffic in open mineral wagons to the sugar refineries at Ely, Kings Lynn and Bury St Edmunds on nearly all the local freights, while

special trains are run as required. Locos are sent from Cambridge to shunt the yard at the Ely plant. There are also special block loads from Ely and Bury St Edmund to Silvertown Thameside, London.

Timber: A fair amount of timber traffic is dealt with, particularly on Bletchley trains and for a merchant near Chesterton Depot. The traffic is probably imported through the small East Anglian ports.

General merchandise is moved in a considerable number of vans and containers, particularly from the light industries in NE London; two important and named freight trains are:

'Lea Valley Enterprise' – the 14.55 Tottenham to Whitemoor is a comparatively new venture introduced to serve the expanding industries in the Lea Valley. It picks up wagons at

Fig. 82: Mildenhall branch line train at Platform 4, Cambridge; 8 December 1954.

Fig. 82

stations from Tottenham to Broxbourne, whence it runs non-stop to Whitemoor to connect with many services from there. Its importance is demonstrated by the fact that it is allocated two engines, that it keeps very good time, and that it is given a clear road via St Ives. Lea Valley Enterprise is followed later by a series of express freights with important connections at Whitemoor including a through service from the large freight depot at Spitalfields, London.

'Fenland Freighter' is a more recently named-train, starting at Kings Lynn and picking up traffic for London, CAM usually providing a fairly large contribution.

In the Up direction there is less merchandise traffic and more empty-van working.

Fig. 83: Down mixed freight approaching Mill Road bridge north of Cambridge; 22 July 1948.

Fig. 83

Chapter 16

A GOODS PORTER ON CAMBRIDGE STATION – 1958 TO 1964

I n the Introduction I explained that part of my interest in, and knowledge of, Cambridge Station was much stimulated when I worked there as a goods porter. Many of my friends doubted my good sense in 'playing with trains' but I knew that there was much more to the operation of a large station than 'playing'. I have never fully understood the fascination which the working railway had – and still has – for me but I know I am not alone. Indeed, as I write this in early July 2016, the 9-15 July *Radio Times* offers three nights of live trainspotting. I have never liked the term 'trainspotting' because the popular image of 'collecting engine numbers' never appealed to me but today the term is in more general use.

One of the presenters, Dr Hannah Fry is quoted in the *Radio Times* as explaining:

'Trains are part of all our lives – part of our social and political history. … There's something really romantic about trains that appeals to all sorts of people … There are lots of people who enjoy trains who wouldn't stand out as trainspotters.'

Perhaps some of those people are reading this book so let me explain a little of the reality of the romance of trains – and Cambridge Station – as I experienced it. Although I had been recommended by Mr George Docking, District Operating Officer, I first had to attend for an inteview with the Station Master, Mr Baxter. I still recall him as a smart, gentlemanly, courteous man – in his sixties, I guessed (he retired in 1969) – who asked me about my reasons for wanting to work at his Station, my physical strength, and my readiness to work shifts including a night shift sometimes. I must have satisfied him because he asked his clerk to take me to the Down End Inspectors' Office and introduce me to the Inspector who would 'set me on'.

The Down End Inspectors' Office is marked A in **Fig. 84** and also contained the Station Announcer. The Inspectors – for there were several depending on shifts and other duties – were gods as far as porters were concerned. Some wore black bowler hats and overcoats that looked as if they would stand up on their own when taken off. The Inspectors gave us instructions and, I think, determined which goods porters were on which shift week-by-week.

B in **Fig. 84** was the Down End Porters' Room – our Mess Room – which was a

Fig. 84

Fig. 84: The head end of bay Platforms 5 and 6 and showing Down End Inspectors' Office, Down End Porters' Room, and doorway to Gentlemen's urinals and WC.

smallish square-shaped room containing a central table, benches and chairs, and a gas cooker on which stood a large kettle and a tea urn in which tea of extraordinary thickness and potency brewed all day. Around the room at just above head height was a shelf for mess kit, bags, overalls and whatever else

was stowed there. The shelf produced occasional suprises like a steady rain of live, wriggling, maggots which told us that Porter D's tin of fishing bait had overturned.

C was a Gents' urinal which was usefully near our Mess room – almost *en suite*!

I remember the Porters' names with whom I worked but I will identify them like 'Porter D' to avoid any unintentional offence. I was made welcome and learned a lot, especially from the older men who were happy to share their long knowledge of the railway, Cambridge Station and how to do jobs that sounded simple but often were not.

Generally, goods porters, if not given special jobs by the Duty Inspector, were general labourers, loading and unloading the extensive parcels traffic that was in the brake compartments of most trains and sometimes in special vans attached to passenger trains.

The Station Parcels Office was at the Up end on Platform 3 and was managed by Chief Parcels Porter, Harry Plumb. There was also an Up End Porters' Room on Platform 3 and sometimes I was rostered for an Up End shift so saw something of the whole station. Indeed, an incident – for which I was entirely culpable – happened on an Up End shift and on Platform 3. It was a quiet Saturday in September 1963 and I had already noticed a Travelling Post Office (TPO) vehicle temporarily stabled at the head shunt. The Great Train Robbery had occured in August 1963 so TPOs were very much in the news.

The TPO on Platform 3 was open, and empty, so being curious and 'spare' on that quiet day I got in. I knew where the master switches for carriage stock lights were located but could find no switches in the TPO. Finally, noticing several cord pulls hanging down over the sorting areas, I pulled one. I should have known that the pulls were alarms. Immediately the most clangorous bells I had ever heard began to ring. If I could not find the master switch for lights I certainly could not find a switch to quell the alams, which by then – I learned – were being heard throughout the station. Fortunately an Inspector quickly arrived, peace was restored, and I was reported to the Station Master.

Mr Baxter saw me in his office on Monday morning. He was curious to know of my interest in railway vehicles like the TPO so I was rightly reprimanded

and I apologised, but he then talked of some of his experiences with TPOs. A gentlemanly telling-off!

A job that sounded simple, but was not, was an Inspector's order to unload a prize calf on a down express and take it to a vehicle waiting near Platform 3 entrance door (**Fig. 33**, page 60). Inspectors' orders were often brief so the first I knew of this one was: 'Bob, calf on the next Lynn; take it to the Fish Dock; bloke there for it.'

I soon learned not to bother an Inspector with questions but to talk to one of the older goods porters on my shift. Porter E explained that the calf's legs and lower body were likely to be in a sack: 'May be shit as well, Bob – should 'ave an 'alter round its neck.' Unless it was a very small calf it was probably better to remove the sack, wipe off any shit, and help the calf to walk off the train restraining it if necessary with the halter which would be a choke-fastening round the calf's neck.

Fortunately my calf was clean and looked to be quite small, even when standing. What I had not anticipated was the considerable strength that such a smallish body can have. Once on the platform, and despite the choke halter, it went romping up the platform pulling me behind it. Then, before I could stop it, the calf dived under a trestle table set-up by the WH Smith bookstall and lifted its head, and the table-top. This caused a rain of books onto the platform which quietened the calf but not the flustered passengers round the table nor the Smith's manager who was not pleased.

No reprimand that time and the Royal Fish was an easier job. Duty Inspector again: 'Bob, Royal Fish, on the Lynn front brake; check the sawdust.' This time Porter F explained that the Queen was at Sandringham so I must wait at the country end of Platform 4 to meet the down express from Liverpool Street to Kings

Fig. 85: Cambridge North Signal Box, 31 August 1965.

Lynn. I set off with a bucket of sawdust to find two large wooden fish boxes marked 'HM THE QUEEN' and labelled 'Salmon'. There was a circle of sawdust around the boxes which contained fish and ice and the boxes were weeping slightly into the sawdust. I added more sawdust and grinned as I said to myself, 'I hope you enjoy them, ma'am.' I heard nothing from Sandringham!

Both the Up and Down Porters' Rooms were entertaining places at times because several of the older porters were interesting characters. We used to have our sandwiches while sitting round the table – as long as the maggots were back in their bait tin. I have already mentioned the Free Library on the corner of the City Council's Hooper Street Yard and I was a regular user of the Rock Road Free Library

Fig. 86

Fig. 86: 0-6-0 45843 at the north entrance to Cambridge Loco Shed, 8 December 1954. Bay platform 6 is behind a wall on the left so just out of picture.

near my home. Fortunately, Porter R did not use my library. He was a rather morose and very determined man who periodically removed from the Porters' Rooms' walls any pictures of which he disapproved. There were very few such pictures but one day I was alone with him in the Down End Room as he began a purge so I asked him why he was so concerned. 'They are filth,' he said, 'filth and they should not be allowed, especially for young men like you. Cambridge libraries are the same.'

I asked him what he meant – perhaps imagining I was missing something in my library. 'Many of the books are unsuitable,' he said, 'so I carefully work through them at home, tear out any unsuitable pages, then return them to the library.' I said no more!

The clue to a more strenuous job than the Royal Fish is in **Fig. 85** and the job came, for once, with slightly more explicit instructions from the Duty Inspector. 'Bob, you're a tall lad' (I thought this was a sinister beginning!); 'get a coaling ladder and a shovel from the Loco. There's a 16T up against the stop by North Box; shovel out a good quantity of coal and see if the Bobby wants some more in his Box.'

Interesting job; the strenuous bit came a little later. First a walk to the country end of Platform 6 then round the corner and into the Loco Shed, which was a shadow of its former busy life, and closed in 1962.

Fig. 86 is what I would have seen in 1954 but, because it was so busy then, a goods porter looking for a ladder and a shovel might not have been welcome. Even in the late 1950s, I was very aware of railway 'territories' and the platform staff were not welcome away from 'their' platforms and certainly not in the Loco.

I found a ladder and a shovel then set off to Cambridge North Box and the 16T mineral wagon which had been shunted

Fig. 87

up to the buffer stop in **Fig. 85** – the 'clue' to which I referred earlier – but when I arrived there was no coal left under the buffer stop.

I climbed up to the Signal Box door, knocked, and entered the Bobby's domain. Fortunately I knew that the universal railway slang for a signal man was 'bobby,' from the railway policemen who were the first means of controlling trains (**Figs 44**, **45, 46**, pages 54, 55) and from them back to Sir Robert (Bobby) Peel who introduced uniformed police in the UK that were initially nicknamed 'Peelers.'

Fig. 87 is the interior of South Box in the early 1970s, so a little after my time. South Box was very similar to North Box and the reason for using this picture is to illustrate the characteristic pot-bellied coal-burning stove in the corner of the box. That is why the coal was required and, 'Yes please, mate, and a good bit under the stop, please' was the answer to my question about needing coal in the box coal scuttle.

I knew that the down main line ran past the box, and is visible in **Fig. 85**, which is why the box's coal store is tucked away under the buffer stop. So no ladder to gain access to the 16T mineral wagon on that side! I checked that the wagon handbrake lever was pinned down then propped my ladder against the end of the wagon and climbed up onto the coal. Fortunately the wagon was full so I could see where to pitch the coal and I began shovelling. Not surprisingly, coal dropped from about 12ft above ground level, does not form a neat heap. I was noisily reminded by a passing Permanent Way (PW) man to, 'Keep that bloody rubbish off the main, mate.'

I smiled ruefully to myself and reflected that this was developing into a strenuous *and* a difficult job! I climbed down again and, carefully watching for any movements on the down main, shovelled back the coal that had strayed to there.

Back up the ladder again and more shovelling, this time to the other side of

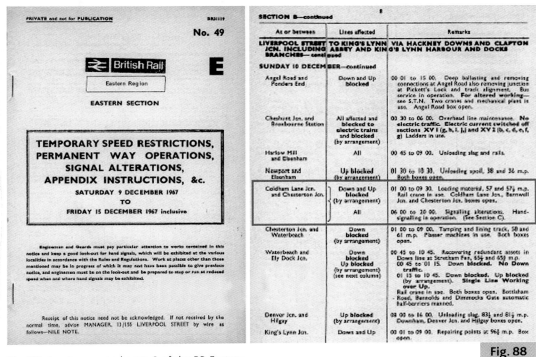

Fig. 88: Front cover and page 8 of the BR Eastern Region Eastern Section Notices Saturday 9 December to Friday 15 December 1967.

the wagon but that, too, was potentially hazardous because, as in **Fig. 85**, a diesel locomotive was stabled alongside my siding so ground-space was limited. And, of course, the coal beside my truck had then to be shovelled again to a neat pile under and around the buffer stop.

Welcome relief came from the Bobby in the box. I filled the box coal scuttle and was offered a short sit down (not much space for that!) and a cup of tea which was very welcome.

Another strenuous job which I much enjoyed was to take the Down End Notices to wherever they were required and relevant. I walked from a mid-point opposite Cambridge Station in the carriage sidings to Coldham Lane Diesel Depot nearly one mile north, and back. I enjoyed this job partly because of the exercise but

even more because I was seeing a portion of the working railway at ground level and meeting people doing a variety of jobs.

Railway 'Notices' in the 1950s and 1960s were the equivalent of twenty-first century emails and text messages. They were distributed daily, and sometimes hourly if significant changes were happening, to all operating centres – like signal boxes; offices; signing-on points and meeting places like mess rooms and trackside bothies. The Notices constituted the working railway's 'bush telegraph'.

As soon as new Notices arrived the old ones were discarded unless the new Notice was an amendment to part of a previous Notice in which case the amendment was pasted over the relevant deletion. Fortunately for this book, a retired railway signal engineer who was interested in railway history and worked in the BR Eastern Region found me an example of a surviving Notice

Fig. 89

Fig. 89: Cambridge 45 ton capacity steam breakdown train, 1960s. This crane remained the only working steam vehicle on the Station site until the early 1970s. As the lettering on the jib shows it was made by Cowans Sheldon in Carlisle and it came to Cambridge in 1940. The LNER No. was 961606 and the subsequent BR No. was 133. Breakdown cranes were sometimes used for civil engineering work – as may have been the case here – because they had easy access to railway sites.

from December 1967. **Fig. 88**i is the cover of a 60 page A5 stapled booklet. It was principally for signalmen but, in **Fig. 88**ii, is information for all staff working in the area if they needed to be on the permanent way. I have highlighted the section which relates to the area in which I delivered Notices: Coldham Lane Junction Signal Box was almost the furthest point of my walk and I would also deliver a copy to Coldham Lane Diesel Depot.

The Notices state that both Down and Up tracks were blocked and a rail crane was working in the section. The size of crane is not specified but it may have been the Cambridge steam breakdown crane which was stabled near Cambridge North Box and was always in steam in readiness for any calls.

As happened periodically on my Notices walk, I have been diverted a little by recalling the breakdown crane. But steam breakdown cranes always interested me as items of railway machinery. I often saw the Cambridge crane near North Box during a Notices walk and, once, I was invited to: 'Come aboard mate.' Steam crane drivers, and the whole breakdown crew, were experienced, courageous

and very skilfull men. The driver on this occasion saw my interest and was happy to share his knowledge and pride in 'his' crane with an interested listener. As **Fig. 89** shows, the driving position of a steam crane is a relatively narrow space with the boiler behind the driver and his controls for derricking; crane hoisting; slewing and travelling are in front of him. The steam cylinders, one on each side, are outside the driving space.

I mentioned earlier that my Notices walk took me to some unusual places, like the bothy amongst the carriage sidings, and most of them were good for a cup of tea and listening to some current railway gossip. An unusual 'find' was Mill Road Junction signal box, long disused but preserved, as illustrated in **Fig. 90**, as a base and mess room for PW men and some civil engineering labourers. I received a strong cup of tea there and bits of interesting PW history from some of the older men.

And a final memory of unusual, or different, jobs is about Chipperfield's Circus elephants and an elephant-knowledgeable BT Police Sergeant. Chipperfields were touring in the 1960s and claimed on their posters to have 'Europe's Greatest Elephant Herd'. The Circus usually toured by rail in the UK and, as the Up End Duty Inspector told me on an otherwise quiet Sunday duty: 'Bob, sixteen of 'em coming down Platform 3 this afternoon; you need a bucket and shovel to clear up the Station forecourt after 'em.'

The elephants, each trunk holding the tail of the elephant ahead, ambled out of the former GN Station doorway (**Fig. 33**, page 60) and into the forecourt. I stood, back to the wall of the Station. Fascinated by these delightful creatures, I waited – bucket and shovel poised – and suddenly realised that the line of elephants, led by a tusker and a mounted mahout, was wandering from a straight line and was

coming ever closer to us. Fortunately the BT Police Sergeant saw the problem. 'It's all right lad,' he said authoritatively, 'I'll deal with this'. He drew a truncheon and took a vigorous poke at a grey flank that was brushing us close to the wall while saying loudly to the elephant in his best BT police manner, 'move over there'. To my relief the elephant gently moved over and the line behind similarly swerved a little away from us. We were saved and I was greatly indebted to my police colleague!

Fortunately, my bucket and shovel were not required so I thanked the sergeant for 'rescuing' us. I have always admired the work of the BT Railway Police force and I can thank him again today!

Fig. 90 - Mill Road Junction Signal Box, 1960s.

Fig. 90

Chapter 17

BR MODERNISATION PLAN AND THE 'BEECHING REPORT':

The Reshaping of British Railways

*T*he Reshaping of British Railways was published in March 1963. Commonly known as the 'Beeching Report', after its author Dr Richard Beeching, Chairman of the British Railways Board, it is remembered chiefly for its proposals to close 2,363 passenger stations and withdraw all services from about 5,000 route miles. Most of these closures took place during the succeeding decade.

Beeching has been more reviled than most public servants and the criticisms of his work were bitter and sustained. One historian calls Beeching's appointment, '… a tragedy for the nation … one of the major aberrations of the Macmillan government.'

Beeching was typically seen as having callously ignored the social consequences of closures, falsified figures, studied the railways in isolation from transport as a whole, and was variously accused of co-operating with an anti-rail conspiracy or simply being wrong. We, and the railways, are now nearly sixty years further forward than publication of the 'Report' and a number of books published in the last decade have taken a more measured and balanced view of

Beeching's work. A retrospective *tour d'horizon* of the UK railways in the later 1940s – after a long and damaging world war – and the 1950s helps to explain what the Government expected of Beeching.

Nationalisation in 1948 created British Railways (BR), one of the largest 'business' organisations in the UK, employing 648,740 staff. I have placed 'business' in inverted commas because BR needed to become business-like. But it was placed under the control of civil servants who had no experience of running a business and little knowledge of the rail industry.

Rail managers on the nationalised railway had to obtain prior approval from the Government for capital finance towards new projects or for urgent post-war maintenance and repairs. If consent was given, BR usually had to borrow funds and thus pay interest whether it made a profit or loss on the projects. BR paid its way until 1952, but then losses rose, increasingly. Under the accountancy system in use, for 1961 there was an operating loss of £86.9M and a further £49M interest and central charges to be paid. In 1962, the loss was more than £100M and interest on the railways' debts added another £50M.

In order to reduce these losses and introduce modern management techniques into BR, Ernest Marples, the Minister of Transport, brought in Dr Beeching from outside the industry. His *'Reshaping'* Report showed how he intended to alter the rail industry; it concluded:

'If the whole Plan is implemented with vigour, much of the Railways' deficit should be eliminated by 1970.'

Beeching recommended in his Report that the railways had to concentrate on carrying the traffic for which they were best suited with increasing efficiency, while cutting out that which did not pay. This meant investing in the transport of large loads over long distances, while withdrawing many stopping-train passenger and pick-up freight services (in other words local passenger or freight services stopping at every station). Lines on which no other traffic was carried could never be profitable and should be closed. In short, the railways should behave like a business.

The Report proposed savings estimated at up to £147m per annum but withdrawal of local passenger and freight services would save only 28 per cent of this figure. The closure of unremunerative lines should have created savings in the BR revenue budget, but costing proposed closures and calculating the anticipated savings was very difficult and vigorously contested. The 'hardship' created by rail closures was a defence against many closures but defining 'hardship' was a social services and legal minefield.

For instance, in Cumberland, a farmer complained to his MP that if he was no longer able to see the branch train passing in the afternoon he would not know when it was time to go home for his tea. He was advised to get a watch. In a Norfolk branch line example, the taxpayer had been paying over four times as much to operate the service as its passengers had been paying to use it. Such expenditure could not be justified when so few benefited but the 'hardship' case identified people marooned in a formerly rail-served village: two schoolteachers and a pupil would have to wait until 6.45pm for a bus back to their homes; some rural residents were reliant on the train to reach doctors, dentists and chemists in their nearest small town

These very genuine complaints resonated in the local areas but were not arguments that would influence Treasury officials, or a Government, unless substantial public service subsidies for the railways were agreed and implemented.

The Beeching Report proposed several activities that should produce significant savings and generate more revenue income including: continuing locomotive conversion from steam to diesel; introduction of 'Freight Liner' trains; concentration of sundries traffic to about 100 main depots; introducing Red Star parcels services; attracting extra freight traffic to rail.

But it was the list of passenger closures that received most comment when the Report was published, and subsequently. The sombre list of proposed closures immediately inspired a *Guardian* editorial, entitled 'Lament', which utilised some of the more interesting station names and ended, 'Yorton, Wressle, and Gospel Oak, the richness of your heritage is ended. We shall not stop at you again for Dr Beeching stops at nothing.'

In a similar vein, later the same year Flanders and Swann produced their valedictory song, *Slow Train*, which to a large extent involved setting to music the list of stations Beeching proposed to close. East Anglia was not forgotten:

'I'll travel no more from Littleton Badsey to Openshaw;

At Long Stanton I'll stand clear of the
doors no more.

No whitewashed pebbles, no Up and no
Down.

. . .

I won't be going again
On the Slow Train.'

The Cambridge district, however, received
less publicity about proposed closures
than other parts of the country except,
perhaps, for the closure of the Cambridge-
Oxford line via Sandy, Bedford and
Bletchley. **Fig. 91** is a 'Beechinged' version
of the Railways to Cambridge map, **Fig.
27**, page 53, which illustrated Chapter
8. It shows that Cambridge is still a busy
entrepôt but the rural railways, the goods
yards and the parcels traffic from the
Platform 3 Parcels Office, have all gone.

However, an article in *The Economist*
on 16 April 2016 suggests that railway
development in East Anglia and related to
Cambridge is still flourishing:

'A museum in the centre of Wisbech, a
Georgian town of 30,000 souls in East
Anglia, proudly displays the original
manuscript of Charles Dickens's *Great
Expectations*. Those were days in which
Wisbech prospered. The frenzy of
railway building in the nineteenth
century gave the town three stations;
now it has none. The last passenger
train left in 1968, five years after
the report by Dr. Richard Beeching,
Chairman of British Railways, on the
future of rail, which led to the closure of
nearly a third of Britain's 17,000 miles
of track and a third of its 7,000 stations.
Wisbech has suffered economically.

'Yet Wisbech, like many towns cut off

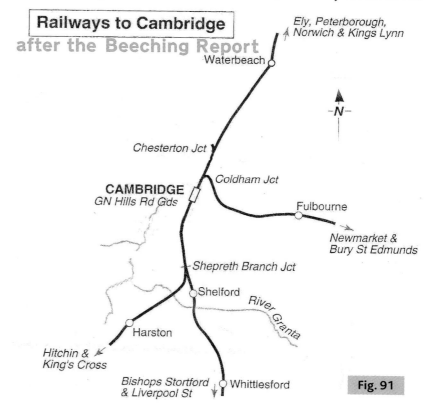

Fig. 91

from the rail network, is now expecting great things. In recent years several hundred miles of railways around the country have been restored. As roads clog up and urban house prices climb, commuters, environmentalists and local politicians are pushing for more old lines to be re-opened.

'It is a remarkable new trend. After the war, many thought that roads would rule and rail would go the way of canals. When Milton Keynes, a new town, was built 55 miles north of London in the 1960s, it was deemed not to need a station. One was at last opened in 1982. In 2015 6.6M journeys started or ended there. Traffic on other restored lines has boomed, too. The track that re-opened in 2015

from Edinburgh to the Borders – the Waverley Line – expected 650,000 journeys in its first year. 500,000 were made in the first 5 months.

'The process of re-opening is laborious. Feasibility studies take years. But with rail journeys doubling in the past 2 decades, Whitehall now realises it may be easier and cheaper to add rail capacity this way than through pharaonic projects such as HS2, a high-speed link north from London, set to cost over £45 billion ($64 billion).

'It is the growth of Cambridge, 40 miles to the south of Wisbech. and a centre for high-tech, that has provided the impetus for re-connecting Wisbech. A new station is opening at the Cambridge Science Park and it is hoped that the old line to Oxford will be restored by 2024. The Wisbech rail link would halve travel time to 40 minutes. Cambridge has lots of jobs and Wisbech has cheap houses (the average

Fig. 92: An entertaining fragment of social history but very pertinent: 'We send all our goods by road.' Dr Beeching might respond: My *Reshaping* Report echoes Mr Goodley's comment.

WISBECH & UPWELL TRAMWAY

Opened for all traffic:	**Monday 20 August 1883**
Closed to passenger traffic:	**Saturday 31 December 1927**
Closed to all traffic:	**Friday 20 May 1966**

Mr F Goodley of Basin Farm, Outwell, told the *Wisbech Advertiser* in May 1996:
The passenger days were a bit before my time, but I did have a ride on the tram. We used to take our fruit to the tram, and it always frightened the life out of the horses .... Its closure will make no difference to me. We send all our goods by road. But we used to like the old tram, especially the steam one.

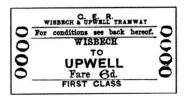

Fig. 92

price is around £150,000 compared with £398,000 in Cambridge), with a recent local plan proposing 10,000 more. If the link goes ahead, the Government would meet most of the £100m cost.

'Britain is not expecting another Dickensian railway boom. Perhaps 700-800 miles of lines closed by Beeching will be restored in total ... But sometimes small amounts of investment can make a big difference.'

Chapter 18

CAMBRIDGE STATION AND THE PRIVATISATION OF BRITISH RAILWAYS

British Rail (BR) was privatised in a process initiated by the Railways Act 1993 and completed by 1997. A track authority – initially Railtrack and from 2002 Network Rail (NR) – was set up to own and manage the infrastructure. For operational and administrative purposes NR created ten geographical sectors across the country. Cambridge Station and most of the areas referred to in this book are in Anglia. When introducing the Bill which became the Railways Act, the Secretary of State for Transport said:

> As an organisation, BR combines the classic shortcomings of the traditional nationalised industry. It is an entrenched monopoly. That means too little responsiveness to customers' needs, whether passenger or freight; no real competition; and too little diversity and innovation' (House of Commons Debates, 2 February 1993:124)

'No real competition' was the essence of the Conservative government's case for privatisation. 'Competition' was to be achieved by a number of separate private companies set up to operate railway passenger and freight services. The passenger train operating companies – TOCs – bid for a franchise to run a service and, if successful, pay access charges to NR for paths on the lines served by their franchise.

Privatised freight business was originally handled by six freight operating companies (FOCs) but amalgamations and changes have currently created five FOCs. The largest – and a reflection of the growth of European business in the UK – is DB Schenker Rail UK, a subsidiary of Deutsche Bahn.

Most passenger and freight rolling stock, and locomotives, are owned by three Rolling Stock Leasing Companies (ROSCOs).

And finally, in overall control of this competitive complexity is the Office of Rail and Road. ORR's website explains:

> 'The Office of Rail and Road is the independent regulator for Britain's rail industry and monitor of Highways England.
> 'We are the economic regulator for railway infrastructure (Network Rail and HS1); the health and safety

regulator for the rail industry as a whole – including mainline, metro, tramways and heritage railways across Britain; and the industry's consumer and competition authority.

'We monitor Highways England's management of the strategic road network – the motorways and main A roads in England.'

Cambridge Station, like most of the former BR Stations, is owned by Network Rail. Eighteen of the biggest and busiest stations are also managed by NR. Most of the remainder, including Cambridge, are managed on a day-to-day basis by the principal TOC operating services to and from that station.

I have spent a little time briefly explaining the current *modus operandi* of the UK's privatised railways because it is yet another change in the history and operation of Cambridge Station. To create a little continuity in this story I shall start ten years before privatisation was effected by BR.

I have already mentioned William Parker, a retired senior BR officer who has kindly helped me for this book with memories of his service on the Great Eastern Line. He subsequently became Divisional Manager, King's Cross when KX took over the former GN lines which embraced Cambridge. Bill outlined for me some of the developments which were taking place in the 1980s and 1990s:

> GN / GE Joint Line, closed

> New power signal box for Cambridge in 1982

> Many branches and small goods depots closed

> Despite the reduction in freight traffic, significant customers remained at:

  01 Ketton Cement Works near Stamford

  02 Chivers at Histon

  03 Sugar Beet factory at Bury St Edmunds

  04 Three breweries at Kings Lynn, Bury St Edmunds and Wisbech

  05 New large chemical factory south of Shelford

> Improvement to service quality, shunting and wagon examination at Ketton Cement Works

> Extensive increase in passenger business

> Central PO depot built near Cambridge Station

> Almost total closure of Whitemoor and New England marshalling yards

> Closure of most of Wisbech rail area except freight services to Metal Box and several smaller companies

> Preparation for electrification from Royston and Bishop's Stortford to Cambridge and Kings Lynn

> Expansion of Kings Lynn and Saffron Walden car parks – and gaining reluctant planning permission for them from District Councils using pressure on them by local MPs, Henry Bellingham and Alan Hazelhurst.

> Improvements to carriage cleaning facilities at Coldham Lane

> Improved punctuality to Liverpool Street:

  01 Right-time starts from Cambridge Station

  02 Better train regulation at Shepreth Branch Junction and at Ely junctions

  03 Improved timings to Liverpool Street

    a. Initial thinking of potential new stations at Chesterton and for

Addenbrooke's Hospital; a new island platform at Cambridge; park-and-ride at Whittlesford

b. Most main road level crossings reconstructed as auto-barriers but there were problems – as occurred nationally – with vehicle drivers evading the lights. This generated a purge on offenders in association with British Transport and County Police. Accommodation crossing irregularities still persisted so another purge was initiated jointly by County Police; BR Operating & Traction Inspectorate and BT police.

I have included this extensive list because it shows that BR in the Anglia Region was planning ahead so privatisation did not suddenly provoke extensive changes.

After privatisation, infrastructure management was carried out by Railtrack and, subsequently, by Network Rail. Many readers may know that Railtrack failed financially and operationally in 2002 so was replaced by a government-controlled not-for-profit company, Network Rail. This, as is much of the privatisation story and its success or failure as a means to operate British Railways, is a story outside the objectives of this book. As far as I know, this story of Cambridge Station's history, development and operation was not materially affected by the Railtrack to NR change.

Cambridge Station's status post-privatisation is illustrated by NR's categorisation of 2,520 UK stations for planning and operational purposes. The categories are from A to F; Cambridge is a Regional Hub or National Interchange Station and category B. NR explains that:

'66 stations provide major interchange opportunities both between trains and other forms of public transport such as trams, buses and taxis. They should also offer major car parking and cycle hub facilities. National Interchange Stations usually have more than 2M trips per annum and a ticket revenue greater than £20m.'

Chapter 19 illustrates the changes which are still currently (2016) in progress for Cambridge Station but it is relevant here to mention the categorisation of other stations already mentioned or illustrated on maps:

Important Feeder 'C' Stations

275 stations provide important rail feeder services on a busy trunk route. These stations are sub-divided into C1 (city or busy junction) and C2 (other busy railheads). 'C' stations will usually have 500,000 to 2M trips per year and ticket revenue between £2M and £20M

01 Bishop's Stortford **C2**
02 Bury St Edmunds **C2**
03 Hitchin **C2**

Medium Staffed 'D' Stations
298 stations
Small staffed 'E' stations
675 small staffed stations which typically have only 1 member of staff in attendance at any one time. Many stations will only be staffed for part of the day. Trips will be typically up to 250,000 per annum and revenue up to £1M.

> Whittlesford Parkway
Unstaffed 'F' Stations
1,192 unstaffed stations which form almost half the total number of stations. The 'F' stations are further sub-divided into F1 (basic) and F2 (below 100,000 journeys per annum) to avoid the provision of unnecessary facilities at the very small stations. Trips

are typically up to 250,000 per annum and ticket revenue up to £1 million.

> Newmarket – **F1**

> Waterbeach – **F2**

Currently (in 2016) three TOCs are providing electric, and some diesel, services to and through Cambridge Station which can be summarised:

Cross Country	Birmingham to Stansted Airport via Cambridge
Great Northern	London King's Cross to Cambridge and north to Kings Lynn
Abellio GreaterAnglia	London Liverpool Street to Cambridge
	Cambridge to Ely and Kings Lynn
	Cambridge to Norwich
	Cambridge to Ipswich

And finally, there is now an island platform again at Cambridge, although the scissors crossing and the long platform remain. The platforms are still generally used in the 'traditional' way with London-bound Up services at the southern end and north-bound Down services at the country end. However, the intensity of services through the Station now require more platform faces for swift loading and unloading.

Abellio GreaterAnglia TOC won the franchise from February 2012, initially to July 2014 then to October 2016. On 24 August 2016, the Department for Transport formally announced it is awarding the franchise to the current operator, Abellio, to 2025. From October 2016, it will be called Abellio East Anglia

The Abellio TOC is rightly proud of its achievements and it is appropriate to end this chapter with quotations from the Company's website in July 2016 including **Fig. 93**:

'… our passengers will benefit from refreshed rolling stock between Norwich and London, more local services on the Abellio network, and twice as many weekday off-peak services between Stansted Airport and Cambridge. The upgraded connection between Cambridge, a global centre of technological expertise, and Stansted Airport, will boost the city's links with the rest of Europe.

'The package of enhancements builds on the progress made since Abellio started running the franchise in February 2012, including: improved punctuality; re-painting of stations; refurbishment of some diesel trains; smart ticket purchase options; better customer information and (in partnership with Network Rail) a major reduction in disruptive weekend engineering work.

'Details of the enhancement programme:

> New off peak services for the Cambridge - Stansted Airport route on Mondays to Fridays from July 2014.

> 1,600 additional standard seats on weekday intercity services by October 2016.

> Over 400 additional cycle parking spaces at stations, and schemes to ensure that all stations will have cycle parking by October 2016.

> 20% funding increase for Community Rail Partnerships.

> Fitting of controlled emission toilets

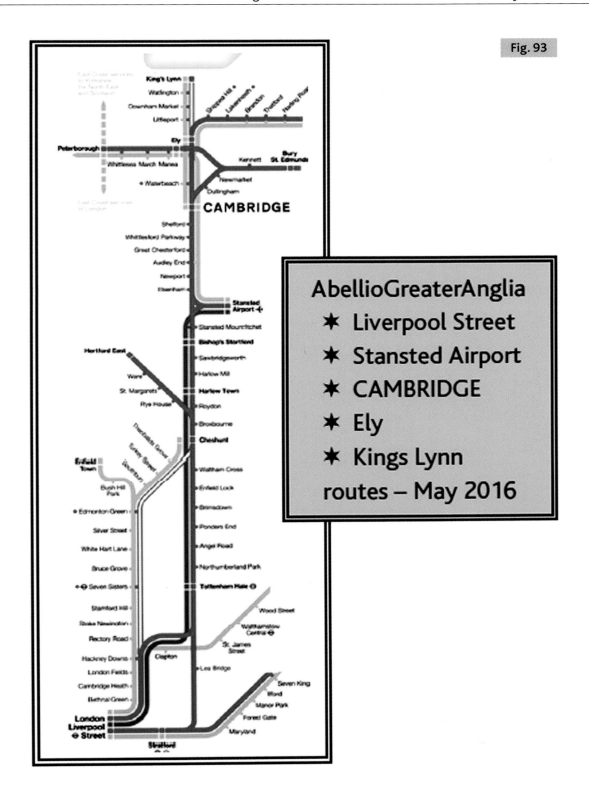

Fig. 93

(CET) allied with a £2M investment by Network Rail to stop waste being flushed onto the tracks.

> Completion of station upgrades at Bishop's Stortford, Cambridge and Chelmsford.'

And finally, again from website information:

'Abellio is a European transport company operating bus and railway systems. Initially, in 2001, it traded as NedRailways and became Abellio in October 2009. The company is the international arm of the Dutch national railway company Nederlandse Spoorwegen. Abellio's Head Office is in Utrecht.'

Chapter 19

RE-SHAPING THE STATION SETTING AND A NEW ISLAND PLATFORM

There have been several drivers in the re-shaping of Cambridge Station site and creating a new island platform. They are: AbellioGreaterAnglia and Network Rail – creating a more user-friendly access within the Station buildings and platforms; and developer Brookgate and Cambridge City Council – creating CB1 which is the umbrella name for the re-development of the Station forecourt, the areas around it to north and south and along Station Road.

Fig. 94 shows the 'Station Area' which the City Council was appraising for development in June 2004. I have added A, B and C to identify the railway land which, by that date, was no longer required for railway use:

A was the extensive GER Hills Road sidings and Goods Yard area

B was Tennison Road sidings

C was the Engine Shed site which, with the replacement of steam locomotives by diesels, was closed in 1962

Another large building area which was becoming available was Foster's Mill, the large Roller Flour Mill which is immediately west of the station and was a striking object in many photographs. The mill, owned and capitalised by the Foster family, Cambridge bankers, was opened in 1896 as a state-of-the-art roller flour mill with GER rail sidings and ready access for road deliveries. In 1917, the Foster family sold the mill to Pauls Agriculture and in 1947 Pauls Agriculture in turn sold it to Spillers – to most people in Cambridge it was sometimes still called Foster's Mill, to others it was called Spillers Mill. Spillers were absorbed into Rank Hovis and the mill finally ceased to work in 2002. It was derelict for several years but the local authority planners considered it an iconic building which had important historical associations with the station. Then developers began to create a number of attractive flats from the existing buildings despite severe fire damage during demolition work in 2012.

Fig. 95 shows the Mill in the early 1960s; today the mill building has gone but the former silo, white painted and to the right of the Mill is now flats which are one of the 'keynote' elements of CB1, the post-code inspired name for the whole of the station area development.

Cambridge City Council had been keen to improve and develop the Station area for a number of years. With the run-down

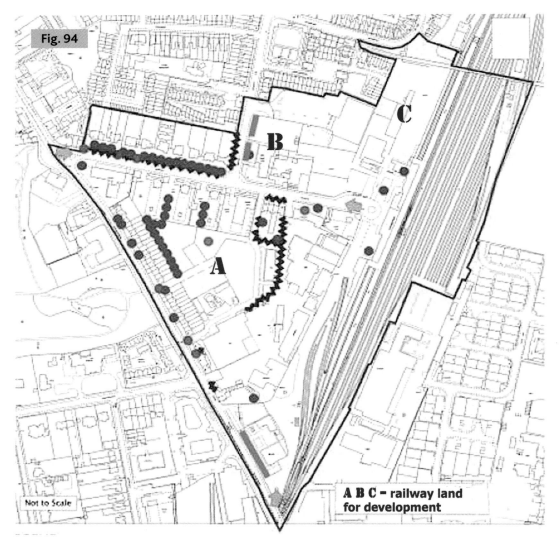

Fig. 94: Colour sketch plan of the 'Station Area' in 2004.

of the railway facilities mentioned above, Foster's Mill closing, and many of the large nineteenth century mansions along Station Road being turned into offices or flats, the 'gateway' to and from Cambridge was unattractive. Car parking spaces were limited; random and opportunist cycle parking obstructed pedestrian routes – **Fig. 96** – and the few bus services which served the station had limited loading and turning space.

AGA could also make a strong case for improvements to the Station itself and, with NR, to the trackwork and platforms. AGA's *Cambridge Station Regeneration* publication (July 2014) illustrates how busy the Station is:

> footfall 9M+ p.a. (27,000 per week)

> 800,000 interchanges p.a.

> only 450 car parking spaces

Fig. 95

> 1,400 cycles parked in 1,100 spaces

> Over 500 cycles on peak trains

> space required for a Guided Bus terminus

The 'Cambridge Effect' – the expansion of the City – needed good communications. The new Cambridge Science Park will be served by Cambridge North Station to open in 2017 which will be likely to change the balance of rail use at Cambridge Station.

AGA's proposals to improve the Station included:

> Four entrance doors from Station Square

> Relieving ticket hall congestion by enlarging the hall, creating an 'open style' ticket desk with eight positions and ten ATMs

> Extended gateline (ticket barriers)

> Five access doors to and from platforms

> Improved circulation on the platforms

> More retail space and an improved retail offer including a new pub with entrance from Station Square

> New restaurant in restored GN Station building (on Platform 3) and with an entrance from Station Square

> Relocated and enlarged toilets plus a new disabled toilet

> improved connectivity between rail services and parking / public transport offer in Station Square.

Network Rail's principal contribution to these improvements has been the creation of a new island platform. **Fig. 97** shows the new Platforms 7 and 8 in use and the potential problems that any flights of steps – to the new footbridge – produce. A lift,

Fig. 96: Temporary road signs and extensive cycle parking in the Station Forecourt, 2014.

too, is an integral part of the footbridge structure.

And, finally, CB1 which creates the landscape and transport interchange setting for the twenty-first century Cambridge Station. A Master Plan for the whole Station Area in **Fig. 94** was commissioned from the Rogers, Stirk Harbour & Partners (RSHP) architectural practice and was completed / approved

Fig. 97: Passengers queue for the steps on NR's new island platform.

by 2007. The RSHP website – www.rhs-p. com – explains the philosophy of the Master Plan:

'… [a] 26-acre site - centred around the Victorian [railway] station and historic Foster's Mill. The area had long been due for regeneration and the Station itself, already the busiest in the East of England, has struggled to cope with nearly 10M passengers p.a. that pass through its ticket hall.

'The new mixed-use development provides a new transport interchange with a remodelled Station Square at its heart, and provides Cambridge with the world-class gateway that it deserves.

'The RSHP scheme … includes more than 53,000sqm of office floor space, 331 residential units, accommodation for over 1,000 Anglia Ruskin University students, 5,255sqm of retail space, a hotel and art workshop.'

Fig. 98 is a visualisation of the completed scheme published by Brookgate, the Cambridge-based developer which is creating the various elements of the Project due for completion in 2017. Particularly relevant to this book is the Master Plan's outlining of the Transport Hub which CB1

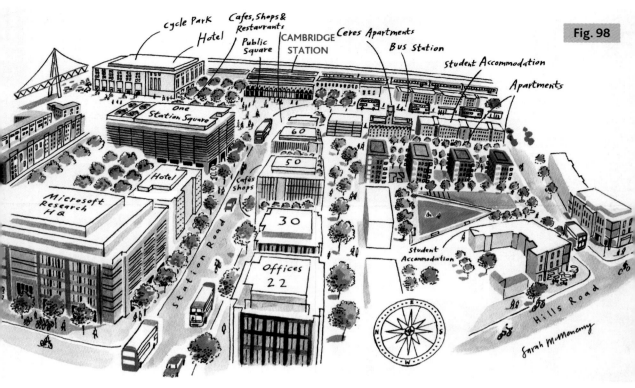

Fig. 98: Visualisation of completed CB1 redevelopment of the 'Station Area'.

and the AGA + NR developments will create:

TRANSPORT HUB

Situated directly in front of the main line station, an all new transport interchange will include bays for buses and drop-off and pick-up for taxis, new cycleways, and the route for the new Cambridgeshire Guided Busway – ensuring efficient and environmentally sound links to other parts of the city including the park and ride. At CB1 you will be within easy reach of local, national and global destinations –

Train: Cambridge Station itself provides fast train services to King's Cross, Liverpool Street, Stansted airport and the region.

Bus: The new Cambridgeshire Guided Busway has four separate routes offering quick and easy transfer to the Science Park, Addenbrooke's Hospital and many other parts of the city. A large number of conventional buses serve all parts of the city and the region.

Cycle: Cycling, traditionally the Cambridge transport of choice, now has proper provision with a 3,000 cycle park, the largest in the UK. …. the city centre [is] less than 1 mile

Travel times via rail – **Fig. 99**:

> King's Cross Station
> 45 minutes

> Liverpool Street Station
> 1 hour 10 minutes

> Stansted Airport
> 30 minutes

> Heathrow Airport
>   1 hour 55 minutes

> Access to Cambridge by road:
>   there is easy access to major roads,
>   including M11, M25 and A14, so
>   fast links to London and the rest of
>   the UK.

Fig. 100 from the Brookgate CB1 Website shows One the Square, fronting the new Station Square. It is an impressive focal point which forms a 'welcome' to people arriving at Cambridge Station. One The Square is the landmark address of the whole development, with a building to match. It has been designed as a modern interpretation of classic design proportions to compliment the Grade-2 listed Cambridge Station façade. It is the largest and most prominent space available in the city centre, with 137,000sqft of purpose-built office space.

As a Cambridge man and a railway-man I am delighted that the rather run-down and partially derelict 'Station Area' is acquiring a new look and a new buzz. Though I never needed to 'park' my cycle at the station, the fact that 3,000 cycles can now be parked at the Hotel is a reflection of changing times and needs.

It seems appropriate to end this

Cambridge

30 MINUTES

45 MINUTES

London Stansted

London King's Cross

Fig. 99

chapter with **Fig. 101**-which illustrates the diverse and mixed-use development and epitomises the intentions of the RSHP

Fig. 100: One the Square fronting the new Station Square in CB1.

Fig. 100

Master Plan. Lord Rogers introduces the Plan in the Brookgate CB1 brochure:

'At the heart of our urban strategy lies the concept that cities are for the meeting of friends and strangers in civilised public spaces surrounded by beautiful buildings.'

Enjoy Cambridge Station Square and CB1!

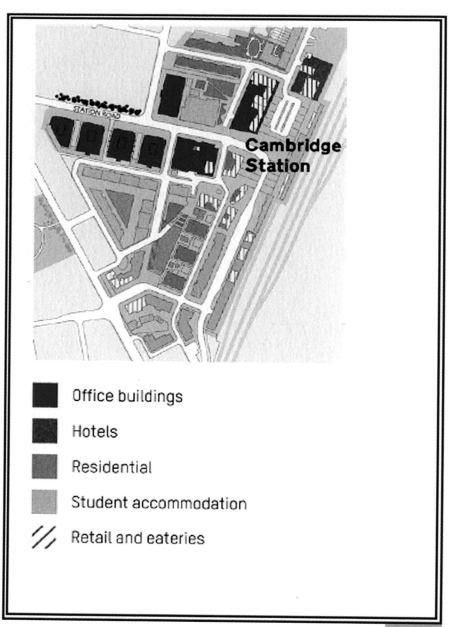

Fig. 101: Diagram of mixed use development for RSHP Master plan in CB1.

Office buildings

Hotels

Residential

Student accommodation

Retail and eateries

Fig. 101

Chapter 20

CAMBRIDGE STATION AND RAIL SERVICES TODAY

f you Google 'Cambridge Station,' the plan in **Fig. 102** comes up on the National Rail Enquiries website. Acknowledging the plan copyright, I have reproduced it here, with the addition of CB1 Cambridge Square name, as the most informative and easily available map of the new Cambridge Station. It shows the access and Ticket Hall improvements mentioned in Chapter 19 and the new island – Platforms 7 and 8 – linked by a footbridge to the existing and original main platform.

Presumably, because the plan is intended specifically for passengers, it simplifies the trackwork. The scissors crossover, which enables the long platform to be Platform 1 and 4, is missing as is the bi-directional through line. **Fig. 103,** which was part of my fieldwork at the station in mid-November 2015, shows the trackwork near the scissors crossing, looking south from the new footbridge. Platform 4 is on the right and the new Platforms 7 and 8 on the left.

Smarter Cambridge Transport (SCT) –

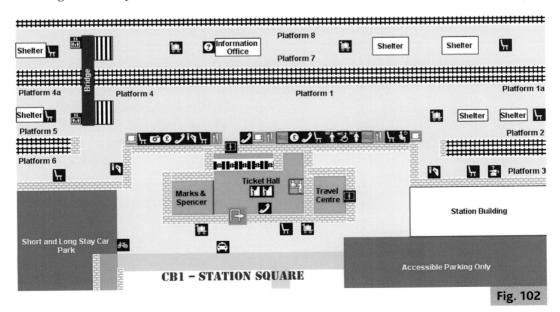

Fig. 102

Fig. 103

Fig. 103: The scissors crossover serving Platforms 1 and 4 – from footbridge to Platforms 7 and 8 on the new island platform.

has two map / diagrams of rail links to and from Cambridge – **Fig. 104** and **Fig. 105** – that are an up-to-date conclusion to my researches. The SCT website displays these map / diagrams and explains the purpose of the organisation:

'Smarter Cambridge Transport comprises a team of impartial, unpaid volunteers. The group has no political or commercial allegiance and its agenda is transparently about seeking out, developing and promoting the best transport-related ideas for making Cambridge and the surrounding region a great place to live, work and study.

'Smarter Cambridge Transport is an unincorporated association governed by a constitu:ion adopted on 24 April 2016.

'We started life as *Better City Deal*. We believe our new name better captures our focus and ambition, not just within the context of the City Deal, but for the future of transport across the region.

The first of the two diagrammatic maps– **Fig. 104** – illustrates the current rail services to and from Cambridge in 2016. The second, **Fig. 105**, illustrates proposals for the future which nicely summarise the re-openings of branch lines; the recognition that centres like Wisbech and Haverhill need railways again; and that there should be a renewed East-West link by re-opening a railway to Oxford via Bedford and Sandy.

There are two new stations proposed for Cambridge; Cambridge North at the Chesterton Junction site for Science City and Cambridge South to serve the new and hugely expanded Addenbrooke's Hospital. On the former Newmarket Railway is a joint station proposed to serve Cherry Hinton and Fulbourn. These adjoining villages have expanded greatly and are likely to develop more if they can be rail-served again.

I believe these SCT proposals are a pragmatic response to the growth and importance of Cambridge; to the financial investments promised in the Greater Cambridge City Deal (June 2014); and to the nationwide realisation that we need a platform to promote better rail services. Smarter Cambridge Transport is providing a platform and becoming an engine for progress. I wish them all well.

It would have been helpful, as a comparator, if a contemporary Traffic Survey – like the CURC 1961 Survey summarised in Chapter 15 – was available today. However, the working railway uses computerised Working Timetables and I am very grateful to Geraint Hughes of AGA for supplying a PDF of Up and Down trains to and from Cambridge on Mondays to Fridays 14 December 2015 – 13 May 2016.

I have chosen a busy morning, two hours, Up and Down, from 08.43 to 10.51 on **Fig. 106** and **Fig. 107**. For readers not familiar with such documents here is a brief key:

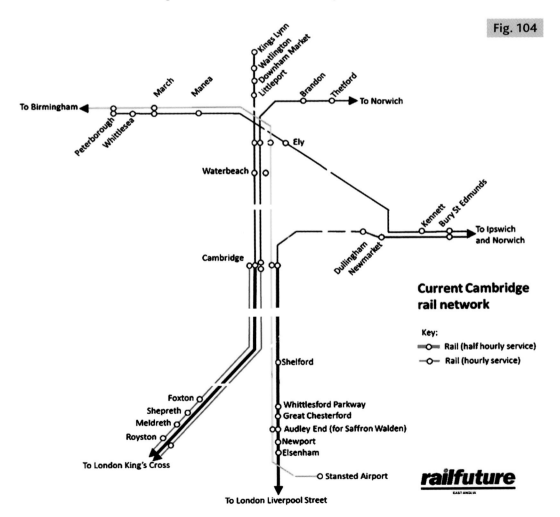

Fig. 104: Colour diagrammatic map of current Cambridge Rail Network.

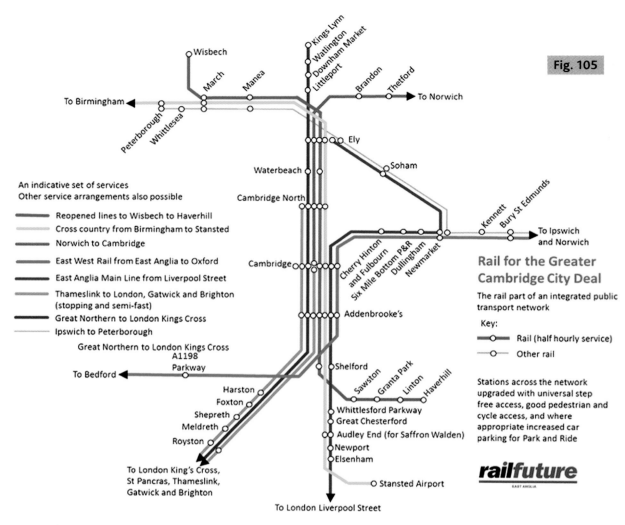

Fig. 105

An indicative set of services
Other service arrangements also possible

— Reopened lines to Wisbech to Haverhill
— Cross country from Birmingham to Stansted
— Norwich to Cambridge
— East West Rail from East Anglia to Oxford
— East Anglia Main Line from Liverpool Street
— Thameslink to London, Gatwick and Brighton
   (stopping and semi-fast)
— Great Northern to London Kings Cross
— Ipswich to Peterborough

Great Northern to London Kings Cross
A1198
Parkway

Rail for the Greater Cambridge City Deal

The rail part of an integrated public transport network

Key:
—O— Rail (half hourly service)
—O— Other rail

Stations across the network upgraded with universal step free access, good pedestrian and cycle access, and where appropriate increased car parking for Park and Ride

railfuture EAST ANGLIA

Fig. 105: Diagrammatic map of proposed future rail network around Cambridge Station – Rail for the Greater Cambridge Deal.

TRAIN: this column shows the train identification number, or headcode; a 4-character identification code.

SBJ: Shepreth Branch Junction

WB: Waterbeach

CL: Coldham Junction

cs: Carriage sidings

Remarks/Works: railway working information – for instance Train 2H12 Liverpool Street Down to Cambridge arrives in Platform 1 @ 09.55 then, as

Train 5H12. moves to carriage sidings @ 10.00. As Train 5H23 it leaves the carriage sidings @ 10.13 and arrives at Platform 4 at 10.18 to become Up Train 2H23 for Liverpool Street leaving Cambridge @ 10.21;. This is the train time in the public Timetable.

The services shown are illustrated in the first diagrammatic map, **Fig. 104**. The frequent Up trains to London King's Cross or Liverpool Street are approximately half-hourly on a regular-interval basis.

The Stansted Airport trains are hourly and likewise the return workings to Birmingham so there is now a good Midlands connection.

TRAIN	ORIGIN	DESTINATION	SBJ	LINE	CAMBRIDGE arrive	Pl	CAMBRIDGE depart	CL	WB	DIAGRAM	Remarks / Notes
2K62	Cambridge	Norwich				5	09.12	09.14		603	off 1K61
2H10	Liverpool St	Cambridge	09.20		09.25	4				47 46	5H10 09.30cs
2C06	Kings Cross	Cambridge	09.23	DSL	09.30	3				068	2C41 09.55 Kings Cross
1T08	Kings Cross	Lynn	09.26		09.30	1	09.35	09.37	09.41	052 051	SPLIT 1T19 to attach
1H00	Liverpool St	Cambridge	09.33		09.38	8				26 25 24	5H00 0956 cs 2H21 10.04 Liverpool Street
2W11	Cambridge	Ipswich				6	09.44	09.46		606	off 2W06
2H12	Liverpool St	Cambridge	09.49		09.55	1				34 35	5H12 10.00 cs
1N49	Stansted	Birmingham	09.52		09.58	4	10.01	10.03		211	
1C46	Kings Cross	Cambridge	09.57		10.03	7				070	1T57 to attach
1C10	Kings Cross	Cambridge	10.00		10.06	1				057 056	1C21 10.15 Kings Cross
2H14	Liverpool St	Cambridge	10.03	DSL	10.09	3				61 31	2H25 11.04 Liverpool Street 2H27 11.21 Liverpool Street
1K66	Cambridge	Norwich				5	10.12	10.14		604	off 1K65
2C08	Kings Cross	Cambridge	10.23	DSL	10.29	2				097	2C43 10.55 Kings Cross
1T12	Kings Cross	Lynn	10.26		10.30	1	10.35	10.37	10.41	065 064	SPLIT 1T23 to attach
2H62	Stansted	Cambridge	10.30		10.35	8				39	5H62 10.41 cs
2W13	Cambridge	Ipswich				6	10.44	10.46		621	off 2W08
2H16	Liverpool St	Cambridge	10.46		10.51	8				44	5H16 11.04 cs

CAMBRIDGE DOWN TRAINS — MONDAYS – FRIDAYS 14th December 2015 to 13th May 2016

Fig. 106 and 107: Tables showing Cambridge Down and Up trains, 09.00 to 11.00 from the current (2016) Abellio Greater Anglia Working Timetable.

Fig. 106

TRAIN	ORIGIN	DESTINATION	WB	CL	CAMBRIDGE arrive	Pl	CAMBRIDGE depart	DIAGRAM	Remarks / Notes
1T15	Lynn	Kings Cross	08.36	08.41	08.43	1		079	attach to 1T04 split
2H17	Cambridge	Liverpool Street				2	0.848	37 38	off 2H06
1T15	Lynn	Kings Cross				1	08.51	060 079	
1K61	Norwich	Cambridge		08.51	08.55	5		603	2K62 09.12 Norwich
2C39	Cambridge	Kings Cross				3	08.55	101	off 2C04
1L28	Birmingham	Stansted		09.05	09.08	7	09.10	314	
1T17	Lynn	Kings Cross	09.08	09.12	09.15	1		073	attach to 1T06 split
2H19	Cambridge	Liverpool Street				8	09.18	21 22	split off 1H98
1T17	Lynn	Kings Cross				1	09.21	085 084 073	
1C55	Cambridge	Kings Cross				3	09.27	074	off 1C44
2B61	Cambridge	Stansted				2	09.31	39	split off 2H08
2W06	Harwich	Cambridge		09.35	09.38	6		606	2W11 09.44 Ipswich
1T19	Lynn	Kings Cross	09.38	09.42	09.45	1	09.51	051 066	attach to 1T08 split
1K65	Norwich	Cambridge		09.51	09.55	5		604	1K66 10.12 Norwich
2C41	Cambridge	Kings Cross				3	09.55	068	off 2C06
2H21	Cambridge	Liverpool Street				8	10.04	24 25	split off 1H00
1L30	Birmingham	Stansted		10.07	10.09	8	10.11	312	
1C21	Cambridge	Kings Cross				1	10.15	056 057	off 1C10
5H23	10.13 cs	Cambridge			10.18	4		26 23	2H23 10.21 Liverpool Street
2H23	Cambridge	Liverpool St				4	10.21	26 23	off 5H23
1T57	Ely	Kings Cross	10.17	10.21	10.24	7		083	attach to 1C46
2B65	Cambridge	Stansted				2	10.26	40	split off 2H08

CAMBRIDGE UP TRAINS — MONDAYS – FRIDAYS 14th December 2015 to 13th May 2016

Fig. 107

Fig. 108

Fig. 109

Fig. 110

Railway to Guided BusWay – Histon Station (St Ives Loop) 1976 and 2016

Fig. 108 Histon Station, already closed to passenger traffic in January 1976; track lifted 2007.

Figs. 109 and **110** Buses on the Cambridge Guided BusWay Route C passing Histon Station, 23 July 2016

POSTLUDE

A Postlude is a final or concluding piece of music or, more specifically for my interests, the end of an organ recital. So, after an extensive 'recital' about Cambridge Station which opened with a Prelude, I am finishing with some memories of Cambridge Station that friends have contributed.

Railways, and therefore railway stations, were a new and exciting social phenomenon in the nineteenth century. In Thomas Hardy's novel *Jude the Obscure*, published in 1895, Jude suggests to his girlfriend, Sue, that they sit in the cathedral to talk. She replies, 'I think I'd rather sit in the railway station. That's the centre of the town life now. The Cathedral has had its day!'

A percipient girl – but Cambridge, though without a cathedral, does have Kings College Chapel probably known world-wide for the Christmas Eve Nine Lessons and Carols Services. It seems appropriate to begin the Postlude with this memory from Richard Hill: Songman Emeritus, York Minster Choir:

'During my late adolescence, family holidays were often taken at Hunstanton, on the North Norfolk Coast, which, given the fact we lived in Leeds, seemed a million miles away from that war-torn city, both geographically and in tone.

'On Sunday 23 June 1963, my father and I undertook a railway journey from Hunstanton to Cambridge, via Kings Lynn, in order to attend 3.30pm Evensong in King's College Chapel. I remember passing Wolferton Station – still sumptuously maintained as it had once been for Queen Victoria's journeys from there to Sandringham House. We had to change trains at Kings Lynn so the whole journey to Cambridge took over two hours, then a bus to Drummer Street bus station, then a walk through the centre of Cambridge to Kings College and the magnificent Chapel.

To our initial disappointment, we discovered that Evensong that afternoon was sung by the Choral Scholars only and not the boy choristers. Father suggested an immediate return to Hunstanton but I persuaded him to stay and we heard wondrous singing from a superb group of young men. And we also enjoyed the Chapel's magnificent Harrison & Harrison organ.

'Cambridge, still to this day, excites me when I return. I never had the academic finesse to be able to study there but, many years later, I was able to derive vicarious pleasure from coaching young men attending Ampleforth

College, for choral scholarships at King's, St John's, Jesus and Girton colleges. That rail journey was, for me, formative in so many ways. It gave me the determination to work towards becoming a professional singer, an ambition I duly fulfilled.'

Another memory which embraces King's College, classical pipe organs and Cambridge Station is from James Lancelot, Organ Scholar, Kings College and now Master of the Choristers and Organist, Durham Cathedral:

'In my undergraduate days (1971-74) there was a 9.30 train to King's Cross which still included a Gresley buffet car, one of the last wooden-bodied vehicles in passenger service; when funds permitted, full English breakfast was a welcome treat. The coach worked back on an evening train, and again a full meal was served.

'My postgraduate year brought time to join Cambridge University Railway Club, my position as College representative entitling me to a free pass each term (Winchester to Thurso was the final one, I remember). The CURC sadly no longer took over a branch line for annual engine-driving tuition, but we did visit Coldham Lane signal box, and enjoyed a brake-van ride over the St Ives branch, over which I had travelled as a passenger before its unfortunate closure.

'End of term brought a homeward journey … sometimes changing at Ely on to the Harwich – Manchester boat train (the beat of another Gresley buffet car, reputed to serve the best meals on British Rail). It was while waiting in the front seat of a connecting DMU for Ely in the northern bay at Cambridge that we were delayed while the signalman attempted to pull the starter off, hindered by the presence

of a lampman cleaning the semaphore arm. The lampman was either blissfully, or wilfully, unaware of our impending departure. At length, after much jiggling of the signal arm and a fanfare from the DMU driver on the klaxon, we got the road and headed northwards!'

Memories of Cambridge Station have often been of delays, or the extreme cold as a wind 'straight from the Urals' used to scythe along the platform. But some friends had happier memories. Professor Malcolm Brown, who was at St John's College 1965-73 and Downing College 1973-74 told me:

'I used Cambridge Station over a lot of years but I mainly tried to spend as little time as possible there and have to confess to not giving it a great deal of attention! However, I do recall that Cambridge trains typically ran to time and my research collaboration in Cambridge from 1991 to 2006 meant travelling from and to my home in Stroud. I used to reckon that every other time I went I would experience a critical delay – but it was never at the Cambridge end!

And another memory from George Potter, Associated British Cinemas (ABC) Senior 2nd Projectionist in Cambridge in the 1950s and 1960s, is complimentary about the railway's ability to deliver parcels swiftly. George was working at Central Cinema, in Hobson Street, when one day the first afternoon film did not arrive from London. Urgent phone calls to the London distributor promised delivery to Cambridge Station off a Liverpool Street-Kings Lynn express.

George booked a taxi to and from the Station and waited on Platform 4. The front brake guard was ready for him and George then ran with a box containing ten 10-minute reels past the ticket check – the Ticket Inspector had been alerted – to the waiting taxi. Back to Hobson Street, up to the Projection Room and lacing-up the first reel off a flat plate with a central spigot into Projector 1. 'In at the top of the projector' George explained to me. 'through the gate and out of the bottom'. Meanwhile the remaining reels were spooled, the next spool was laced into Projector 2 and the film started only 3 minutes late – 'thanks to BR,' said George.

Another memory shows how railwaymen could be helpful before privatisation and Network Rail made the agile lady's experience in this story from Michael Perrins, railway Archivist and Librarian no longer permissible:

> 'One Sunday evening, probably in the Spring of 1985, during ECML electrification works south of Peterborough I was returning to London King's Cross from Leeds. The train consisted of Mk 1 coaches hauled by a class 47 loco. We ran up the main line as normal until Peterborough then were diverted via March and Cambridge to Hitchin.

Our driver knew the road from Peterborough to March and from Cambridge to Hitchin but not the vital link in between. We were therefore held at March because no pilot man was available so we had to wait for one to arrive from Cambridge and be persuaded to do another round trip instead of signing off and going home.

> 'While we were waiting, a lady passenger came to March station, wanting to travel to Cambridge. Although our train was not booked to stop there it was obvious that we would have to stop, briefly, to set down the pilot, so the station staff introduced her to the Guard who settled her in the compartment next to the brake and ensured that the loco crew knew what was happening.

> 'All went well until we pulled into Cambridge on the through goods lines. Fortunately, the lady was reasonably fit and agile. The Guard got down onto the ballast first, then helped her down and escorted her across the tracks to the ramp at the end of the platform.

> 'After all this we carried on southwards: I cannot remember any more problems that night.'

The University brought many students to Cambridge Station and here is the memory of Peter Hollindale. Reader in English, University of York, from 1953, when as a stranger from Chesterfield he was bound for Jesus College:

> '[My] first time ever in Cambridge – Scholarship Exams, December 1953.

> 'Local connecting train from Kettering, stopping at many local stations such as Raunds. My compartment full of local countrymen, each with a dead rabbit, and one of them with a ferret, very much alive. They spoke a dialect almost as incomprehensible to me as Geordie. Strange stuff for a town boy.

> 'Then Cambridge, into a bay at the northern end. And a walk down a seemingly interminable main platform. As a former train spotter I was a connoisseur of station platforms and this was the longest I'd ever come across. In a cold, wispy Cambridge fog, it was intimidating.'

And another memory, from the same source, which echoes the Thomas Hardy suggestion that a railway station was a centre of town life:

> 'On 6 February 1958, I attempted to hitchhike back to Cambridge after a visit to Chesterfield. It was bitter winter weather and one of the days when nothing goes right. After being stuck without success on the far side

of Nottingham, I decided to abandon the journey, return to Chesterfield, and travel to Cambridge by train the next day.

At Mansfield bus station there were placards reading 'Manchester United plane crash'. This was the disaster at Munich when BEA flight 609 crashed on its third attempt to take off from a slush-covered runway. Manchester United football team – the Busby Babes – were on board and a number of famous and admired young players were killed, and others badly injured. All were only a little older than me.

> 'The next day I went back to Cambridge by train. At Cambridge Station it was snowing. Somehow the place is bleaker than most stations in such weather … it felt like Russia. But what I remember is that nobody was talking. Papers with Munich crash headlines were lying about or being read, because this was the day the news sank in. It was the 1958 equivalent of Princess Diana in 1997, but with a 1958 reaction – no overt emotion, just a general, private, appalled silence. At that time football wasn't a hyped-up global business, but the domestic working man's game, and on Cambridge Station that day working men, railwaymen and passengers, were in shock.
>
> 'For people my age it was a harsh *memento mori*. I remember that arrival in Cambridge as one of the bleakest moments of my life.'

A nicely whimsical memory of Cambridge Station, Anglican church organ music and choral settings is from James Lancelot again. James reminded me that Sir Charles Villiers Stanford was educated at Cambridge and appointed organist to Trinity College in 1873. Although Stanford made a rich contribution to music in Cambridge James believes that he took

umbrage because he was never given a Fellowship.

Subsequently, and occasionally, when tutoring his students, he declined to enter the environs of the University and instead gave supervisions in the waiting room at Cambridge Station. Access in those days, long before ticket battiers, to a station waiting room was free or not more than a 1d platform ticket. Stanford believed that this was far enough away from Trinity College and any University influence. Perhaps he was unaware that the site of the Station had been purchased from Jesus College!

I have been quite strict in this book about limiting descriptions of the locomotives that worked Cambridge trains but the memories in this chapter allow me a little more latitude. I can also recall more friends I have made in a busy and enjoyable career.

Rev Alan Cliff, born in Morecambe, Lancashire in 1936, became a Methodist minister in 1960. He also married Rosemary, his wife, in 1960. He served in Norfolk, Edinburgh and, in 1974, moved to Wales to take charge of the Wrexham circuit. Alan had to take early retirement in 1987 on health grounds, moved to Rhyl, and developed a busy and health-improving career as a writer. In 1990 he self-published *British Makers of 0 gauge, 1890 - 1990*, which sold 1,200 copies. Since then he has written over 300 articles for model railway magazines and a series of children's books about *Jack the Station Cat*. He has been a railway enthusiast all his life and has always had model layouts of different gauges lurking in various corners of the house and garage. Alan was elected as a full member of the Welsh Academy (the National Society of Writers in Wales) in 2006.

> 'I was a student at Cambridge October 1958 to June 1960, having for the previous four years been a student at

Fig. 111: 3-rail 0 gauge model of ex GER D16 4-4-0 2618 carrying her 1946 LNER number.

Oxford. So I cannot lose the Boat Race and I did travel on the whole of the Oxford Cambridge railway link that sadly no longer exists.

'I mentioned when we talked of the 'glory day' of an ancient ex-GER D16 4-4-0. I am pretty sure the loco was 62618 a former 'Royal' engine and a Claud Hamilton design. The event took place, if I remember correctly, in my first term at Cambridge. I was seeing Rosemary off on a train from King's Lynn to Liverpool Street which left Cambridge sometime around 7.15PM.

'Rosemary, then my fiancée, had been visiting me for the weekend. The train was late and I noticed, waiting at the south end of the station, a B1 4-6-0 so I suspected an engine change was imminent. Finally, wreathed in smoke and vapour, the train clattered in headed by D16 4-4-0 62618. The old engine's smokebox was dull red from her exertions and steam poured out of all manner of places. Believe it or not a huge cheer went up from the would-be passengers and particularly those escorting them.

'The grinning crew acknowledged

the greeting as the veteran clanked down the platform and pulled up at the south end. There was a rush forward and many fiancées and girlfriends were temporarily bereft of their men folk as we rushed to congratulate the old lady and her crew. The loco was uncoupled and melted away into the night. The waiting B1 4-6-0 duly took her place and hurried the train off to London.

'Animated groups of railway enthusiasts left the station doubtless offering theories to one another about the appearance of a 'Claud' on a crack London express. I have no doubt several young ladies on the train were bemoaning the fact that they were temporarily jilted in favour of an old battleaxe!!

'I have a 3-rail 0 gauge model of 2618 carrying her 1946 LNER number.' (**Fig. 111**).

Alan still has a delightful sense of humour, not least about his Methodist ministry, his time reading theology at Cambridge University and training at Wesley House on Jesus Lane. Alan recalled for me another, and perhaps spiritual dimension, for the importance of Cambridge Station and the railways around it:

'Part of our training involved conducting services at Methodist churches in Cambridgeshire, other parts of East Anglia, and beyond. It was College policy that students travelled, wherever possible, to their appointments by train. In those days Cambridge was ideally placed.

'Thus I found myself travelling from Cambridge to stations on the loop line to Ely via St Ives, such as Histon, Oakington and Long Stanton. Returning from an appointment at Histon one cold wet night I was invited into the signal box by the kindly signalman.

Stations on the ex LNWR line to Bedford such as Potton and Gamlingay were in regular use. I think it was an appointment on that line where I had an encounter with an ancient tortoise stove to keep the congregation warm. The thing smoked worse than Cambridge loco shed and my congregation, who needless to say sat at the back, were scarcely visible!!

'The Mildenhall branch was not used. Mainly because there was no Sunday service on the branch and the country chapels were near enough to Cambridge for lifts by car to be arranged.

'Peterborough and stations on the Ely, March line thereto were regular appointments for Wesley House students. I went to Peterborough once. Here I was treated by the Sunday School children to a rather unusual rendering of, 'I will make you fishers of men'. Their revised version was '… fishy old men!'

'All the other lines that still exist were in regular use by Wesley House students:

> the ex GNR line to Hitchin, though I think Baldock was the furthest station used.

> the ex GER line to Liverpool Street as far as Great Chesterford and Audley End.

> the line to Newmarket (famous for its shunting horse used to marshal horse boxes), Kennet and Bury St Edmunds.

> 'Thus, the railways radiating from Cambridge played an important part in the lives of those training for the Methodist ministry at Wesley House in the late 1950s!'

And the railways around Cambridge Station played a noisy part in many Cambridge dwellers' lives, as in this extract from *Period Piece. A Cambridge childhood*, Gwen Raverat's memoir of her 1890s upbringing among the eccentric Darwin family, first published by Faber and Faber in 1952:

'… when we were in bed we could hear, a long way off, the trucks being shunted at the Station and the whistling of the engines on the line …'

And in the 1940s & 1950s I remember the same sounds when I was lying in bed, 'in the quiet of the night,' at my home in Cherry Hinton Road. Sounds that conjured ideas and dreams – like Lytton Strachey who regularly used the railway to and from Cambridge when he was at Trinity College from 1899 to 1905:

'… one was in a special (a very special) train, tearing along at break-neck speed – where? One could only dimly guess – one might be off the rails; or at Timbuctoo; or in Heaven – at any moment.'

My dreams never took me to Timbuctoo – perhaps because my geographical knowledge told me that there was no station at Timbuctoo. But they did eventually bring me to the 'Heaven' of the National Railway Museum in York – and to writing this book!

A long journey and another student memory of Cambridge, and the classical pipe organ which this Postlude is still remembering. David Pipe was Organ Scholar at Downing College 2002 - 2005 and is now Director of the Organists' Training Programme & Cathedral Organist, Diocese of Leeds:

'My only real memories of Cambridge Station involve getting a train at an ungodly hour in order to give a lunchtime organ recital in Ripon. I think the train was to Peterborough; then another train from Peterborough to York; a third train from York to Harrogate and finally a bus to Ripon ... It felt like quite an adventure!'

An adventure which illustrates the transport connectivity (a horrible contemporary word!) which twenty-first century Cambridge Station still offers. And which leads me to a penultimate memory by Canon Roger Bradshaigh Lloyd (1901-66) recounted in his book 1951, *The Fascination of Railways*, now sadly out of print. Canon Lloyd was a graduate of St John's College and was a prodigious writer, mainly on matters theological, but he was fascinated by railways and followed his first railway book by two more: *Railwaymen's Gallery* (1953) and *Farewell to Steam* (1956).

Cambridge features in Chapter 7 – Station Sauntering – from *Fascination* and the edited passage below reflects his enthusiasm; his sense of wonder in observing the working railway; the operating excitements of the long platform, the scissors crossover and four different railway companies managing to work together:

'At Cambridge the station is still further distant [than at Oxford] from the nearest college but the road which joins them is not quite so dispiriting as at Oxford. First, the traveller passes the railway sidings [Tennison Road visible

on the right from a double-decker bus] ... then ... a region of rather dim little shops and garages, and it is only after one has passed the vast Roman Catholic church of St. Mary that one sees anything in the least congruous with what a University town might be expected to show. [Downing College on the left]. Oh, the places we choose for our stations in England!

'However ... Cambridge station has two features, one absolutely unique, and one nearly so –

'[I know no] other station ... of comparable importance which has only the one through platform. You enter it and you expect to see the [at least one more platform] platform on the other side [of the tracks] after the traditional manner but instead you look out upon a sea of railway lines [including extensive carriage sidings] There is absolutely no other platform except the one on which you stand. As this has to serve the needs of both up and down trains, and as very often both an up and a down train use the same platform at the same moment, there is some very pretty and dexterous intricacy of working to see.

'The second and nearly unique feature is that in only one other station, Carlisle [which was served by L&NWR, Caledonian, Midland, G&SWR, NER, NBR, M&C], could one see every day the engines and trains of quite so many of the old companies.

'When I was an undergraduate [in the early 1920s] it was still a Great Eastern station. But the Great Northern regularly used it for its trains from King's Cross via Hitchin; the London & North Western had perhaps six trains a day to and from Bletchley [and Oxford]; and the Midland drove a single line to it from Kettering by way of Huntingdon. Thus there were engines and the rolling stock of these four railways to be seen, so that Cambridge Station was very prodigal in its [colour and] variety.

'What is more, there was one hour in the twenty-four when you had the comings and goings of all four railways within slightly less than sixty-minutes, and this hour was the very convenient one of 3.30 to 4.30 in the afternoon.

'At 3.30pm the consciousness of the station was plainly directed towards the arrival of the [Up] train to London from Norwich and Ely; and a whole series of traffic movements began which the fact that this important train was shortly due had set in motion.

'First of all a new engine backed out of the [Loco Shed] at the north end and moved slowly down to the tiny bay at the south end, where relieving engines always waited for their trains. Nearly all the trains to and from London changed engines at Cambridge; and they still do.

'... no sooner was the relieving engine safely stowed out of the way in its bay than a train of four of the old clerestory 6-wheeled coaches of the Great Eastern ... from Mildenhall [came into Platform 1] and poured out its passengers and parcels in a tearing hurry. It was standing where the express must come to rest and it had not long to get clear. Most of its passengers and parcels were for London, but some passengers always walked ... [across to Platform 2] ... where the 4-o'clock for Bletchley was waiting. Its coaches were still chocolate and white (they gradually changed to red while I was at Cambridge) and it might be pulled by a 2-4-2 tank engine or else by a 'Precursor'. It was always a well-filled train. Schoolboys going home to villages with exciting names like Old North Road and Lord's Bridge used it, and there were always plenty of people making for Bedford or Birmingham.

'The really long-distance travellers to Lancashire or Scotland went by the 6.20pm Bletchley where they caught a train which got them to Crewe at about 11-o'clock at night. One of the 'Precursors' which haunted Cambridge in those days was *Sirocco*, which is now the sole survivor of its class; and if *Sirocco* was on the train that day one went up and inspected her all over and greeted her like an old friend.

'But even as one was doing that there was an indefinable stir on [Platform 1] which always heralds the approach of an express, and is set in motion by the wiseacre who keeps his eye on the appropriate signal and murmurs to a friend, 'She's signalled.' And who is always over-heard, and suitcases are picked up, and everybody takes one step forward or two to the side as though that mystic and instinctive drill somehow helped to get a better seat in a train not yet in sight. We all do it, however irrational.

'That meant it was time to get back to the very centre of the [long] platform, opposite the Booking Hall. That was the exciting place and the peculiar arrangement of Cambridge Station made it so. I have said that Cambridge has ... only one platform to serve the needs of both Up and Down traffic. It is long enough for two full-length trains, one [Up] for London and the other [Down] for Norwich, to stand tail-to-tail at the same moment at the same platform. But an Up and a Down train often arrive within a few minutes of each other and when they do it is obviously impossible for either to travel the length of the platform by the platform line. So at the centre of the station there is a [scissors] crossover [and a through line parallel to the platform line].

'Now this particular [Up train to

London] was followed soon after by a [Down] train from London and therefore it always used the cross-over. So one took care to stand at a point just a yard to the south of the actual centre of the crossing.

'You heard the [Up] train before you saw it; the driver generally whistled as he crossed the River Cam a mile away. Then [up] she came, headed by her blue Holden engine, going fast – far too fast, as it always seemed, to get over that crossing safely.

'It must have been a point of honour with those Cambridge drivers to take it as fast as they dared. I have seen them do it scores of times, and never without a second's holding of my breath. Always the thought came, 'He'll never get over it at this speed,' but he always did. The train came fast down the track. She arrived at the points, and did a quick jerking lurch as the bogey took them. Then all those heavy wheels thudded and crashed over the diamond centre, and the coach wheels followed suit, their normal time rhythm broken into [a] syncopation; and it always seemed to me, and still does, the most satisfactory of [railway] noises,

'There the Up train was, at rest [on platform 1] at last, but one could never see the engine that had brought it for it came off at Cambridge and the Cambridge firemen never wasted a second in uncoupling their engines, running them back to the [Loco Shed along the through line] and getting away to their tea. They never left time [for us watchers] to walk the length of the train.

'It was now about 4.14pm and so far as I can remember the Down train from London was due at 4.25; but before it came [into Platform 4] something much more interesting was due – the Midland branch-line train from Kettering [via St

Ives]. But exactly where it would arrive was always rather a gamble. If the Up train to London got smartly away there was just time to nip the little Midland train in over the central crossing onto Platform 1 … before the Down train from London arrived and claimed that same crossing. But there was also an empty bay at that time of day at the north end, and often they brought the Midland in there [to Platform 5 or 6]. But it was pleasantest when it followed the express over the crossing into the platform 1, for as it took the points it repeated all the thuds and bangs of the express, but pianissimo, as it were a faint echo.

'It was not possible to watch both the [Midland] 4.20 from Kettering and the [Great Eastern] 4.25 to Norwich, but my own choice was for the Midland train every time. The 4.25 was simply a duplication of the express which had just left for Liverpool Street. But the 4.20 from Kettering was an exceedingly individual little train. Normally it had just two coaches – very elderly Midland but of that company's best vintage. The train had meandered its slow way through a succession of villages with intriguing names like Raunds, and had arrived at Cambridge by way of Huntingdon and St Ives.

'It was nearly always drawn by what was even then nearly, if not quite, the oldest class of engines in regular service in Britain, the Kirtley 2-4-0. They had two of them at Kettering and they treated them as working museum pieces should be treated; they kept them clean and they polished their brass parts till they shone. But the gaze of the beholder was at once riveted not on the brass but on the phenomenal height of the chimney. The cab, too, seemed minute; and such of its roof as there was, which was not much, seemed designed to protect the front parts of a dwarf. But the man who often drove it was no dwarf: far from it, he was something of a giant, and he seemed to have great difficulty in tucking his head under that cab roof. I remember him still, an elderly man with long and streaming white moustaches, looking like a taciturn but venturesome pirate of the railway age. He and the old Kirtley engine were working out their declining years together but the engine lasted longer than he did.

'By this time, the London and Norwich trains have both gone, the Midland has backed out into the yard, and *Sirocco* has departed to Bedford and Bletchley. On the main platform a local [stopping train] to Liverpool Street is standing with a 'Claud Hamilton' at its head. But there is still one more sight to behold before we call it a day and go off to tea.

'I said at the beginning that Cambridge was the only place where you could see the engines of no less than four of the old companies and so far we have only seen three. But a signal at the south end is down and the points are set for the bay near the flour mill, and there she comes, the 4.40 [Down] from King's Cross and Hitchin, with its authentically Great Northern teak coaches, and headed by one of the Ivatt 4-4-2 Atlantics. In their heyday – 1902 to 1910 – [they were] the most famous express engines in the country, but already superseded and relegated to local running from places like Hitchin. But I have a very deep personal affection for those engines for it was on one of them that I rode on the footplate for the first time. There was a certain Hitchin driver who seemed to tolerate importunate undergraduates and if I happened to be about when he brought a train in he would invite me into the cab and let me stay there while he took the engine out into the yard to do a little shunting and to be turned at the turntable. If he happened to be on the 4.40 when I was there I always missed my tea, but it was worth it.

'Such was the rich menu of one hour's station sauntering at Cambridge. It was fun all the year round but best of all in early December on a fine day. The light gradually faded and dusk had come when the platform ticket was handed to the collector at the barrier. And there waiting was the Ortona bus – a green [open top] double-decker with solid tyres and no roof, to take me back through the lit streets of Cambridge to [St John's] college to a firelit room high up under the rafters and muffins by the fire for tea ...'

Canon Lloyd was not forgotten by subsequent writers, including Gilbert Thomas, father of David St John Thomas whose memory lives on in the publisher he started: David & Charles of Newton Abbot, now owned by F&W Media International Ltd.

Gilbert Thomas, in *Window in the West* (Epworth, 1954) offers some very relevant concluding comments for this book and my own fascination for railways and steam locomotives:

'For Canon Lloyd as for countless others the spell of railways is easier to feel than to define. It is, I suppose, the many-sidedness of railways that breeds so many devotees. People love them for different reasons [but] one common link is the affection for the steam locomotive ... The steam locomotive is the one really civilised machine devised by man. It is safe and dependable in all weathers; it is powerful enough to be slightly awe-inspiring yet tame and gentle enough to be friendly; it

Fig. 112

CAMBRIDGE

1958
"What Was Cambridge"
A B1 61300 on a stopping train to London

has living and visible breath; ... it is companionable.

Still, the love of railways will survive the eventual passing of steam, and it extends to the modern young ... like us elders for whom in childhood the railway held a monopoly [amongst other forms of transport] and was therefore associated with our early exploration of the world.

It was the railway that took us from home and opened new horizons ...

Gilbert Thomas was writing more than sixty years ago and I am not sure that twenty-first century 'modern young' think of the railway as opening new horizons

for them. But I hope I have shown that Cambridge Station is still a living entity which has grown, expanded, and created new travel opportunities.

It certainly opened my young eyes to a wider world and it has offered me job opportunities and experiences which I still treasure and am pleased to share in this book.

And one final memory. When I met George Potter he showed me a drawing made by his son, Derrick, of the London end of Cambridge Station in 1958. The title is Derrick's and it illustrates some of the motive power and railway operation changes in this book. Thank you Derrick, and George...

LIST OF ILLUSTRATIONS

From my time working for BR in the 1950s and 1960s, then my time at the National Railway Museum (1987 – 1994) and as an active member of the Railway Study Association (1988 –) I have been a keen photographer and collector of railway photographs. I have tried to contact all possible copyright holders and have checked any unacknowledged images with forensic image search engines. If any have been missed would those concerned please contact me.

Fig.xx	Summary of title / caption and © acknowledgement
Front cover	View northward beside Cattle Market railings towards the south (Down) end of Cambridge Station with overhead electrification wiring in place, 1988. © Anthony Kirby.
Fig.1	The splendid architectural facade of Cambridge Station (1846) . . . . with letters LNER above the centre. © Kidderminster Railway Trust. 162647. undated.
Fig.2	Cambridge Motor Omnibus Company open-topped double deck bus on 'STATION MARKET HILL service, c1890s. © Midland Railway Study Centre
Fig.3	Map of UK Regions – East Anglia. Author's collection. Re-drawn from map of UK Regions with additions for this book.
Fig.4	Map showing River Cam plus tributaries and River Ouse illustrating Cambridge as a geographically favoured route centre. Author's collection. Re-drawn and edited for this book from: Steers. J.A. (Editor). The Cambridge Region 1965. British Association for the Advancement of Science 1965.
Fig.5	The growth of Cambridge built-up areas. Author's collection. Redrawn with additions for this book from: Jones. David. *Hideous Cambridge – a city mutilated*. Thirteen Eighty One LLP.2013.

Fig.xx	Summary of title / caption and © acknowledgement
Fig.6	Table showing passenger numbers and ticket income generated on ECR in six months ending 4 January 1851. Author's collection.
Fig.7	Table showing ECR train services timetable between London and Cambridge in 1859. Author's collection.
Fig.8	Plan for two semi-detached villas in Station Road on land sold by Jesus College, Cambridge to GNR. Jesus College Archives. Reproduced by kind permission of the Master and Fellows of Jesus College, Cambridge.
Fig.9	Plan accompanying Agreement between ECR and Jesus College, Cambridge indicating land owned by the College and sold, with the authority of the Master, to ECR. Jesus College Archives. Reproduced by kind permission of the Master and Fellows of Jesus College, Cambridge.
Fig.10	Cambridge Station. Illustration from Illustrated London News 2 August 1845 page 73 – THE EASTERN COUNTIES RAILWAY – OPENING OF THE LINE TO CAMBRIDGE AND ELY
Fig.11	Map showing sites proposed for railway stations at Cambridge 1834 – 1864. © The Oleander Press Cambridge 1976
Fig.12	B& W photograph of 'railway houses' beside parapet of Mill Road bridge. From: Wilson. Caro. *124-134 Mill Road Cambridge. Mill Road History Project. Building Report. Mill Road Bridges. 2013*
Fig.13	Colour picture of Victorian villas in Station Road, Cambridge. © Anthony Kirby.
Fig.14	Sketch Plan of Great Eastern Railway from LNER Encyclopaedia online. Edited with additions for this book. Author's collection.
Fig.15	GER 'Claud Hamilton' D15 Class 4-4-0 1858 (re-numbered 8858 by LNER then 2549 in 1946 heading a London passenger train on Platform 1, Cambridge Station circa 1920. © Kidderminster Railway Trust.
Fig.16	GER Heraldic device. Author's collection
Fig.17	GER Old Comrades Association badge. Author's collection
Fig.18	Sketch plan illustrating the ambitious and largely unrealised proposals of the Newmarket & Chesterford Railway Company. Re-drawn and edited for this book from: Barnard. E.A.B (Editor). *Proceedings of the Cambridge Antiquarian Society October 1928 – October 1930.* Bowes & Bowes 1931. *A derelict railway being the history of the Newmarket & Chesterford Railway* by Kenneth Brown. Paper read 14 November 1927.

Fig.xx	Summary of title / caption and © acknowledgement
Fig.19	ECR Timetable 1853 – Newmarket Railway. Author's collection
Fig.20	B&W photograph of north (DOWN) end of Cambridge Station showing Newmarket Branch c1890. Author's collection
Fig.21	Plan illustrating track layout for Cambridge Station junction to Newmarket Railway for BoT Accident Enquiry 1884 [based on OS 1888 Town Plan at 1:500] Plan drawn by Ian Strugnell for GER Society 1993; re-lettered and slightly amended for this book.
Fig.22	Cambridge as the centre of a web of railway lines. Edited, re-labelled and prepared for this book. Author's collection
Fig.23	B&W photograph of Mildenhall branch train at Barnwell Junction c1950. © John Coiley; courtesy to author by Mrs P. Coiley 2016.
Fig.24	B&W photograph of LNER Class B12 hauling an up passenger train passing Norman Cement Works near Cherry Hinton, 1950s. © Anthony Kirby.
Fig.25	Map showing the number of licensed stage coach coaches running between principal centres in East Anglia in 1834. © Gordon D.I. *The Railways in the Eastern Counties. A Regional History of the Railways of Great Britain Volume V*. David & Charles. 1968
Fig.26	Colour photograph of the remains of a painted sign advertising Marsh & Swan horse-drawn traffic services. Author's collection.
Fig.27	Map from: *Of Great Public Advantage – Aspects of Cambridge and its railways 1845 – 2005*. Geoffrey Skelsey LVO. *BackTrack* July & August 2005. © Pendragon Publishing
Fig.28	Diagrammatic plan: MR running rights over GER tracks, Cambridge. © Midland Railway Study Centre
Fig.29	Diagrammatic plan of Cambridge Station: track layout for platforms and Newmarket branch. Author's collection
Fig.30	Diagram of Passenger Running Lines, Cambridge Station 1908. Cecil Allen. © Railway Magazine 1908
Fig.31	Engraving c1845, of original Hills Road bridge looking north and UP end of 1845 Station building. Cambridge collection.
Fig.32	Colour photograph of site of carriage lamp room at Cambridge Station. Author's collection.

Fig.xx	Summary of title / caption and © acknowledgement
Fig.33	B&W photograph of GN gates leading directly from Cambridge Station forecourt to Platform 3. © Kidderminster Railway Trust. 162650. undated.
Fig.34	Copy of first page of hand-written letter from ECR Cambridge Line Office, Shoreditch to Master of Jesus College, Cambridge. 13 January 1847. Jesus College Archives. Reproduced by kind permission of the Master and Fellows of Jesus College, Cambridge.
Fig.35	Plan from ECR Engineer's Office of site of Cambridge Station including some track and buildings and indications of additional land to be purchased from Jesus College Cambridge. Handwritten dating, February 1861 then March 1862. Jesus College Archives. Reproduced by kind permission of the Master and Fellows of Jesus College, Cambridge.
Fig.36	Edited and Adobe Photo shopped crop from Fig.35 showing Station buildings and trackwork. Jesus College Archives. Author's collection
Fig.37	Edited and Adobe Photo shopped crop from Fig.36 showing detail of Station buildings, and 1861/1862 labelling. Jesus College Archives. Author's collection.
Fig.38	B&W photograph – c1912 – of a surviving Ticket Platform at the GNR Spalding Station. Courtesy GNR Society Collection
Fig.39	'Plan marked B' otherwise untitled and undated. Shows Cambridge Station site, some track and a number of labelled buildings. Crop Adobe Photoshopped from larger plan of Cambridge Station site dated 1860 in Jesus College Archives. Author's collection
Fig.40	Edited and Adobe Photo shopped crop from GER Plan of Cambridge Station site, 1873. Jesus College Archives. Reproduced by kind permission of the Master and Fellows of Jesus College, Cambridge.
Fig.41	B&W photograph of LNER Booking Hall at Cambridge Station, 1920s. From: *Up to Cambridge*. Paul Anderson. *British Railways Illustrated*. Vol 21 No 9 - 12 June to September 2012. Courtesy Chris Hawkins, Editor BRI.
Fig.42	Land purchase negotiations and record plan between Jesus College, Cambridge and GER / GNR; undated, so probably 1870s. Edited and Adobe Photo shopped crop from larger plan. Jesus College Archives. Author's collection.

Fig.xx	Summary of title / caption and © acknowledgement
Fig.43	Jesus College Station Building Estate Plan, Cambridge 1925. LNER Station, track layout and goods yards. Jesus College Archives. Reproduced by kind permission of the Master and Fellows of Jesus College, Cambridge.
Fig.44	
Fig.45	B&W pictures of nineteenth century hand signal men – often called 'Policemen.' Author's collection
Fig.46	
Fig.47	Plan showing GER / GNR track work and Cambridge Mechanical Signal Boxes. Enlarged, edited, and enhanced from one part of GER Diagrammatic Map of System 1919. © GERS 1986 and Author's collection.
Fig.48	B&W photograph from the steps of Hills Road Signal Box looking north to the UP end of Cambridge Station c1923. © Kidderminster Railway Trust. 173687. undated.
Fig.49	Colour picture of lower and upper quadrant stop (home) and distant signals. Author's collection.
Fig.50	Cambridge Station signalling plan 1926, shortened, edited and re-drawn for this book. From *The Engineer* 10 December 1926.
Fig.51	Colour picture of LNER colour light signals. Author's collection.
Fig.52	B&W photograph showing Cambridge Station Central Signal Box and some of the semaphore signals it controlled for the scissors crossover. © Kidderminster Railway Trust. 045306 c1905.
Fig.53	Cambridge Station colonnade in the mid-1920s. © Kidderminster Railway Trust. 162648. undated.
Fig.54	E4 2-4-0 2790 (built Stratford Works September 1900) on 10.28 to Mildenhall off Cambridge Station Platform 6. Ken Nunn Collection 0145 30.03.48. Courtesy of John Scott-Morgan
Fig.55	Southern end of Cambridge Station 1927. Ordnance Survey 1:2,500. © OS and PROMAP
Fig.56	Northern end of Cambridge Station 1927. Ordnance Survey 1:2,500. © OS and PROMAP

Fig.xx	Summary of title / caption and © acknowledgement
Fig.57	Contrived example of a typically pretentious Invoice from eight-and-a-half mile long three-foot gauge Southwold Railway. Author's collection
Fig.58	Colour photograph of LNER Warning to Trespassers notice; Author's collection
Fig.59	B&W photograph of Devonshire Road sidings serving a typical mid-C20th Coal Yard. From: *Up to Cambridge*. Paul Anderson. *British Railways Illustrated*. Vol 21 No 9 - 12 June to September 2012. Courtesy Chris Hawkins, Editor BRI.
Fig.60	B&W photograph of Hills Road sidings showing a fixed crane on the left; the jib of a mobile crane on the right; a Class 04 0-6-0 diesel shunter in the background; and 2 containers. Probably mid-60s. From: *Up to Cambridge*. Paul Anderson. *British Railways Illustrated*. Vol 21 No 9 - 12 June to September 2012. Courtesy Chris Hawkins, Editor BRI.
Fig.61	B&W photograph showing BOXER horse shunting at Cambridge in January 1957. The GNR goods shed is on the left and the GER goods shed on the right. The horse driver is Sidney Arthur Plumb and the picture is recording BOXER's retirement from railway work. © National Railway Museum/Science & Society Picture Library
Fig.62	B&W photograph showing a view south from the hump at Whitemoor including the retarders and the Control Tower at the North End of the Yard. Coal wagons, which constituted much of the railway traffic into East Anglia, are being divided into the various sidings for onward transit. Author's collection
Fig.63	B&W photograph of L&NWR/LMS Goods Station on the Hills Road / Brooklands Avenue corner and labelled London Midland & Scottish Railway. c1935. © National Railway Museum/Science & Society Picture Library
Fig.64	B&W photograph of Hills Road facade of the L&NWR / LMS Good Station (copied from **Fig.63**) showing E. Pordage & Company Ltd.'s warehouse. c1935. © National Railway Museum/Science & Society Picture Library
Fig.65	B&W photograph of north-facing open front of Cambridge Loco Shed. c1950s. From: *Up to Cambridge*. Paul Anderson. *British Railways Illustrated*. Vol 21 No 9 - 12 June to September 2012. Courtesy Chris Hawkins, Editor BRI.

Fig.xx	Summary of title / caption and © acknowledgement
Fig.66	B&W photograph showing ash pits beside Cambridge Loco Shed. c1950s. From: *Up to Cambridge*. Paul Anderson. *British Railways Illustrated*. Vol 21 No 9 - 12 June to September 2012. Courtesy Chris Hawkins, Editor BRI.
Fig.67	B&W photograph showing coaling tower working at King's Cross. Author's collection.
Fig.68	Colour picture of a sectioned 4-4-0 steam locomotive and tender illustrating the basic working principles of a steam locomotive and the work of disposal which is explained in the text. Author's collection.
Fig.69	B&W photograph showing ash pits, coaling tower and extensive sidings beside the Cambridge Loco Shed. From: *Up to Cambridge*. Paul Anderson. *British Railways Illustrated*. Vol 21 No 9 - 12 June to September 2012. Courtesy Chris Hawkins, Editor BRI.
Fig.70	B&W photograph showing an extract from the 1938 edition of <u>Railway Clearing House Official Handbook of Stations including junctions, sidings, collieries, works &c</u>. Page 109; Cambridge sidings. Author's collection.
Fig.71	OS map extract showing Corporation (Cambridge City) Siding near Mill Road bridge. OS 1926-1927 1:2,500. © OS and PROMAP
Fig.72	B&W photograph showing partially dismantled 0-6-0ST built by Kitson (Leeds, 1932) and used at Fisons Fertiliser Works in Burwell, off the Mildenhall branch: Chalked on boiler is :TO / R DUCE HOOPER ST SIDING CAMBRIDGE. © Kidderminster Railway Trust. 28 March 1959.
Fig.73	OS map extract showing Cambridge Gas Works and the Gas Works siding near Coldham Lane Bridge. OS 1926-1927 1:2,500. © OS and PROMAP
Fig.74	B&W aerial view photograph of Cambridge Gas Works with annotations showing Gas Company's sidings and the site of Richard Duce scrap works adjoining Coldham Lane bridge. Author's collection
Fig.75	B&W photograph of Sentinel steam loco: 0-6-0, chain-driven, vertical 2-cylinder double-acting 80HP steam engine; nicknamed 'Gasbag.' © Tim Edmonds 04 September 1967
Fig.76	Table showing the principal categories of entries for the 1894 and 1922 Cambridge Royal Shows. Author's collection.

Fig.xx	Summary of title / caption and © acknowledgement
Fig.77	Plan of temporary Station for Royal Agricultural Show Traffic, erected by the GER, 1922. Edited and enhanced from Plan published in *The Railway Gazette*, 14 July 1922. Author's collection.
Fig.78	Coloured plan showing the 'Showground' in an edited and enhanced C21st planning proposals map, c1980s. Author's collection.
Fig.79	B&W photograph of south end of Cambridge Station looking north from Hills Road bridge. © John Coiley; courtesy to author by Mrs P. Coiley 2016.
Fig.80	Table 4G: Bletchley Line Passenger Trains (BLY & CAM) – DOWN and UP. © CURC Report.
Fig.81	Table 4Jiii: UP starting freights from CAM © CURC Report
Fig.82	B&W photograph of Mildenhall branch line train off Platform 4. © Kidderminster Railway Trust. 8 December 1954.
Fig.83	B&W photograph of Down mixed freight approaching Mill road bridge. © Kidderminster Railway Trust. 28 March 1959.
Fig.84	B&W photograph of head end of bay Platforms 5 and 6 and showing Down End Inspectors' Office, Down End Porters;' Room and doorway to Gentlemen's urinals and WC. Cropped and edited from: *Up to Cambridge*. Paul Anderson. *British Railways Illustrated*. Vol 21 No 9 June 2012. Courtesy Chris Hawkins, Editor BRI.
Fig.85	B&W photograph of Cambridge North Signal Box. © Kidderminster Railway Trust. 31 August 1965.
Fig.86	B&W photograph of 0-6-0 45843 at north entrance to Cambridge Loco Shed. © Kidderminster Railway Trust. 8 December 1954.
Fig.87	B&W photograph of interior of Cambridge South Signal Box. © Kidderminster Railway Trust. July 1975.
Fig.88	**Fig.88i** Colour picture of front cover of BR Eastern Region Eastern Section Notices. Saturday 9 December to Friday 15 December 1967. Author's collection. **Fig.88ii** Colour picture of page 8 from Fig.88i Notices. Author's collection.
Fig.90	B&W photograph of Cambridge steam Breakdown Crane – 45ton, Cowans Sheldon; 1960s. Author's collection

Fig.xx	Summary of title / caption and © acknowledgement
Fig.91	B&W photograph of Mill Road Junction Signal Box; 1960s. Author's collection.
Fig.92	Map showing Railways to Cambridge after the closures recommended in the Beeching Report. Author's collection.
Fig.93	B&W photograph of information about the closure of the Wisbech & Upwell Tramway. Author's collection.
Fig.94	Colour picture of diagram illustrating AbellioGreaterAnglia routes. May 2016. © AbellioGreaterAnglia. Courtesy of Geraint Hughes
Fig.95	Colour sketch plan of the 'Station Area' being appraised by Cambridge City Council in 2004. © Cambridge City Council. Courtesy Brookgate and Geraint Hughes AGA
Fig.96	Colour picture of south end of Cambridge Station including Cambridge North Signal Box and Foster's [Spillers] Roller Flour Mill. Author's collection
Fig.97	Colour picture of temporary road signs and extensive cycle parking in the Station Forecourt, 2014. © AGA courtesy Geraint Hughes
Fig.98	Colour picture of NR's island platform in use. © AGA courtesy Geraint Hughes
Fig.99	Colour visualisation of completed CB1 redevelopment of the 'Station Area.' © Brookgate.
Fig.100	Colour diagram of train service frequencies from Cambridge to London King's Cross and London Stansted. © Brookgate
Fig.100	Colour picture of One the Square fronting the new Station Square in CB1. © Brookgate.
Fig.101	Colour diagram of mixed use development for RSHP Master plan in CB1. © Brookgate
Fig.102	Colour diagram of developments at Cambridge Station. © National Rail Enquires Website via Google search.
Fig.103	Colour picture showing the scissors crossover serving Platforms 1 and 4 – from footbridge to Platforms 7 and 8 on the new island platform. Author's collection

Fig.xx	Summary of title / caption and © acknowledgement
Fig.104	Colour diagrammatic map of current Cambridge Rail Network. Courtesy Paul Hollinghurst (Railfuture) Cambridge
Fig.105	Colour diagrammatic map of proposed future rail network around Cambridge Station – Rail for the Greater Cambridge Deal. Courtesy Paul Hollinghurst (Railfuture) Cambridge
Fig.106 Fig.107	Tables showing Cambridge Down and Up trains, 09.00 to 11.00 from the current (2016) AbellioGreaterAnglia Working Timetable. Courtesy Geraint Hughes AGA
Fig.108	Colour picture of Histon Station, already closed to passenger traffic, January 1976; track lifted 2007. © Tim Edmonds
Fig.109 Fig.110	Colour pictures of buses on the Cambridge Guided Busway Route C passing Histon Station, 23 July 2016. © Tim Edmonds
Fig.111	Colour photograph of 3-rail 0 gauge model of ex GER D16 4-4-0 2618 carrying her 1946 LNER number. Courtesy Rev Alan Cliff.
Fig.112	Photograph of drawing 'What Was Cambridge' showing B1 61300 at Platform 2 with 'a stopping train to London in 1958. Courtesy George Potter; picture drawn by his son Derrick.
Fig. 113	LMS Class 4F 2-6-0 M3004 leaving Cambridge Platform 3, probably with a Bletchley and Oxford train. Ken Nunn Collection 7425 30.03.48. Courtesy of John Scott-Morgan
Fig.114	A Royal Train (the 4 lamps on the front indicate that the Monarch is aboard) leaving Cambridge for London in 1954. Locomotive is ex-LNER B17/4 Sandringham class 4-6-0 No 61671 'Royal Sovereign.' © Kidderminster Railway Museum Trust. Photo: 142665
(Fig 115) rear cover	Edited colour scan of the Cambridge area from Railway Clearing House Official Map of the East of England. 1922. Courtesy of Michael Perrins

NOTES

Chapter 5: GER and the Newmarket Railway Company's Cambridge branch

01 This account is edited from:

    01 Barnard. E.A.B (Editor). *Proceedings of the Cambridge Antiquarian Society October 1928 – October 1930*. Bowes & Bowes 1931. *A derelict railway being the history of the Newmarket & Chesterford Railway* by Kenneth Brown. Paper read 14 November 1927.

    02 Voisey, Francis (January 1994) *Accidents On The Great Eastern 28. Great Eastern Journal 77 Vol 8.7* © Great Eastern Railway Society. I have drawn extensively and express my thanks.

    03 Rose, Colin (October 1998). *The Newmarket & Chesterford Railway. Great Eastern Journal. No. 96. Vol.10.6* © Great Eastern Railway Society.

Chapter 8: 'Four Railway Companies in a tangle of mutual inconvenience'

01 I have acknowledged *BackTrack* © for this map in the details of **Fig.27** but can acknowledge here the support from Michael Blakemore, Editor of *BackTrack* and owner of Pendragon Publishing, and from Geoffrey Skelsey. Geoffrey has told me that 'we were in fact at Cambridge Station at the same time, as I worked there semi-officially (possible in those days!) in the summer of 1963 when I was an undergraduate.' I recommend to the interested reader of this book Geoffrey's article in *BackTrack* Vol. 19 (2005) Nos 7 and 8, July pp 100-406 and August pp 501 – 506.

02 Cecil J Allen (1886 – 1973) qualigfied as a Civil Engineer and joined the Engineer's Department of GER in 1903. Fig.30 is Allen's sketch plan for his 1908 *Railway Magazine* article: *Notable Railway Stations No 42 – CAMBRIDGE (GREAT EASTERN RAILWAY)*

Fig.113: LMS Class 4F 2-6-0 M3004 leaving Cambridge platform 3, probably with a Bletchley and Oxford train, 30th March 1948.

Fig.114: A Royal Train (the 4 lamps on the front indicate that the Monarch is aboard) leaving Cambridge for London in 1954. Locomotive is ex-LNER B17/4 Sandringham class 4-6-0 No 61671 'Royal Sovereign.'

SELECT BIBLIOGRAPHY

ADDERSON, Richard and KENWORTHY, Graham, *Eastern Main Lines – Cambridge to Ely including St Ives to Ely* Middleton Press, 2005.

ALLEN, Cecil J and JOHNSON, H C, *Great Eastern Railway* Ian Allan, 1961

BODY, Geoffrey, *Railways of the Eastern Region:1 Southern Operating Area, 2 Northern Operating Area* Patrick Stephens, 1989

BONAVIA, Michael, *The Cambridge Line* Ian Allan, 1995

BRODRIBB, John, *LNER Country Stations* Ian Allan, 1988

ESSERY, Bob, *Railway Signalling and Track Plans* Ian Allan, 2007

FELLOWS, Reginald B, *London to Cambridge by Train 1845 – 1938* Fellows & Walter Lewis, Cambridge, 1939

FELLOWS, Reginald B, *Railways to Cambridge: Actual and Proposed* Oleander Press,1976

GREAT EASTERN RAILWAY SOCIETY JOURNAL SPECIAL No 5, *Eastern Counties Railway 150th Anniversary* GERS, 1989

GORDON, D I, *A Regional History of the Railways of Great Britain – Volume V: The Eastern Counties* David & Charles, 1968

HAWKINS, Chris and REEVE,George, *Great Eastern Railway Engine Sheds – Part II – Ipswich & Cambridge Districts* Wild Swan Publications,1987

KITCHENSIDE, Geoffrey and WILLIAMS, Alan, *Two Centuries of Railway Signalling* (Second Edition) Ian Allan, 2008

LLOYD, Roger, *Fascination of Railways* George Allen & Unwin,1951

MOFFATT, Hugh, *East Anglia's First Railway: Peter Bruff and Eastern Union Railway* Terence Dalton, 1987

OCCOMORE, David, *Along the Line. Railway connections between Newmarket, Ely and Bury St. Edmunds* Occomore, 2010

PARR, Harry and GRAY, Adrian, *Life and Times of the Great Eastern Railway* Castlemead Publications, 1991

PORTER, Enid, *Victorian Cambridge – Joseph Chater's Diaries* Phillimore 1975

RUSSELL, Cohn and JESSE, Ronald *Cambridge Railway Station* Book-on-demand, Miami, 2015

SIMPSON, Bill, *Oxford to Cambridge Railway – Vol II: Bletchley to Cambridge* Oxford Publishing Company, 1983

WARREN, Alan and PHILLIPS, Ralph *Cambridge Station – A Tribute British Rail* Eastern Region, 1987

INDEX

The list of CONTENTS on pages 5 and 6 is a useful guide to the whole book. Because the specific subject of the book is Cambridge Station that is not one of the Index subjects except for one 'Cambridge Station' entry which leads to the proposed sites for the Station.

Similarly, because Chapter 14 is specifically about the Royal Shows in Cambridge 'Royal Show,' is not an Index subject.

A suggestion for enjoying the Index as well as using it for reference is to glance through the entries and follow up one or two which seem to be unusual or whimsical:

3.000 cycle park; 369 rabbits; 'Busby Babes;' Clayhithe sluice; Drummer Street; Elephants; Horatio Love; *Jack the Station Cat*; Library censorship; Ortona; Royal Fish; 'She's signalled;' Charles Villiers Stanford; Ticket Platforms; Timbuctoo.

Explore, and enjoy!

AbellioGreaterAnglia (AGA) –
  Working Timetable   7 140
  142 143 155 **Fig.94 Fig.106**
Addenbrooke's Hospital   139
  148 152 **Fig.5**

Backs. The (of some Cambridge
  Colleges)   28 **Fig.5**
Barnwell / Barnwell Junction   17
  48 52 171 **Fig.23**
Bateman Street (Cambridge)   15
Bedford *(see also Oxford)*   48 52 112
  116 120 134 152 163 165 167
Billingsgate Market (London)   22
Bishop's Stortford   16 18 52
  87 90 116 138 139 142
Bishopsgate Station (see also Eastern
  Counties Railway Company)   16 20
Booking Hall (Cambridge Station)   55
  66 67 165 172 **Fig.41**

Botanic Garden (Cambridge)   16
  Fig.5 Fig.11
Brandon (Norfolk)   18 27
  39 **Fig.14 Fig.18 Fig.25**
British Railways / BR / Privatisation of BR
  – Chapters 17 and 18   90 16 132 - *et seq*
British Transport Police
  (BTP)   130 131 139
Brookgate (see Chapter 13)   8 143 - *et seq*
Bury St Edmunds   20 27 39 41
  47 78 83 116 121 138 139 163
  Figs.14 18 22 25 27 104 105
'Busby Babes'   161

Cambridge City Council   103 143 – *et seq*
Cambridge Gas Works   89
  104 **Fig.73 Fig.74**
Cambridge Station – proposed
  sites   24 – *et seq* **Fig.5 Fig.11**

Cambridge University Railway Club
(CURC) – Chapter 15   115 – *et seq*
Cambridgeshire   19 22 35 37 114 148 163
Cattle Market (Cambridge)   65 83 96
    116 169 (**Front cover**) **Fig.43 Fig.114**
CB1 (Development of Station
    area) / Station Square –
    Chapter 19   143 – *et seq*
Cecil J Allen   52 179 **Fig.30**
Cecil Fane (Chairman, Newmarket
    Railway Company)   39
Chappel & Wakes Colne Station   49
Charles H Parkes (Chairman GER)   32
Chelmsford   13 41 83 142
Cherry Hinton / Cherry Hinton
    Road   17 41 49 52 55 153 163 **Fig.24**
Clayhithe Sluice   18
Coal (Cambridge Station) – Chapter
    11   12 14 18 21 22 32 68 88 89 92
    93 94 96-101 103 104 120 121 127-
    129 **Fig.56 Fig.59 Fig.62 Fig.67**
Coal fields   10
Coke Stage (Cambridge Station)   68 **Fig.42**
Colchester   13 19 27 41 49 83
    110 116 **Fig.14 Fig.18**
Colchester, Stour Valley, Sudbury
    & Halstead Railway   49
Coldham's Brook   17
Coldham Common   46 49 55 **Fig.5**
Coldham Junction   42 89 154 **Fig.27**
Colne Valley & Halstead Railway   49
Cycle Park   148 **Fig.98**

Doncaster   31 32 93
Dr Richard Beeching / – BR
    Modernisation Plan
The Beeching Report – Chapter
    17   132 - *et seq*
Drummer Street (Cambridge
    Bus Station)   17 158

East Anglian Railway   19 27 **Fig.18**
East Road (Cambridge)   17 **Fig.5**
Eastern Counties Railway Company
    [ECR] – Chapter 2   2 10 18 – *et seq* 24
    26 27 30 31 32 35 36 37 39 40 41 48 51
    52 58 59 60 61 62 63 65 66 68 79 89 95

Eastern Union [Railway]   19 30
ECR Board   20 24 31 63
Elephants – Chipperfield's Circus
    at Cambridge   11 80 130-131
Ely   14 19 21 27 39 47 48 50 51 52
    78 83 116 121 138 140 163 165
    Figs 4 14 38 21 22 27 104 105
Engine [Loco] Shed[s] – Chapter 12
    (see also Motive Power Depots)   53
    80 95 – *et seq* **Figs 28 30 36 37 39
    42 43 47 55 56 65 66 69 86**
Essex   13 14 22 34 35 50 120
Exning Halt   49

Fen Ditton Halt   49
Fordham Junction   48
Fulbourn / Fulbourn Station   17
    41 44 52 153 **Fig.105**

Gainsborough   31
George Docking – District
    Operating Officer   11 123
George Hudson (Chairman ECR)   32 39
Gerard Fiennes   11
Girton   17 159
Goods [Freight] / Goods Shed[s] /
    Goods Traffic – Chapter 11   19
    52 80 - *et seq* **Figs 27 36 39 42 43
    46 48 55 60 61 62 63 64 82 83 92**
Goods Porter (Cambridge Station)
    – Chapter 16   123 - *et seq*
Granchester Meadows   **Fig.5**
Great Eastern Railway [GER] – Chapters
    4 5 6 and 8   20 22 30 – *et seq* 66 80
    87 94 96 97 **Fig.14 Fig.27 Fig.42**
GER D15 Class 4-4-0 'Claud Hamilton'
    Locomotives   33 **Fig.15**
GER Coat-of-Arms   34
Great Eastern Railway Society   22 179 181
Great Northern Railway [GNR]   18
    25 27 28 31 48 52 53 56 59 60 65
    66 67 79 80 91 93 94 95 96 108 111
    163   **Figs.18 27 28 30 33 40 42**
GN&GE Joint Line   31 138
Great Yarmouth [also Yarmouth]   13
    20 21 22 27 39 52 83 **Fig.14**
Guildhall (Cambridge)   11

Harston   14 **Fig.27**

Harwich / Harwich Parkeston
   Quay   20 32 83 159

Haughley Junction   41

Haverhill   15 49 52 116 152

Hills Road (Cambridge) / Hills Road
   bridge   17 25 29 57 65 89 90 91 93
   96 117 143   **Figs.11 28 30 31 39
   40 43 47 50 55 60 63 64 77 79**

Histon / Histon Station   52
   83 138 163 **Figs.109 110**

Hitchin   28 48 52 116 139 160 164
   167 **Fig.14 Fig.22 Fig.27**

Horatio Love (Chairman ECR)   20

Horses – cartage and shunting (Cambridge
   Station) / racehorses   37 49 50
   68 87 91 – *et seq* 104 108 **Fig.61**

Illustrated London News / ILN   25
   26 57 58 59 95 Fig.10 Fig.31

Industrial Sidings (Cambridge
   Station area) – Chapter 13   102
   - *et seq* **Figs.70 71 72 73 74 75**

Island Platform (Cambridge Station) –
   Chapter 19   59 63 65 68 108 139 140 143
   – *et seq* 151 **Fig.37 Fig.97 Fig.102 Fig.103**

Ipswich   13 16 20 34 35 41 47 52 83 116
   120 140 **Figs.14 22 25 93 104 105**

Jack the Station Cat   161

Jesus College (Cambridge) / Jesus College
   Archives – Chapter 9   10 17 24 25
   27 29 46 55 57 – *et seq* 95 96 160 161
   Figs.8 9 13 34 35 36 37 39 40 42 43

Jockey Club (Newmarket)   37

Kettering   47 160 164 166

King's College Chapel   158 159

King's Cross (London)   7 47 56
   98 116 138 140 148 154 159 160
   164 167 **Fig.22 Fig.27 Fig.47**

King's Lynn   13 83 162 **Fig.4
   Fig.14 Fig.25 Fig.27**

Lending Library censorship
   (Cambridge)   127

Lightly Simpson (Chairman GER)   32

Lincoln (city of)   28 31 41 93 111

Liverpool Street Station (London)   16 20
   31 35 47 49 75 111 116 118 125 138 140
   148 154 159 162 163 166 167 **Fig.27 Fig.47**

London, Midland & Scottish Railway
   / LMS   (see Midland Railway)

London & North Eastern Railway /
   LNER   10 22 33 49 67 71 76 80
   89 90 – *et seq* 96 97 103 104 130
   162 **Fig.1 Fig.43 Fig.53 Fig.54**

London & North Western Railway
   / L&NWR   48 52 89 93 94 96
   108 111 117 164 **Fig.27 Fig.28
   Fig.30 Fig.43 Fig.47 Fig.55**

London   13 14 16 – *et seq* 25 26 27 29 31 –
   et seq 37 39 41 44 47 49 50 52 54 55 56 60
   67 71 90 93 94 110 116 118 120 121 122
   135 140 149 154 159 160 162 164 165 166
   167 168 **Fig.3 Fig.18 Fig.19 Fig.25 Fig.47**

Long Stanton Station (cut flower
   traffic)   83 93 95 134 163

Lord Claud Hamilton
   (Chairman GER)   32 36

Lord Cranbourne (Chairman GER)   32

Lord George Manners (Chairman,
   Newmarket Railway Company)   37 40

Lowestoft   13 22 83

March   14 15 32 92 94 116 120 160
   163 **Fig.14 Fig.104 Fig.105**

Market Place (Cambridge)   16 17 24

Marquess of Salisbury KG PC
   (Chairman GER)   32

Mechanical Signal Boxes (Cambridge
   Station) – Chapter 10   72 – *et seq* **Fig.47**

Messrs. Marsh & Swan – horse
   drawn traffic   51 **Fig.25 Fig.26**

Middlesex   34 35

Midlands   14 16 120 154

Midland Railway / MR / LMS   7 10
   52 53 54 67 89 93 94 96 111 120

Mildenhall branch   48 103 118
   120 163 **Fig.23 Fig.82**

Mill Road (Cambridge) / Mill Road
   bridge   17 28 29 52 53 103 107
   108 116 130 **Fig.12 Fig.28 Fig.47
   Fig.50 Fig.56 Fig.71 Fig.83 Fig.90**

Motive Power Depot (See also Engine Shed[s]) – Chapter 12   27 52 67 95- *et seq* 117 120

National Railway Museum - NRM   12 97 101 163
Network Rail (NR)   7 68 137 138 139 140 142 143 145 160
Newmarket & Chesterford Railway – Chapter 5   37- *et seq*
Newmarket branch accident at Cambridge 1883   43- *et seq*
Newmarket Road (Cambridge)   17
Newmarket / Newmarket Race Course   19 37 39 41 42 43 – *et seq* 47 49 52 55 63 65 78 90 116 117 118 140 152 163 **Fig.18 Fig.19 Fig.20 Fig.21 Fig.22 Fig.24 Fig.27**
Newnham   17
Norfolk   13 14 18 22 24 27 35 50 83 133 158 161 **Fig.3**
Norfolk Railway   19 30 39
Norman Cement Works near Cherry Hinton   49 **Fig.24**
Northern & Eastern Railway   18 27
Norwich   13 16 20 21 22 23 27 34 35 39 50 52 83 93 94 110 116 140 165 166 167 **Fig.14 Fig.25 Fig.27 Fig.104 Fig.105**

Ortona [Bus Company]   121
Oxford / Cambridge – Oxford line via Bletchley, Bedford and Sandy   28 48 52 56 93 96 112 116 120 134 135 152 162 164 **Fig.113**

Parcels traffic (Cambridge Station) see Chapter 11   80 - *et seq*

Peterborough   21 35 48 93 116 160 163 164 **Fig.14 Fig.18 Fig.27**

Rabbits (at Royal Show in Cambridge)   108 **Fig.76**
'Railway Mania'   37 58
Railway Notices   129
River Cam   13 14 16 28 89 104 166 **Fig.4 Fig.5 Fig.11**
River Stort   22

Romsey Town / 'Railway Town' (Cambridge)   16 17 **Fig.5**
Royal Fish – salmon fish boxes for HM The Queen   125-126

St Andrew the Less Parish, Cambridge   71 **Fig.42**
Samuel Laing MP (GER Board Member)   32
Sancton Wood (Architect)   2 26 **Fig.1**
Sawston   15
Scissors Crossing (or crossover) (Cambridge Station trackwork)   54 65 67 77 140 151 **Fig.47 Fig.50 Fig.103**
Shelford / Shelford road   17 48 49 52 112 **Fig.27**
Shepreth Branch Junction   48 **Fig.22**
'She's signalled.'   165
Shoreditch Station (ECR Head Offices, London)   60
Signals & Signalling (Cambridge Station) – Chapter 10   72 - *et seq*
Six Mile Bottom   41 46 **Fig.18 Fig.19 Fig.105**
Smarter Cambridge Transport (Website) – Chapter 14   151- *et seq* **Fig.104 Fig.105**
Southwold Railway Company   85 **Fig.57**
Spalding / Spalding Station (Ticket Platform)   31 65 **Fig.14 Fig.38**
Stables – horses for cartage & shunting (Cambridge Station)   50 51 90-93 **Fig.38 Fig.61**
Stanford. Sir Charles Villiers   161
Stansted Airport   140 148 154 **Fig.93 Fig.99 Fig.104 Fig.105**
Station Road (Cambridge)   2 8 16 24 25 29 36 65 91 103 143- *et seq* **Figs.13 40 42 43 55 56 94 98 101**
Stowmarket   41 83
Stratford   16 116 **Fig.54**
Suffolk   13 14 22 35 47 50 83 **Fig.3**

Tennison Fields Sidings (Cambridge Station)   67 107
Thetford   27 39 83 **Fig.14 Fig.18**
Timbuctoo (Lytton Strachey)   163
Ticket Platform[s]   44 45 46 63 65 **Fig.37**

Travelling Post Office (TPO)   125
Trumpington / Trumpington Temporary
    Station – Chapter 14   17 108 – *et seq*

University of Cambridge   7 89

Way & Works   16 68 **Fig.39 Fig.42**
Whitemoor Marshalling Yard,
    March   92 120 **Fig.62**

William French DD (Master of
    Jesus College)   24 60 **Fig 9**
Wisbech / Wisbech & Upwell
    Tramway   14 20 83 116 134 135
    138 152 **Fig.14 Fig.92 Fig.105**
Worlington Golf Links Halt   49

Yorkshire   14 32 41 93 120

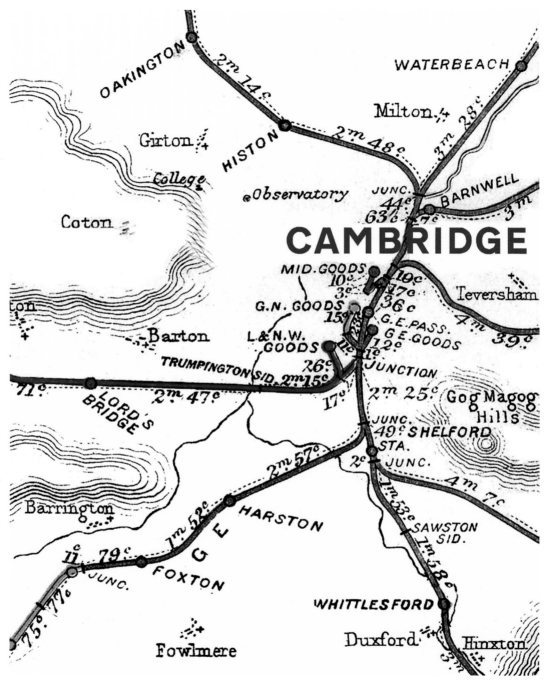

Edited colour scan of the Cambridge area from Railway Clearing House Official Map of the East of England. 1922. (Courtesy of Michael Perrins)